John Song

STUDIES IN
WORLD CHRISTIANITY

The Nagel Institute for the Study of World Christianity
Calvin College

Joel A. Carpenter
Series Editor

OTHER BOOKS IN THE SERIES

Christianity and Catastrophe in South Sudan
Jesse A. Zink

The Rise of Pentecostalism in Modern El Salvador
Timothy H. Wadkins

Global Christianity and the Black Atlantic
Andrew E. Barnes

The Making of Korean Christianity
Sung-Deuk Oak

Converts to Civil Society
Lida V. Nedilsky

Evangelical Christian Baptists of Georgia
Malkhaz Songulashvili

China, Christianity, and the Question of Culture
YANG Huilin

The Evangelical Movement in Ethiopia
Tibebe Eshete

John Song

Modern Chinese Christianity and the Making of a New Man

Daryl R. Ireland

BAYLOR UNIVERSITY PRESS

Cover design by Kasey McBeath
Cover image: "The Great Meeting to Establish the Zhangzhou Evangelistic Teams, November 1934." Courtesy of the Joint Archives of Holland.
Book design by Baylor University Press

Figure 1.1 (Diary of Song Shangjie, March 15, 1927, John Sung Papers [record group 263]) and figure 1.2 (Diary of Song Shangjie, April 11, 1927, John Sung Papers [record group 263]) are held at Special Collections, Yale Divinity School Library. Used by permission.

Hardcover ISBN: 978-1-4813-1270-7
Library of Congress Control Number: 2020937633

Printed in the United States of America on acid-free paper with a minimum of thirty percent recycled content.

To Cisca, who listened, laughed,
and labored alongside me—again!

Series Foreword

It used to be that those of us from the global North who study world Christianity had to work hard to make the case for its relevance. Why should thoughtful people learn more about Christianity in places far away from Europe and North America? The Christian religion, many have heard by now, has more than 60 percent of its adherents living outside of Europe and North America. It has become a hugely multicultural faith, expressed in more languages than any other religion. Even so, the implications of this major new reality have not sunk in. Studies of world Christianity might seem to be just another obscure specialty niche for which the academy is infamous, rather like an "ethnic foods" corner in an American grocery store.

Yet the entire social marketplace, both in North America and in Europe, is rapidly changing. The world is undergoing the greatest transregional migration in its history, as people from Africa, Asia, Latin America, and the Pacific region become the neighbors down the street, across Europe and North America. The majority of these new immigrants are Christians. Within the United States, one now can find virtually every form of Christianity from around the world. Here in Grand Rapids, Michigan, where I live and work, we have Sudanese Anglicans, Adventists from the Dominican Republic, Vietnamese Catholics, Burmese Baptists, Mexican Pentecostals, and Lebanese Orthodox Christians—to name a few of the Christian traditions and movements now present.

Christian leaders and institutions struggle to catch up with these new realities. The selection of a Latin American pope in 2013 was in some respects the culmination of decades of readjustment in the Roman Catholic Church. Here in Grand Rapids, the receptionist for the Catholic bishop answers the telephone first in Spanish. The worldwide Anglican communion is being fractured over controversies concerning sexual morality and biblical authority. Other churches in worldwide fellowships and alliances are treading more carefully as new leaders come forward and challenge northern assumptions, both liberal and conservative.

Until very recently, however, the academic and intellectual world has paid little heed to this seismic shift in Christianity's location, vitality, and expression. Too often, as scholars try to catch up to these changes, says the renowned historian Andrew Walls, they are still operating with "pre-Columbian maps" of these realities.

This series is designed to respond to that problem by making available some of the coordinates needed for a new intellectual cartography. Broad-scope narratives about world Christianity are being published, and they help to revise the more massive misconceptions. Yet much of the most exciting work in this field is going on closer to the action. Dozens of dissertations and journal articles are appearing every year, but their stories are too good and their implications are too important to be reserved for specialists only. So we offer this series to make some of the most interesting and seminal studies more accessible, both to academics and to the thoughtful general reader. World Christianity is fascinating for its own sake, but it also helps to deepen our understanding of how faith and life interact in more familiar settings.

So we are eager for you to read, ponder, and enjoy these Baylor Studies in World Christianity. There are many new things to learn, and many old things to see in a new light.

Joel A. Carpenter
Series Editor

Contents

Note on Spelling

In 1979, *hanyu pinyin* became internationally recognized as the preferred way to romanize Chinese characters. Alternative spellings disappeared rather quickly; Peking became Beijing almost overnight. A few names escaped the conversion. Chiang Kai-shek, for example, had been an internationally recognized figure, and people feared readers might not know that Jiang Jieshi was the same person. Now those concessions are disappearing. Chinese names and places are being universally transliterated using *hanyu pinyin*. If necessary, alternative spellings are put in brackets.

This book has done the same. Few will protest these alterations, except for maybe one: the decision to change the name John Sung to John Song. I have followed the broader academic convention and taken a recognized and even beloved spelling and put it into *hanyu pinyin*. The goal is to make it possible for anyone working in Chinese to be able to find Song, not just the few who know the name used by missionaries over eighty years ago. That name, John Sung, seldom appears in the historical record. In China he was referred to as Dr. Song Shangjie, Song being his family name.

Preface

"Have you heard of John Song?"

"No . . ." I dragged out the word while I ransacked my memory. Finding nothing, I added quickly, "At least, I don't think so." The answer was not ideal during an interview to study Chinese Christianity in a doctoral program, but it was the best I had to offer.

"Not a big deal," the professor replied kindly, as if he did not expect me to know *all* the minutia of Chinese Christianity. I relaxed. "An interesting character, though." He proceeded to rehearse the outline of Song's career: he grew up in China, but went to college in America; he earned a Ph.D. in chemistry, and then moved to New York City to study at Union Theological Seminary; in the midst of the modernist-fundamentalist controversy, Song had an old-time religious conversion, and Union was so terrified of it, they had him removed from the premises; Song was put into an insane asylum, but after his release, he returned to China and became the nation's preeminent evangelist; after ten years, Song had led more Chinese people to believe in Jesus Christ than any other person in history. Sound vaguely familiar?

It didn't.

My embarrassment may have initiated this project, but it is not what sustained it. Curiosity took over. Who was this [John] Song Shangjie, and why did I know nothing about such a man? Some answers came quickly. Like many others, I had to admit my knowledge of Christianity had a distinct Western bias, but that did not explain everything. After all, China's own church history textbook, which goes to great lengths to tell the story of *Chinese* believers, is altogether silent about its most traveled, visible, and popular Christian.[1] What makes him so elusive?

For one thing, primary sources have been sparse. Song never took time to write books or articles. Even his two autobiographies were dictated, not written. He had different priorities than preserving his ideas in the forms favored by historians. Tantalizingly, Song did keep a personal diary, and excerpts started leaking out in the 1990s. However, since his daughter controlled what was seen or published, and because it was clear that she was carefully curating the materials for the spiritual edification of her readers, it remained difficult to know what to make of his journals, or of Song himself.

The secondary sources were technically abundant, but difficult to compile. The news reports, testimonies, transcriptions of his sermons, audio-taped memories, photographs, letters about meetings with Song, and so forth were scattered across three continents. To make matters even more complex, they were preserved in different languages. The pieces necessary to understand John Song were yet to be assembled.

Thus, with only a splotch of information here and a blob of an anecdote there, Song's fragmented story had turned into something of a Rorschach test. People could see in it what they wanted.[2] If I were to understand John Song, and not just the predilections of his biographers, I would need to get my hands on fresh sources.

To begin, it seemed critical to know what happened at Union Theological Seminary. Unfortunately, "It is not UTS's policy to retain the student files of students who stayed less than a year and did not complete courses."[3] Hoping to find tangential information in other files, I traveled to New York anyway, only to be stunned when Song's records were handed to me. I was the first researcher to see the complete record of how Union experienced John Song, and so remain indebted to Ruth Tonkiss Cameron for putting that file together. It was the beginning of everything else.

---

[1] Luo Weihong, *Christianity in China*, trans. Zhu Chengming (Beijing: Wuzhou, 2004).

[2] Daryl R. Ireland, "John Sung's Malleable Conversion Narrative," *Fides et Historia* 45, no. 1 (2013): 48–75.

[3] Ruth Tonkiss Cameron, correspondence quoted in Jonathan Seitz, "Converting John Sung: UTS Drop-Out, Psychiatric Patient, Chinese Evangelist," *Union Seminary Quarterly Review* 62, no. 1–2 (2009): 80.

The other major discovery was Song's diary. Today, his journals are available at Yale Divinity School, but when I first set out to study Song, the only way to see the 6,000-some pages of his daily diaries was to go to Trinity Theological College in Singapore. When I arrived, however, the collection was closed. No one was allowed to view the digitized journals. For a week I sat in the library, half-heartedly skimming various periodicals and church reports about Song's revivals, as Bishop Hwa Yung worked behind the scenes to secure permissions for me to open the files. I still do not know what was said nor all who were involved, but I am extraordinarily grateful to the Bishop as well as to Song's family. It was an honor to be the first researcher to work with John Song's own notes, and they provided the second serious breakthrough in putting this story together.

In between the visits to UTS and TTC, I was assisted by a host of generous people and institutions around the world. Collectively, these librarians and archivists helped build an 11,000-foot-long paper trail (if you laid one page after the other). Thanks to them, I have been able to follow John Song.

However, the closer I seemed to get, the more sources I managed to accumulate, the fuzzier Song appeared to me. I puzzled as I listened to Song (and others) tell the same stories, but never the same way twice. Contradictions compounded. What was true, or truer? Which elements might be reliable, and which parts should I disregard? I despaired at ever knowing what Song was like as a child, or even as a man. Despite all the sources, Song's life remained shrouded in mystery.

That is until I changed the question. Instead of asking, "What happened?" like a conventional biographer, I needed to ask, "How come so many versions?" Why was Song obsessed with reinvention? What was dissolving his past and making it so fluid? The answers did not, and could not, produce a biography. Readers who come to this book for an intimate portrait of his relationship with his wife and children or a travelogue of his many journeys will be disappointed. What a person can find, however, is a study of Song as a crucial but overlooked piece in the puzzle of modern China and modern Chinese Christianity. Song was an innovator. In the 1930s, he pioneered a style of Christianity that delivered to China what its urban inhabitants most desperately wanted: a way to be different, a chance to become new. This book examines how Song initiated an alternative path to China's modernization. In his services he worked out answers to his nation's most pressing questions about how to break with the past and start afresh. Although his revivals initially operated on the fringes of Chinese Protestantism, their features eventually came to dominate and almost define the movement. Today, to look at John Song is to see and understand how modern Chinese Christianity first emerged and why it has grown so dramatically.

Acknowledgments

Typing is a solitary affair, but not writing. This book is the fruition of years of conversations and collaborations. It bears the marks of numerous readers and respondents. Steadfast friends have rescued me from dead ends, mentors have offered guidance and encouragement, librarians and archivists have been indefatigable in tracking down sources, and sharp-eyed editors have not only honed my language but forced me to tighten my thinking. It is a joy to thank them for their contributions.

My earliest debt is to Michael McClymond. He first suggested there might be a story behind the story of John Song. When I found evidence that he was right, Margaret Bendroth helped me shear the wordy description of my findings at Union Theological Seminary so that their import might be clear. Dana L. Robert was generous in guidance and keen in insight as I turned those earliest discoveries into a dissertation at Boston University. Daniel Bays, Mark Noll, and Lian Xi each interacted with certain portions of this work. Their encouragement and feedback inspired me to keep going and to dig deeper.

Unearthing sources required constant assistance. In Europe, Brian Stanley opened the University of Edinburgh's Andrew F. Walls library for me, even though it was supposed to be closed. In the Netherlands, Cornelis van der Laan sent me all the issues of the Pentecostal periodical *Gouden Schoven* in which Song was mentioned. Meanwhile, Huub Lems of the Mission Foundation of the Protestant Church in the Netherlands, granted me access to a wide range of mission files stored in the Utrecht Archive.

In Asia, Irene Wong and Mandy Liu worked tirelessly to track down a variety of sources housed at the Hong Kong Baptist University. Siu Chao Lee of the Bethel Mission helped me locate historical records of that organization. In Singapore, not only did I enjoy the hospitality of Michael Poon, Michael Mukunthun, and Eunice Low at Trinity Theological College, but I also received help from Wong Siew Yun of the Chin Lien Bible School, Ernest Lau of the Methodist Archive, and Lieu Heng San and Teek Bing Yeo from the Telok Ayer Methodist Church. One of the most delightful trips was to Sibu, Malaysia. There, Francis Wong, Wong Meng Lie, Tie King Tai, Thomas Lau, and Su Chii Ann collaborated to unearth an enormous collection of Song material before I even arrived. Zheng Jincan made important introductions for me in China and provided tours of the area where Song Shangjie grew up. He was most generous with his time and knowledge. The staff of the Shanghai Municipal Archive was likewise prompt, congenial, and helpful in sorting through the amazing collection of Christian materials housed in their collection.

I also had the benefit of working with knowledgeable and wise archivists in the United States. Ruth Tonkiss Cameron from Union Theological Seminary, Kara Jackman at Boston University, Meri Jansen from the Church of the Nazarene Archives, Marisa Louie of the National Archives in San Francisco, Kevin Haire from the Ohio State University Archives, Geoffrey Reynolds of the Joint Archives of Holland, Michigan, Dale Patterson of the United Methodist Archives and History Center, and Martha Smalley of the Yale Divinity School Library are particularly important to single out. Each one went an extra mile to find scattered materials in their collections about John Song.

Earlier publications gave me chance to try out what I was uncovering. Portions of chapter 1 and 2 are adapted from "John Sung's Malleable Conversion Narrative," *Fides et Historia* 45 (Winter 2013): 48-75. Chapter 6 is expanded from an article first published in "Becoming Modern Women: Creating a New Female Identity through John Sung's Evangelistic Teams," *Studies in World Christianity* 18 (January 2012): 237-253. "The Legacy of John Sung," *International Bulletin* 40 (October 2016): 349-357, synthesized ideas that reappear in various parts of this work. I am grateful to the publishers for permission to build on that material. I would also like to thank the Rev. Timothy Wang for allowing me to add something special to this publication: images from his grandfather's diary.

Joel Carpenter and the team at Baylor University Press have been fabulous. Combined with the two anonymous readers, they provided the kind of feedback an author both loves and hates to receive. It caused me to do much more work and to think more carefully, but the result—I hope—will reveal how much I appreciated their wisdom.

Finally, I need to thank friends and family. Jessica Williams [Ding Huijun] became the world's foremost authority on Song's almost illegible scrawl. She spent scores of hours and suffered countless headaches as she helped me make out which characters Song was scribbling. Her transliteration of significant portions of Song's diary make this work possible. My father, Herb Ireland, traveled with me through seven countries to collect materials on Song. He was a buoyant companion and stalwart supporter. Not to be outdone, my mother, Carolyn Ireland, helped comb through and organize the piles of material that I gathered in Europe and Asia. My wife and son, however, were the ones who worked with me on John Song not for weeks at a time, but for years. Whether I was happy, frustrated, or exhausted, they let me talk it out over lunch and dinner. Their patience and questions birthed some of the sharpest insights. Thank you, Cisca and Alexander.

Introduction

The Quest to Become New

The day started cool, but before it was over it would turn incendiary. The university students who gathered in the early afternoon were flushed, but not from heat. They were burning with an excitement that the breeze, and their intoxicating defiance, only fanned. In disobedience of the Ministry of Education, they clustered together at Tiananmen, the Gate of Heavenly Peace. At first the hundred or so pupils attracted little attention in Beijing's enormous central park, but as more and more students arrived, their giddy enthusiasm and outburst of cheers that greeted new arrivals began to gather a crowd of curious onlookers. What they observed were now thousands of students unfurling funeral flags with the names of sitting government officials written on them. One banner, written in a student's own blood after biting his finger, distilled the students' demands: "Return our Qingdao!"

The Paris Peace Conference of 1919 had revealed backroom deals and secret handshakes. In fulfillment of their unpublicized promise to reward Japan for its naval support, France, Great Britain, and Italy concluded World War I by announcing plans to hand over the German-controlled areas of China to Japan. China's contribution of one hundred thousand men to the Allied effort on the European front and its claim to territorial sovereignty were not so much being ignored as they were dismissed. The clandestine arrangement with Japan preceded China's claims made in Paris. Parties like the United States were dismayed by what was happening but found it in their own self-interest to uphold the technicalities of international law. The strategic port of Qingdao, along

1

with the rest of Germany's holdings in China, would belong to Japan after the signing of the Treaty of Versailles.

The news mobilized over three thousand students from thirteen universities in Beijing. Appalled by the reports filtering back to China, they gathered in the early afternoon of May 4 with the purpose of marching to the foreign legation, where they hoped to submit their grievances to foreign ambassadors who might convince their governments to reconsider this abomination. The young intellectuals set out from Tiananmen and moved through the streets in orderly fashion, waving their banners and handing out tracts that explained their actions to those lining the streets. Written for the masses, not in rarefied classical Chinese, the message was simple. China could not survive as a nation if it could not even hold its own territory. "We urge our country's industrial and commercial sectors to rise up and organize a national assembly, to fight for sovereignty abroad and to drive out the traitors at home."[1]

Two hours of negotiations proved futile. Students were not allowed to enter the foreign quarter. The experience was a reenactment of China's national humiliation: Chinese people could no longer control their own land. In a burst of righteous indignation, the crowd marched to the home of the Minister of Communications, Cao Rulin, who four years earlier, having few political or military options at hand, had notoriously conceded to Japan's Twenty-One Demands and handed over large chunks of China's land and resources. Now, demonstrators shouted for him to give an accounting for his traitorous behavior. Police efforts to quell the mob only fueled its fury. Students hurled stones and flagstaffs into Cao's windows, and a few resourceful belligerents managed to climb the compound wall, jump through a window, and open the front gate. As Cao fled out the back, a vigilante force stormed his home, smashed his furniture, and set the house ablaze.

[1] Chen Pingyuan, *Touches of History: An Entry into 'May Fourth'* (Leiden: Brill, 2011), 30. Chen also provides many of the details for what happened on that day. His microscopic study even includes investigations of the weather conditions. Additional details, especially what preceded and happened after the date of May 4, 1919, are drawn from several sources: Chow Tse-Tsung, *The May Fourth Movement: Intellectual Revolution in Modern China* (Cambridge, Mass.: Harvard University Press, 1960); Vera Schwarcz, *The Chinese Enlightenment: Intellectuals and the Legacy of the May Fourth Movement of 1919* (Berkeley: University of California Press, 1986); Jonathan Spence, *The Search for Modern China* (New York: W.W. Norton, 1990); and Jacques Gernet, *A History of Chinese Civilization* (Cambridge: Cambridge University Press, 1996).

By the time the military arrived, the outburst of rage had already dissipated, and the number of students at the scene dispersed along with it. A sweep of the streets managed to put thirty-two young scholars behind bars that night, but their protest had released something new. Students were united. That night undergraduates reconvened to discuss their options. The first priority was to figure out what they could do about their imprisoned classmates. Fear initially chilled the gathering as word spread that those arrested could be executed under martial law. By dawn, though, moral outrage heated their discussions. How could the government condemn a few dozen students when thousands of them were all responsible? They staged a new round of protests and managed to organize sympathetic demonstrations across China. Two thousand people took to the streets in Wuhan, ten thousand gathered in Nanjing, and Shanghai drew close to twenty thousand onlookers as students made speeches condemning not only the government's heavy-handed discipline, but also its timorousness at the Paris Peace Conference. What kind of government would give away its own land?

Framed that way, students easily swayed popular opinion. Chinese newspapers rushed to support the protesters. Political parties, which opposed the ruling clique in Beijing, capitalized on the widespread sympathy for the students' point of view and joined them in criticizing the government. Chambers of Commerce rallied behind the students' patriotic rhetoric of boycotting Japanese goods. It made good business sense. Merchants and industrialists were facing the threat of Japan dumping goods in China to drive down prices and eliminate any Chinese competition. Various parties coalesced in opposition to the government.

Anger and resentment hiked over mountain ranges, spilled down tributaries, and generally pooled in schools across the land. Even Guthrie Memorial High School in Putian, Fujian Province, got pulled into the vortex of events. The isolated Methodist school, immured by the ocean on one side and encircling mountain range on the other, witnessed students organizing political rallies, and the large brick building became the scene of young people shouting and chanting, demanding something better for China.[2] Presumably among them was a short, gangly preacher's kid—a rather indistinguishable pupil in the mob. [John] Song Shangjie, like tens of thousands of others, watched the power of the

---

[2] Kele Paofan, *Xingan Puxian* (Taipei: Hyweb Technology, 2006), accessed February 11, 2020, https://books.google.com.tw/books?id=pbUvAwAAQBAJ.

May Fourth Movement sway an entire nation. In fact, caught up in the patriotic fervor, Song began visiting a local barber in Putian to have his eyeballs scraped and, to hedge his bets, also the Methodist hospital to receive eye drops. He needed to be free of trachoma if he were going to study in America and learn how to rejuvenate his nation.[3] Yet the imaginative teenager, even in the wildest flights of fancy, could not have anticipated what would happen when he returned a decade later. No one could have foreseen that the seventeen-year-old who had stood at the steps of Guthrie Memorial High School calling for China's national salvation would become the nation's premier revivalist, inviting millions of people to accept eternal salvation through Jesus Christ. That was still too far away. In 1919, the young Song, like his classmates, gathered only to add his voice to the growing crescendo of frustration with the government.

His anger, which merged with the national outcry, was one thing, but those in political power recognized *realpolitik* was another. To antagonize Japan was foolish; their neighbor to the east had superior military and economic power. Thus, the president of the Republic of China, Xu Shichang, gave orders to crack down on the spreading discontent. He instructed police to arrest university students who had begun street preaching on patriotism and handing out tracts in *baihua*, vernacular Chinese.

The students never flinched. They simply began taking bedrolls on their backs into the streets so that, when arrested, they would have something to sleep on in the quickly overcrowding jails. In Beijing alone, 1,150 students were imprisoned. The government's attempts at suppression backfired, generating ever-widening circles of sympathy for the May Fourth Movement. Women became involved, marching to the Presidential Palace to demand the release of the young men. Female students started to make speeches on the streets in order to resupply the dwindling ranks of their male counterparts. Factory workers and clerks went on strike. The students even motivated beggars, prostitutes, and singsong girls to refuse to work. It was the first political and patriotic strike in Chinese history. The issue was not wages or working conditions, but a mass protest against the Chinese and Japanese governments.

---

[3] Song Siong Chiat [Song Shangjie], *My Testimony: Being the Autobiography of Dr. John Song (Song Siong Chiat) the Chinese Evangelist*, trans. E. Tipson (Kuala Lumpur: Caxton Press, 1936), 33.

Somewhat to everyone's surprise, the Chinese government capitulated to popular sentiment. By June 28, pro-Japanese cabinet members, including Cao Rulin, were forced to resign, and instructions were sent to Paris for the Chinese delegation not to sign the Treaty of Versailles. That did not mean that China suddenly maintained its rights over Qingdao. With or without its delegates' signatures, international powers would give China's port to Japan. Yet across the nation, those who witnessed or participated in the events of May Fourth and its aftermath knew that, even in failure, the students had succeeded. This was the beginning of something new.

Some believed it was the birth of modern China, others preferred to call it New China, but the idea was the same: henceforth, things could be different.[4] China could change. "We should struggle against society in order to regain the hope that we have lost," wrote a young Mao Zedong shortly after the events of May Fourth. "We should die fighting."[5] But fighting whom? Should the Chinese people target the corrupt politicians in Beijing or focus on the foreign gunboats? Was economic stagnation due to unequal treaties that allowed foreign firms to undersell Chinese goods, or a result of Chinese companies not modernizing? Maybe local warlords were the primary problem, or maybe they were only the result of the vacuum created by widespread political apathy. China had many

---

[4] A number of historians have dated China's modernization to the May Fourth Movement. The truth, however, is more complex. The nation state, urbanization, capitalism, rationalization, reconfigured social relationships, differentiated social spheres, and the like, which Dong-no Kim identifies as critical components of East Asia's modernization, did not first appear in 1919. Those seismic shifts had already been shaking the foundations of China. Furthermore, the May Fourth Movement never self-consciously promoted any one of the features of modernity, except nationalism. In fact, some of the visions for how to strengthen China that emerged after the May Fourth Movement would have stood in opposition to general descriptions of modernization. The point is not that May Fourth initiated China's modernization. Its real significance is that May Fourth standardized the notion that things had to change. Some people in China used the language of becoming "modern" to describe what was required. Most, however, gravitated to the simpler and more generic term: China needed something "new." See Albert Park and David K. Yoo, eds., *Encountering Modernity: Christianity in East Asia and Asian America* (Honolulu: University of Hawaii Press, 2014), 4–5; Kam Louie, ed., *The Cambridge Companion to Modern Chinese Culture* (Cambridge: Cambridge University Press, 2008).

[5] Mao Zedong, quoted in *De gong bao*, November 16, 1919, cited in Spence, *Search for Modern China*, 304.

enemies, but what if the deepest problems were within? In the years following May Fourth, anger turned inward on China's own culture and beliefs. Old China was simply not strong enough to survive in a modern age.

The May Fourth Movement fueled an explosion of public conversations about the future of the nation. Debates and radical ideas, many of which had been simmering in university classrooms for decades, now boiled over. Different and often contradictory ways to save the nation were popularized through the explosion of fresh periodicals. Approximately five hundred new magazines appeared between 1919 and 1923.[6] These journals followed-up on the students' achievement of winning the hearts and minds of the masses through their simple tracts and colloquial speeches. Just as the May Fourth events spread by using *baihua*, so the new journals printed their articles in the vernacular. The change was akin to what happened when European national languages supplanted Latin as the means for expressing philosophical, literary, and social concerns.[7] The ancient distinctions in China between those who did mental and physical labor, and between those who ruled and those who were ruled, began to crumble. Elites sought a new type of relationship with China's workers, industrialists, and farmers. They wanted to create a kind of intimacy and solidarity with the masses that could be leveraged to move them. Their magazine titles emblazoned the imperative to erect something different on each cover: *New China, New Learning, New Masses, New Culture, New Woman, New Atmosphere, New Medicine, New Village*. Titles like *New Reconstruction* even dabbled with redundancy to emphasize the overarching point: everything had to be made new if, as it was expressed in the title of several new journals, the Chinese people were going to *Save the Nation*.

Among other concerns, people worried about the effects of China's rapid urbanization. During the nineteenth century, China's cities grew at rates similar to the national population. After 1900, however, cities started to suck in people from the countryside at ever increasing speeds.[8]

---

[6] Zhou Cezong, *Research Guide to the May Fourth Movement: Intellectual Revolution in Modern China, 1915–1924* (Cambridge, Mass.: Harvard University Press, 1963), 43–129.

[7] Peter Gue Zarrow, *China in War and Revolution, 1895–1949* (New York: Routledge, 2005), 137.

[8] John K. Fairbank, *The Cambridge History of China*, vol. 12 (Cambridge: Cambridge University Press, 1983), 33.

In major cities like Beijing, the population spiked dangerously. In 1919, at the time of the student demonstrations, the city had a population of 600,000. Four years later the city had almost doubled to 1,100,000 people. Infrastructure could not stay apace that kind of growth. Factories and businesses could only employ a fraction of the immigrants dreaming of a better future. Urban poverty became a combustible issue, because alongside China's dire poverty were signs of fabulous wealth. A new class system re-stratified China, but it was free from the moral obligations that tied together village scholars, artisans, tradespeople, and tenant farmers. The bourgeoisie, petty urbanites, the working class, and the destitute were all inventing new social roles for themselves. Owners had to figure out if there were any moral limits to maximizing profits. Those who labored in department stores and factories, where they clocked in and out of work, faced—for the first time in their lives—set hours for leisure. What were they to do with their free time? Others wondered about the emergence of unions, gangs, public and private charities, and the growth of prostitution. Were these necessary byproducts of the modern economic system? Was there something better? Publications provided all kinds of answers, but the nagging question remained. How was a person to live in a modern city?

More specifically, how were women to live? The question of the "New Woman" became an enormous field of inquiry and debate. The May Fourth Movement successfully tarnished China's Confucian principles. Students argued that since Confucian China proved to be no match to the nations of Europe, the United States, and Japan, then Confucius was an insufficient guide for nation building in the modern world. The political and economic systems, as well as the values taught by China's preeminent sage, had to be jettisoned if China was to be saved. Women, for example, were no longer to be identified solely in relation to the men in their lives, progressing from being a dutiful daughter, to a chaste wife, to a good mother. To remain ensconced in those three roles now appeared backward and put the nation at a disadvantage in battling the rest of the world. Without liberating half its population, China would always be fighting with one arm tied behind its back. Intellectuals could agree on that, but many questions remained. How were women to be freed? What were a new woman's responsibilities? What did a modern woman look like?

Appearances were important. They had profound political implications. A growing number of people believed that China was weak as a nation and incapable of getting its will in international affairs because its people were physically weak. Healthy bodies were necessary to create a healthy nation. A new preoccupation with physical appearance and exercise emerged in China after the events of May Fourth, spurring the country to send its first delegation of athletes to the International Olympics in 1924. More important still was the question of how to best heal Chinese bodies. New debates emerged over what kind of health care was appropriate. What could cure China and its people of appearing to the world as "hollow-breasted and humpbacked . . . pale-faced and slender-limbed"?[9] Should China adopt Western biomedicine, which apparently strengthened the world's superpowers, or would real patriots improve and rely upon China's own traditions of healing?

In the decades following the May Fourth Movement, these became questions of life and death. China had to change or face extinction. The priorities were clear, if ridiculously ambitious: everyone had to be made new; the masses had to be mobilized before it was too late; if cities were going to be the doorways to a modern and better society, a kind of heaven on earth, then they needed to stop looking like gateways to hell; women, and their place in society, needed to be reimagined; and all of this reinvention, all of the newness Chinese people clamored for, needed to get instantiated in the body somehow.

These concerns were not irrelevant to Christians. Believers were equally obsessed with the quest to modernize China. A cluster of Christian intellectuals in Beijing immediately waded into the May Fourth debates through the journal *Truth and Life*. The editor, Liu Tingfang [Timothy Tingfang Lew], who was the Dean of Yanjing [Yenching] University's School of Religion, used the periodical to forward a Christian vision of a New Man, a New Woman, a New City, a New Body, and the like. Liu was also active in the Young Men's Christian Association (YMCA) in Beijing and served on the National Committee. The connection was fitting, as the YMCA and the Young Women's Christian Association (YWCA) translated many of the ideas in *Truth and Life* into action. They, too, felt the urgency for a New China. The Y aimed to create a new Chinese person: a cosmopolitan person. To do so, they relied on all sorts of tools to mobilize the masses. Lantern slides and

---

[9] Chow Teh Lin, essay in *Yi yao zhi ye zheng wen ji. Di san jie* [*"Old Style" versus "Modern" Medicine in China: Which Can Do More For the Health and Progress of the Country, and Why?*] (Shanghai: Wei sheng jiao yu hui, 1926), 27.

propaganda posters promoted biomedicine, modern education methods, and political internationalism. Lecture tours by the likes of Sherwood Eddy, John Mott, and Gu Ziren [T. Z. Koo] offered Christianity as the means for wholesale cultural and social renewal. Since the Ys were located in urban centers, change usually started there. The YWCA, for instance, helped female factory workers organize, advocate for better wages, insist on safer working conditions, and challenge the twelve-hour working day. Here was a picture of China's modern woman. She perhaps did not avail herself of all the physical exercise programs that were available to men at the YMCA, but she was as concerned as her male counterparts in protecting and improving her body. Christians were as absorbed as everyone else in modernizing China.

The challenge is to recognize the different patterns. *Truth and Life*, the YMCA, the YWCA, and Christian denominations with a strong social agenda are rather easily identified as playing a role in China's reinvention. It is no wonder. They increasingly devoted themselves to large-scale projects of transformation through education, health, agriculture, and land reform. And as they did so, their work in China came to parallel the Nationalist government's own efforts for modernization. In fact, the two sometimes intertwined. The Guomindang (GMD)—the Nationalist Party—even hired people from these Christian institutions to implement its own programs for reconstruction. The government needed the expertise of Christians like George Shepherd (Congregationalist), John Lossing Buck (Presbyterian), and Yan Yangchu [James Yen] (YMCA), who had pioneered programs to remake Chinese culture, Chinese farms, and Chinese people.[10] The high visibility of these Christian leaders, programs, and institutions in creating a New China has made it easy to see them as the harbingers of modern Chinese Christianity.

Yet outside the government spotlight, tucked inside church sanctuaries, many Chinese Christians were following a different pathway to New Life. Revivals had exploded onto the scene just before the May Fourth Movement, and they burned with ever intensifying heat until the outbreak of World War II. [John] Song Shangjie was not the only revivalist of the period, but he was certainly the most famous. He traveled farther than anyone else, clicking off more than one hundred thousand miles

---

[10] James C. Thomson, *While China Faced West: American Reformers in Nationalist China, 1928–1937* (Cambridge, Mass.: Harvard University Press, 1969), 103–16.

between 1928 and 1940; he spoke more often than anyone else, usually preaching at least three times every single day; and he was more effective than anyone else: more than one hundred thousand people prayed for a new life at one of his meetings. By the end of his twelve-year career in the pulpit, more than 10 percent of all Chinese Protestants in the world had decided to abandon their old lives during one of his revival meetings in order to "transform into a new person."[11] In the forge of his "hot and noisy" revivals, where singing mixed with confession, laughter with groans and tears, Song created a Christianity for New China—a faith that mobilized aspiring urbanites, including women, to choose a new life that could transform not only the heart but also the body. It was a style of Christianity that may have appeared marginal at the time, especially to those looking for changes in larger social structures, but it has since come to dominate the Chinese Christian landscape. This is the story of how [John] Song Shangjie built modern Chinese Christianity amidst the tumultuous years of the early twentieth century.

[11] For numbers, see Lian Xi, *Redeemed by Fire: The Rise of Popular Christianity in Modern China* (New Haven: Yale University Press, 2010), 10. See also Joseph Parker, *Interpretive Statistical Survey of the World Mission of the Christian Church: Summary and Detailed Statistics of Churches and Missionary Societies, Interpretive Articles, and Indices* (New York: International Missionary Council, 1938), 19–20. The number of Chinese Protestants living in China and Southeast Asia is very difficult to establish because statistical tables did not distinguish among ethnicities. Parker counts 567,390 Protestants in China/Manchuria, and 982,761 more in all the other countries Song visited in Southeast Asia. That would mean of the 1,550,151 total Protestants in the region, 6.5 percent converted through Song's ministry. However, unless one assumes that the 982,761 Protestants living in British Malaya, Burma, Formosa, the Dutch East Indies, the Philippines, and Siam were all ethnically Chinese—which they clearly were not—then it seems reasonable to conclude that Song was instrumental in at least 10 percent of *Chinese* Protestants in the region. For the idea of transformation into a new person, see "A New Robe," Boston University's Center for Global Christianity & Mission, Chinese Christian Poster Project, accessed March 23, 2019, https://ccposters.com/poster/a-new-robe-2/.

1

The Dissolution

The emergence of a new, modern Chinese Christianity is exemplified through the life and career of Song Shangjie, but like so many other archetypal figures, the heroes who represent the ideals of a community, the origin story of Song Shangjie is hidden in the oily cloth of myth and obscurity. Virtually no records survive from Song's childhood. The accounts that do exist come decades later and are already pervaded with his new, modern evangelistic agenda. What little that is known for certain about his earliest years is that Song Shangjie was born on September 27, 1901, during the Mid-Autumn Festival. He was the sixth child of Chen Ruolan and the Reverend Song Xuelian, a Methodist pastor in the Xinghua [Hinghwa] Conference of Fujian. From birth, Tian-en, or Heavenly Grace as he was called around the house, was immersed in the life of the young church. The first Methodist Episcopal missionaries had arrived in Xinghua only twelve years before, and his father assumed multiple responsibilities in the nascent Christian community. In addition to pastoring, he was also a district superintendent, a school principal, an editor of the *Revivalist*, and a conference evangelist.[1]

As an adult Song Shangjie tried to obfuscate just how deeply Christianity had imprinted itself on his formative years. He was more interested in emphasizing how radically new Jesus Christ had made him. To suggest his new life had any continuity with the past would threaten to minimize the rupture. Thus, he downplayed anything that might suggest

---

[1] *Zhonghua jidujiao weiligonghui baizhoujiniankan, 1847–1947* [*Methodist Centennial in China, 1847–1947*] (Fuzhou, China: The Editorial Committee of the Centennial Celebration, 1948), 112–13.

he was spiritually alive as a youth. Even so, Song Shangjie could never speak about his childhood without referencing the Christian faith that permeated his life. Efforts to seal Christianity away, to defer Jesus' presence until later in his life, never perfectly held. Stories always leaked into those early, supposedly spiritually barren years.

Song found himself admitting that he heard the gospel at an early age. His father spoke to him regularly of the New Birth, and the description of God's marvelous gift of grace enthralled him. He learned from his parents not only how to pray, but also how to experience its power personally. He recalled, for instance, his mother instructing him to pray for his deathly ill father, who lay in the next room gasping for what sounded like his last breath. Song obeyed, and when he finished his desperate and faith-filled plea with, "In the holy name of the Lord, Amen," his father's breathing instantly normalized, and the man was restored to health. Song was also exposed to the Christian faith outside his home. In fact, every dimension of his life was saturated by Christian institutions and practices. On Sundays he attended church in the morning and Sunday School in the afternoon. On weekdays he could be found at the Methodist school. If Song was sick, he went to the Christian hospital. Later in life, whenever he reminisced about the past, Song inevitably fell into describing his pastimes as climbing a prayer mountain to converse with God, going door-to-door to sell Bibles, handing out gospel tracts, preaching a sermon in a neighboring village, writing an article for *The Revivalist*, or entertaining younger children with songs, stories, and pictures about Jesus. There was a reason people called him the "Little Pastor."[2]

Of course, none of this was useful when Song wanted to emphasize the enormity of the change Jesus wrought in his adult life. So, on the occasions when he caught himself speaking too enthusiastically about his youthful piety, he would quickly qualify it. "My work was as gorgeous as the kingfisher's blue, and as luxuriant as the leaves and flowers, yet at the end it could not produce a single plucking of fresh fruit to give to the Lord Jesus."[3] Or he might dismiss his zeal as disguised pride: "I really took the office of preaching the gospel and used it for exalting myself."[4] In other

---

[2] Song Shangjie, *Wode jianzheng* [*My Testimony*] (1933; repr., Hong Kong: Bellman House, 1991), 18.

[3] Song, *Wode jianzheng*, 26.

[4] Song, *Wode jianzheng*, 18.

words Song tried to convince people that the similarities between his past and his present were superficial at best. Nonetheless, the fact that so many of these inconvenient stories bled into his sermons and books suggests just how deeply embedded Song was in the church, and how completely Christianity oriented the earliest years of his life.

The violent shaking of the May Fourth Movement aggravated Song Shangjie, but it never pushed him outside the Christian community. In fact, the church helped him focus his anger and energy. He returned to his Methodist high school with a redoubled commitment: *dushu jiuguo*, he "studied to save the nation."[5] When he determined it was best to obtain a college degree in America, church connections helped him gain tuition-free admittance to Ohio Wesleyan University (OWU). Chinese church pastors and friends generated the money he needed for his steamship fare, and his bishop personally vouched for Song on his immigration papers.[6]

After Song cleared customs in San Francisco in 1920 at the age of eighteen, more than his own memories enter the historical record. Letters, newspapers, photographs, diaries, and school and hospital records all become available. Although his experiences in America would later receive a radically different varnish, the records from the time paint a picture of a young man utterly devout. Upon entering the United States, Song had little more than his train fare to reach Ohio, but that was never a concern. His riches were immaterial. Prayer, hymns, and the providential hand of God were what saw him through.[7] It never hurt, of course, that he also had irrepressible energy and a quick mind. When he completed his bachelor's degree at OWU a year early, he told the school newspaper that he planned to co-register at Harvard Medical School and Boston University's School of Theology so that, in just three more years, he could have both the medical and theological degrees necessary to become a medical missionary in China.[8] In the end, however, Song enrolled at Ohio State University (OSU) that fall of 1923, where over the next three years his incredible energy did, in fact, earn him two graduate

[5] Song, *Wode jianzheng*, 22.

[6] Song, *Wode jianzheng*, 28–29; "Siong-Ceh Sang," 1926, National Archives Arrival Investigation Case Files, 1884–1944, San Francisco Records, Records of the Immigration and Naturalization Service, record group 85, San Francisco, Calif.

[7] Song, *Wode jianzheng*, 34–46.

[8] "New Phi Betas Plan for Future Careers," *Ohio Wesleyan Transcript*, April 18, 1923.

degrees, including a doctorate in chemistry in March 1926, and the nickname "Peppy" for his indomitable physical vitality.[9]

While accumulating degrees and academic honors, Song also cultivated his faith. At OWU, he participated in a local congregation, and used school vacations to tour with a campus gospel team. At OSU, Song received a local preacher's license from the Indianola Methodist Episcopal Church.[10] He preached regularly, but spent more time leading the International Student Forum (ISF). The ISF, a joint venture of the YMCA and the Methodist Episcopal Church (MEC), aimed "to bring about a better understanding between nations and races by frank and sincere discussions of world conditions and the exchange of ideas."[11] To that end Song organized ISF performances that showcased the cultures of international students and coordinated conversations about pressing global topics, such as the international peace movement, industry and international relations, the place of women in society, and the scourge of racial prejudice. Song was especially sensitive to racial issues, having endured the condescension and paternalism of Americans who either saw him as a laundryman or, as the OSU dean once expressed it, a "boy" who would go back to China as a leading citizen.[12]

In an effort to bring about improved racial relations, Song organized a World Friendship Banquet at his church for OSU students. He used the occasion to promote equality and thunder against the Jim Crowing he witnessed in the United States. He warned those assembled, "[Racial inequality] is the great stumbling block to democratic civilization and it puts America on the same level with nations that are called heathen here."[13] Through his efforts the Interracial Council formed at OSU, focused especially on promoting friendship

[9] *Ohio Wesleyan Magazine*, April 1929, 187.

[10] Siong Ceh Sung to Dean Gilbert, May 25, 1926, administrative file for Sung Siong Ceh, [aka] John Sung, UTS STM incomplete, 1926, 1926–2003, series 10A, box 4, folder 9, UTS2 Union Records, Burke Library, Union Theological Seminary, New York. Hereafter, this file will be referred to as UTS2.

[11] "Forum Will Discuss World Problems," *Ohio State Lantern*, August 22, 1924.

[12] "America Suffers in Comparison to Oriental Nations," *Ohio State Lantern*, November 3, 1924; "Greater Freedom Attracts Foreign Students to U.S.," *Ohio State Lantern*, December 8, 1924; "Chinese Customs Play Large Part in Celebration of Anniversary," *Ohio State Lantern*, October 15, 1923.

[13] "World Friendship Inter-Racial Group Formed by Forum," *Ohio State Lantern*, February 9, 1925.

between white and black students. He even convinced the ISF, comprised almost entirely of Asians, to pay for some of their American classmates to attend the National Interracial Conference in Cincinnati, Ohio, March 25–29, 1925.[14]

Song was rewarded for all this innovative ministry by getting to attend the YMCA's Lake Geneva Conference later that summer.[15] There he heard YMCA luminaries John Mott, Gu Ziren [T. Z. Koo], and the Christian Socialist J. Stitt Wilson speak about "Christian personality and the social order."[16] Inspired by their vision, Song returned to OSU planning to organize a conference of international students from across the Midwest in the spring of 1926 in order to galvanize them around Jesus' call for peace. Sherwood Eddy, Kirby Paige, and Shi Zhaoji [Alfred Sze] were going to be the keynote speakers.[17] The event failed to materialize, however, possibly because Song was deposed from the ISF presidency by his classmates for so flagrantly turning the organization into a front for "church propaganda."[18] However, Song remained undaunted. His own vision of Christian service so obviously mirrored the YMCA's that upon

[14] "Race Groups Organize to Combat Prejudices," *Ohio State Lantern*, March 12, 1925.

[15] "19 to Represent Ohio State at Y.M. Annual Gathering," *Ohio State Lantern*, May 14, 1925; Archives of the YMCA: Student Division, record group 58, box 79, folder 1024, Special Collections, Yale Divinity School. In his autobiography, Song reported that he went to the Lake Geneva Conference in 1923 after he graduated from OWU, and later biographers have followed Song's dating. However, no external evidence exists for his attendance at the 1923 meeting, whereas a photo has him at the 1925 meeting. It is possible that he attended the conference twice. That would explain Song's date of 1923, though it would not bring consistency to his story. For in his account of the event, which he wrote years later, he claimed he withdrew by himself because he found the conference in 1923 too shallow and liberal. If that were the case, why would he return in 1925? Almost certainly the editorial comment about the shallowness of the summer retreat reflects Song's view in 1933 when he wrote his autobiography and not what he was thinking at the time. Thus, it might be possible that he attended twice, though I am inclined to think he only went once: June 12–22, 1925. See Song, *Wode jianzheng*, 50–51.

[16] Lake Geneva Student Conference, *Lake Geneva Student Conference, June 12–22, 1925* (United States: Young Men's Christian Association, 1925).

[17] "Student Forum Decides to Hold Convention Here," *Ohio State Lantern*, August 19, 1925. Despite Song's aspirations, the conference never happened. See "Two Gospel Teams to Be Sent by Center," *Ohio State Lantern*, December 16, 1925.

[18] "The Postman's Pack: Letters from Our Readers," *Ohio State Lantern*, June 5, 1925.

receiving his Ph.D. from OSU he prepared to become a secretary for the organization in China.[19]

Seminary was the next step. Song recognized that a theological education could act as a finishing school for him, supplementing his scientific credentials with the kind of "practical religious or social work" he would need to assume a leadership role in the YMCA.[20] Union Theological Seminary (UTS) was the obvious choice. His pastor had ties to the school; the New York City chapter of the Chinese Students Christian Association, to which Song belonged, was particularly strong; the seminary was becoming a dense node of Chinese intellectuals; and a number of Union's professors had turned toward China.[21] In fact, Song had orchestrated the visit of UTS' Harry F. Ward to speak to OSU students in a talk entitled "The Challenge of China," a fact which Song reminded the controversial Christian Ethics professor of when he applied to the seminary.[22]

Song needed to mobilize Ward's support and anyone else's he could find. His application was late, and he needed financial assistance. The seminary was initially willing to offer him a one-year Oriental Scholarship that provided students like him, who had already obtained advanced degrees, a $200 stipend to cover his tuition and dormitory fees. But a student does not live on books and a bed alone, so Song reluctantly

[19] "Foreign Student Celebrities Rate Honorary Clubs, Kegs, and Offices," *Ohio State Lantern*, February 10, 1926. Later in his life, Song told audiences that he had multiple options upon graduation. Usually he and others suggested he was trying to decide whether he should teach in a state university, do postdoctoral research in Germany, or be the "Chair of Science in Peking University." Jennie Hughes, ed., *Bethel Heart Throbs of Revival* (Shanghai: Bethel Mission, 1931), 23. Yet the material that exists from the time of his graduation suggests he was exclusively thinking about working for the YMCA.

[20] "Foreign Student Celebrities," *Ohio State Lantern*; Gilbert S. Cox to Harry F. Ward, May 11, 1926, UTS2.

[21] Ka-tong Lim, "The Life and Ministry of John Sung: Sowing Seeds of Vibrant Christianity in Asian Soil" (Ph.D. diss., Asbury Theological Seminary, 2009); *The Chinese Students' Christian Association Year Book: Commemorating the Sixteenth Anniversary of the C.S.C.A. in North America* (New York: CSCA, 1925); Christopher David Sneller, "Let the World Come to Union and Union Go into the World: Union Theological Seminary in the City of New York and the Quest for Indigenous Christianity in Twentieth Century China" (Ph.D. diss., University of London, 2015).

[22] "'Chinese Night' Planned by the International Forum," *Ohio State Lantern*, November 5, 1925; S. C. Sung [Siong Ceh Sung] to Professor Ward, May 11, 1926, UTS2.

applied for the three-year bachelor of divinity program because it would at least allow him to participate in field work, by which he could receive a small income for his services. In the end the seminary offered the bright applicant the best of both worlds. He could begin in September 1926 on a one-year Oriental Scholarship, and the school granted him special permission to perform field work at the Church of All Nations in the Bowery, from which he would receive a small gratuity for his services.[23]

Song seized the opportunity and moved to New York expecting to change the world. "It is the will of our Father that I must utilize my scientific knowledge and experience to discover the fundamental truths underlying both religion and science."[24] Such a breakthrough would burn away the thorns that strangled the current world order, clearing a space for a new social reality to grow. Through him, Song explained on his seminary application, God was going to "'cast fire' upon the present organized system of materialism and imperialism."[25]

Despite his subsequent denials, it was Song's own life that went up in flames in New York. Rollin Walker, one of Song's former professors at OWU, sounded the alarm on February 17, 1927. In a hurriedly scribbled message to Union President Henry Sloane Coffin, Walker indicated that he had received a disturbing note from Song that was "beyond all question the product of a strained and for the moment abnormal mind." He emphasized that Song had never before displayed any signs of mental instability. "But," Walker worried, "something has gone wrong."[26] He enclosed Song's letter to illustrate the point.

Song had drawn a diagram of a vision which Walker, by the command of Christ, was to help him spread throughout the world. The continents and principle countries of the world were depicted as the heart, lungs, liver, stomach, and other vital organs of the body. In North

---

[23] Charles R. Gilbert to Rollin H. Walker, May 19, 1926, UTS2; Siong Ceh Sung to the Dean of Students, May 25, 1926, UTS2; Ella Howard, *Homeless: Poverty and Place in Urban America* (Philadelphia: University of Pennsylvania Press, 2013), 20. She observed that in the 1920s the Bowery Mission "expanded its efforts to 'Americanize the immense foreign population' of the neighborhood through children's programs." Song's assignment was likely to do something similar. He later fondly recalled working with Chinese children during his field assignment. Song, *Wode jianzheng*, 72–73.

[24] Siong Ceh Sung to Charles R. Gilbert, May 25, 1926, UTS2. Gilbert was the secretary to the faculty and the dean of students.

[25] Siong Ceh Sung to Charles R. Gilbert, May 25, 1926, UTS2.

[26] Rollin Walker to Henry Sloane Coffin, February 14, 1927, UTS2.

America there was an arrow pointing to Niagara Falls—"Where the blood of Christ flows." Europe was designated as "The stomach of the race where the word of God is digested." Other pictures were entitled "The Cross" and "The Gross of Man." Song strained to explain the meaning of the enigmatic imagery: "This is the living man and the living cross! The mystery of the Cross! Every body is a cell of the perfect man!"[27] Then, abruptly, the letter ended: "By John Love Riter Ring," introducing for the first time the name "John" by which Song Shangjie would become known to English speakers, and which, Song explained at the bottom of his effervescent letter, was "The name which Christ gives me."[28]

Troubled by what he read, Henry Sloane Coffin ordered Walker Alderton, the assistant director of field work, to investigate. Interviews with students confirmed that Song was speaking about visions seen on his dorm room wall and that he believed himself to be a prophet of a new age. Classmates also noted that Song had uttered premonitions of his death and had asked that his special revelations be published posthumously. Alderton unlocked Song's dorm room and, after leafing through the papers on his desk, confiscated the material as evidence. He had seen enough. Drafts of a laudatory book on the social settlement movement were coherent, but more recent "outlines of books" veered toward incomprehension.[29] For example:

PEPPY SUNG[30]

I	Auditing course (difficulty in studying)
II	Man in Maine (spirit calls)
III	Walked down a street
IV	Most interesting courses

---

[27] Walker M. Alderton to Charles I. Lambert, February 17, 1927, UTS2. Song's actual letter to Rollin Walker is no longer extant. It is reproduced in a letter sent to Charles I. Lambert.

[28] Walker M. Alderton to Charles I. Lambert, February 17, 1927, UTS2. In Chinese, Song continued to use his given name, though he would occasionally tell an audience that his name, "according to the flesh, is Song Shangjie, but according to the Spirit, Yuehan [John]." Song Shangjie, "Song Shangjie boshi geren jianzheng [The Testimony of Dr. Song Shangjie]," as recorded by Liao Guotian, afternoon, April 2, 1931, *Shengjie zhinan yuekan [Guide to Holiness]* 3, no. 6 (June 1931): 26.

[29] Assistant Director of Field Work to Dr. Charles I. Lambert, February 17, 1927, UTS2.

[30] Song Shangjie had earned the nickname "Peppy" in college, and he spelled his family name "Sung." This outline refers to himself.

V   Holy ground—locked room
VI   5 o'clock—darkness—faces showing themselves
VII   Write more
VIII Experience with newspaper
        12
        16
        3—to—1
IX   Go round the world
X   Sore here-here-here-4 o'clock[31]

Abnormality was easy to recognize, but somewhat more difficult to explain. Alderton reached for the thin Freudian language he had at his disposal and sent word that Song's writings were "shot through with undoubted sex symbolism," recommending that Union bring in a psychiatrist immediately.[32]

Dr. Charles Lambert hurried to Union. He examined the collected evidence, met Song in an arranged interview, and determined that the student needed to be removed from the seminary. Song initially resisted the suggestion, but Lambert and Professor A. L. Swift Jr. insisted. Song finally signed a self-admittance form to the Bloomingdale Hospital in White Plains, New York, at which time President Coffin was duly notified.[33]

---

[31] Assistant Director of Field Work to Dr. Charles I. Lambert, February 17, 1927, UTS2.

[32] Assistant Director of Field Work to Dr. Charles I. Lambert, February 17, 1927, UTS2.

[33] Walker M. Alderton to Charles C. Webber, July 6, 1927, UTS2. Not long before, the state of New York had changed the law so that someone could enter an asylum "voluntarily." In the 1926 "Annual Report of the Medical Director at Bloomingdale Hospital," this legal provision is explained: "The statute permitting mentally and nervously sick persons to voluntarily enter a hospital for treatment is a most humane provision and has undoubtedly saved from severe and lasting psychosis many persons who less than 20 years ago could not have received hospital treatment no matter how much they had desired it, until they had satisfied a court that they were sick and in need of such treatment. The policy that has been followed has been to resort to legal restriction only when it was clearly required to protect the patient and to furnish legal authority for detention that could not properly be dispensed with." Voluntary admission, therefore, meant bypassing the legal system. It did not mean the patient was free to leave on his or her own volition. According to the archivist of Bloomingdale Hospital, "We believe that a voluntary patient had to be discharged from the hospital by the psychiatric staff." See the Society of the New York Hospital, "Annual Report of the Medical Director

That evening Coffin authorized payment for the costs of Song's hospitalization from the seminary's emergency fund, some sixty dollars per week. Soon thereafter, he sent letters to Song's family in China, his pastor in Ohio, and Rollin Walker, who had first alerted him that trouble was brewing. Coffin explained that Song was now in an asylum and, while the diagnosis was as yet uncertain, assured them that the patient was in no physical danger and the hospital staff was committed to giving him every attention.[34]

If Song was troubled by the transition, he made no mention of it in his diary. He was too busy recording the revelations that ambushed him almost everywhere he looked. God, he marveled, sent him personal messages. They appeared in the *New York Times* crossword puzzles, poems in the *Literary Digest*, and articles in the *National Geographic*. God used them to commission Song to create a "United States of the World," to warn him that Satan was even now descending to the earth to trouble both himself and Jesus, and to explain that he would need to stay in the asylum for 33 days just as Jesus had been on the earth for 33 years.[35] Other people, Song smirked, missed these coded messages: "[I]t seems to us that we alone understand the mystical phrases of these unconsciously written poem[s]."[36] No one else recognized that the letter *b* had a special meaning or that the weaving in the rug stood for holiness.[37] Joy came in seeing past the surface of things, penetrating to the divine secrets that infused even the most mundane objects.

Just a little more than two weeks after being hospitalized, Song had his most significant breakthrough yet. As he perused the newspaper advertisements one evening, he was inspired to huddle over his diary and pen his own plug:

---

of Bloomingdale Hospital, White Plains, New York," New York: Society of the New York Hospital, 1926, Medical Center Archives of New York-Presbyterian/ Weill Cornell; Ronald Carroll, email message to author, February 23, 2010; A. L. Swift Jr. to Henry Sloane Coffin, February 17, 1927, UTS2.

[34] Henry Sloane Coffin to Charles Lambert, February 17, 1927, UTS2; Henry Sloane Coffin to Rollin Walker, February 23, 1927, UTS2; Henry Sloane Coffin to Gilbert Cox, March 15, 1927, UTS2; Henry Sloane Coffin to Rev. H. L. Sung, March 15, 1927, UTS2.

[35] Song Shangjie Diary, February 18 and February 19, 1927, John Song Papers, record group 263, Yale Divinity School, New Haven, Conn. Hereafter referred to as YDS.

[36] Song Shangjie Diary, February 21, 1927, YDS.

[37] Song Shangjie Diary, February 22, 1927, YDS.

Everyman's Guide to Radio

Four volumes in one contains the world's knowledge of radio. Contributed to us by the world's leading radio scientists, without question, the most comprehensive, most interesting and absorbing, and the most complete radio book yet published in any country. It is impossible to give comparison because comparisons do not exist. One must read Mark on the subject of "beamed transmission"; the late Matthew on "waves"; Luke on coils, or John on "Vacuum tubes" before the significance of these writings of the masters of the art can be fully appreciated.[38]

Song's advertisement went on to describe how the Gospels' authors provided exact instructions on receivers, transmitters, coils, and loudspeakers. It even finished with a condensed table of contents before urging the reader to purchase the remarkable set.

The lengthy promotional piece was lucid and first reads like a comedic parody of the genre. But Song was terribly serious. He concluded, "Now I must get busy to read Mark to understand all things concerning the radio."[39] Song became obsessed with the idea that each of the four Gospels contained hidden radio schematics. From dawn until the nurses forced him to bed at the end of each day, he feverishly labored to translate each and every word in the Gospel of Mark by using a dictionary Jesus gave him.[40] The task was tedious and all-consuming. It required every single word in a chapter be grouped in alphabetical order: again, alone, are, argue, at; before, began, boat, but, etc. Then he had to finesse a translation. Was the heavenly meaning of "but" "bought" or "big task" in this context?[41] For weeks his answers were plotted on a graph, bit by bit revealing a radio design that Song, exhausted but triumphant, pointed to as capable of catching the heavenly messages God was transmitting (fig. 1.1).

Initially, what he heard was soporific: "The feast of the Eternal is Eternal; The Eternal one gives you the insight; The Eternal one gives you new life; The spirit is Eternal," and so forth—hundreds and hundreds of lines progressing in a minimalist fashion from one thought to the next.[42] But about a week into the experiment Song recorded something new:

[38] Song Shangjie Diary, March 8, 1927, YDS.
[39] Song Shangjie Diary, March 8, 1927, YDS.
[40] Song Shangjie Diary, March 9, 1927, YDS.
[41] Song Shangjie Diary, March 10, 1927, YDS.
[42] Song Shangjie Diary, March 12, 1927, YDS.

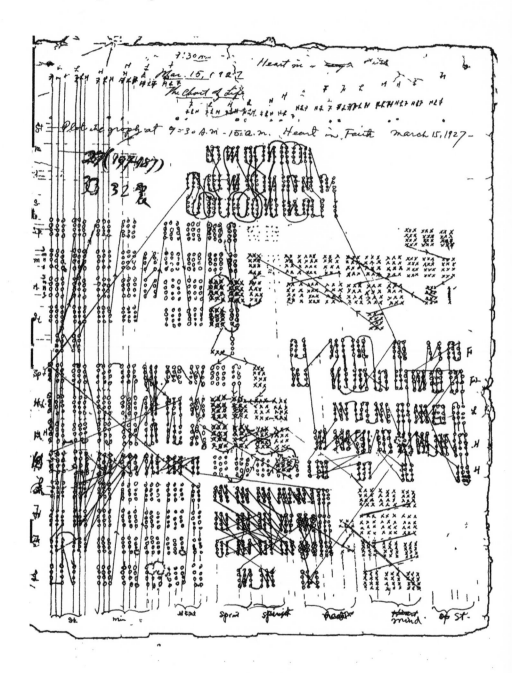

FIG. 1.1

"Mother scolds us for our non-confidence and care and we ask her love and she forgives us . . . it is the great news!"[43]

Song, who never lacked for religious intensity, shifted his zeal to this good news of the Mother, or the Mothers: Mary, the Mother of Jesus; Mary Magdalene, the Mother of Christ; and Mary of Susanna, the Mother of Jesus Christ. This new salvific Trinity eclipsed God the Father, the Son, and the Holy Spirit. It was the Mother "who so loved the world that she gives her only begotten son to them and whosoever believes in him shall have the everlasting life and the sacred love of Mother."[44] To her did Song address his prayers, and she was the one who could forgive sins. Yet this Mother was more than the feminization of the Christian Trinity, for the Mother revealed to Song "the sheer follies of the Bible" and pointed out the failures of Jesus Christ.[45]

Secrets created a profound intimacy between Song and the Mother. For example, he admitted that he lied to the Mother when he told her that he did not want to go to the hospital dance. She, in turn, confided in him her plans to strike the United States with an earthquake on June 21, in which "1/10th of the people will be quaked off."[46] The less they hid things from one another, the more their affection grew. "We love each other so much we hate to quit kissing," Song confessed to his diary.[47] Eventually, before "zeal for mother has almost burnt us up," the two wed.[48] Song described the ceremony in his journal: "Then we have a marriage contract. . . . he trusts his wife as the temporary God of All—the voices of the dead are happy because God and Goddess knows [sic] their pain and suffering. We are immediately engaged and marry in the evening." The service happened in Song's hospital room in the presence of Mary Magdalene, Mary Clopas, and seven thousand chosen ones who were designated as honorary queens. Song and the Mother made pledges of fidelity to one another, celebrating that now, "They

[43] Song Shangjie Diary, March 18, 1927, YDS.

[44] Song Shangjie Diary, March 18, April 2, and August 8, 1927, YDS. It is dangerous to try to make sense out of non-sense, but the context in which Song inserts this modified version of John 3:16 does make it sound like Song identified himself as the only begotten son.

[45] Song Shangjie Diary, April 2, 1927, YDS.

[46] Song Shangjie Diary, April 1 and April 3, 1927, YDS. Despite the Mother's warning, the United States suffered no major earthquake on June 21, 1927.

[47] Song Shangjie Diary, April 3, 1927, YDS.

[48] Song Shangjie Diary, March 31, 1927, YDS.

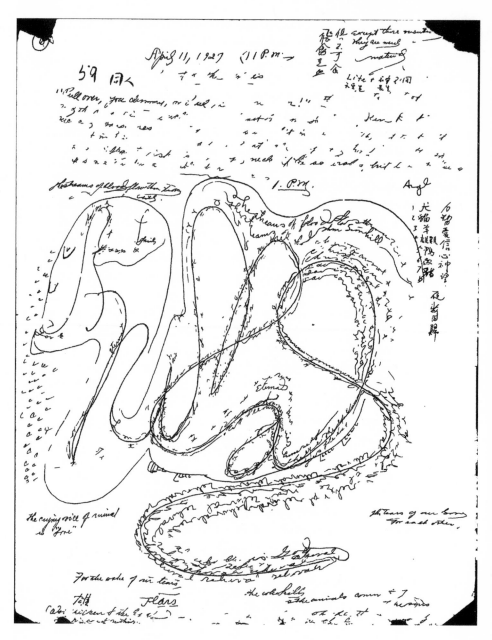

FIG. 1.2

alone are the creators." They consummated the ceremony with a "holy kiss and holy union."[49] Intimate communion was theirs at last.

Communication, on the other hand, suffered. Song found it difficult to write coherently after his marriage to a supernatural being. In subsequent days his thoughts were ever more disordered, incomplete, or disjointed. Finally, he largely abandoned words altogether for what he described as "sky writing."[50] Florid pictures became the vehicle by which he tried to express his spiritual ecstasies (fig. 1.2).

Meanwhile, ten weeks into Song's hospitalization, President Henry Sloane Coffin faced the grim prospect that Union's Oriental Scholar might require permanent care. At the end of April, the doctors at Bloomingdale were still reluctant to advance a diagnosis, the exact nature of Song's malady eluding definition. Yet in the meantime, Union's emergency fund had been tapped for more than $700 and was virtually depleted. Having paid for the equivalent of two new automobiles, the seminary had no more money to offer, but insofar as Song had no family able to claim responsibility for him, it fell to UTS to decide about treatment. With sensitivity toward the escalating tension over immigrants in the United States, Coffin refused to move Song to a public hospital, convinced he would be deported immediately. Besides, Coffin wrote, "To make any change at present would, according to his physicians, be deleterious to his well being."[51] Since Song needed to remain in Bloomingdale, Coffin worked energetically to solve the financial shortfall. On Friday, April 22, he wrote to Rollin Walker explaining the situation and expressed hope that many at OWU, who knew Song better than those at UTS, might contribute generously to his care. On the same day, Coffin also sent letters to Halter Jennings and Edward Sheldon, directors at Bloomingdale, explaining that Union's emergency fund had been emptied and asking for a reduction of their fees for Song's treatment.[52]

Song apparently weighed heavily on Coffin's mind, for that Sunday, April 24, Song's unresolved case seemingly guided Coffin in the selection of his sermon. Electing to preach from an old, familiar manuscript, Coffin pulled from his file a homily based on Deuteronomy 33:13, "The

---

[49] Song Shangjie Diary, April 4, 1927, YDS.

[50] Song Shangjie Diary, April 9, 1927, YDS.

[51] Henry Sloane Coffin to Rollin Walker, April 22, 1927, UTS2.

[52] Henry Sloane Coffin to Halter Jennings, Esq., April 22, 1927, UTS2. Henry Sloane Coffin to Edward W. Sheldon, Esq., April 22, 1927, UTS2.

Deep that Coucheth Beneath." Speaking at Union College in Schenect-ady in the morning and Albany First Presbyterian Church in the eve-ning, Coffin specifically addressed psychosis. "It will not do," he warned the assembly, "to disregard the investigations of painstaking explorers of the depths of our human nature," adding, "Any light which can be thrown upon insanity and 'break-downs' . . . is welcome." He continued, "It makes little difference whether you label the anarchic elements [of the mind] with 'a legion of demons' or 'brute instincts and complexes.' Labels change with fashions of thought. It is all-important that a man deranged by disorganizing factors—passions, phobias, fears—should face the unifying and redeeming Son of God."[53]

Back at Union the following day, president Coffin sent a brief note to Song at the urging of the hospital staff. It echoed the optimistic tone of his sermon and reminded the patient "that we will always have a place for you when you are well enough to work again."[54] Coffin was eager to put the awkward and expensive situation behind him.

Song, on the other hand, was busy complicating the matter. For instance, during that last week in April, Rollin Walker sent word to Coffin confessing, "I received one or two very sane letters from Mr. Sung, but a week or so ago I received a most distressingly abnormal one which made my heart sink."[55] Walker enclosed one hundred dollars of his own money for Song's care, elegantly expressing his own assessment of the situation. At the end of that week Coffin, too, received a note from Song. The letter was visually astonishing—the script was excessively ornate, completely different from his previous handwriting—and the message unclear:

> Our dear president Coffin:—
>
> Spiritually in deepest gratitude to your spiritual love and mystical sym-pathy we pen this epistle of love as our token of gratitude.
>
> Our past misunderstanding has created a spiritual gulf between us. We must learn to forgive each other and follow the wisdom of turtle.
>
> U.T.S. is the best theological seminary in which many prophets are playing the music of love dawning in the spiritual air. Our past spiritual

[53] Henry Sloane Coffin, "Deuteronomy 33:13," Henry Sloane Coffin Collection, Series 2: Sermons, Addresses, Lecture Notes, 1903–1962, box 9, folder 127, Burke Library, Union Theological Seminary, New York.

[54] Henry Sloane Coffin to Liong C. Sung, April 25, 1927, UTS2. See also Henry Sloane Coffin to Rollin Walker, April 22, 1927, UTS2.

[55] Rollin Walker to Henry Sloane Coffin, April 27, 1927, UTS2.

journeys owe mountains of love to spiritual showers of some of your hard fighting prophets.

Trust you will understand desert experiences and say not 'spiritually drunken.'

Thru your love and cooperation we humbly expect to be spiritual [joined?] and mentally tried in our beloved U.T.S. for a period of two years.[56]

The letter continued in a similar vein for some time before mysteriously ending on a conspiratorial note. "Please keep this letter in secret! Silence is the best spiritual cure!"[57]

Song, himself, largely maintained a self-imposed silence in his journal through the rest of the spring, but when he cracked H. G. Wells' massive *Outline of History* in the summer, he once again reached for a pen to record his discoveries. Before Song had even reached the bottom of the tome's first page, he saw things clearly: "[H]istory is the eternal diary" in which divine mysteries were secreted away.[58] In rapturous delight, he took copious notes. Someone had to explain what God had been doing. Wells' book had opened by describing the importance of the star closest to the earth. To put the sun in perspective he had explained that (a) the distance between the earth and the sun was enormous—a bullet would have to travel seven years without losing any speed to reach the sun if shot from the earth; (b) the sun dwarfed the earth—if the earth was an inch in diameter, then the sun would be nine feet across; and (c) the sun spins on its axis, completing a rotation every twenty-five days.[59] Those were the facts, but therein, Song concluded, lay also the mysteries: "It takes seven spirits to explode the sun. The human is one inch in diameter (loyalty) while the sun is nine feet in diameter in comparison (love). Christ commences the actuality at the age of 25."[60] All of history dripped with spiritual significance, Song reiterated. One only needed eyes to see it.

The hospital staff, apparently, were blind to his cabalistic revelations. They were busy seeking the cause of his psychotic break with reality. Some of the doctors suspected he suffered from a "paranoid condition," perhaps "paranoid dementia praecox"—now known as

[56] Siong Ceh Sung to Henry Sloane Coffin, April 27, 1927, UTS2.
[57] Siong Ceh Sung to Henry Sloane Coffin, April 27, 1927, UTS2.
[58] Song Shangjie Diary, August 4, 1927, YDS.
[59] H. G. Wells, *Outline of History* (New York: Macmillan, 1920), 1.
[60] Song Shangjie Diary, August 4, 1927, YDS.

paranoid schizophrenia.[61] At twenty-five years old, Song fit within the standard age range for the onset of schizophrenia, and his vivid description of visions and audible voices, as well as the disordered logic of his book outlines, letters, and diaries, were standard symptoms. Others suggested failed romance as the cause of Song's collapse. William Alderton, the first person at UTS to investigate the reports that Song was acting strangely, offered this interpretation at the very beginning. He reported on February 17, 1927, that he had reason to believe Song experienced "a great emotional shock, and that a recent love affair has not eventuated happily for him."[62] A few months later, he repeated the story of the jilted lover, but told it with less conviction. As best he could put it together, Song's "affair of the heart with a Chinese young lady in this country" was broken off sometime before he moved to New York.[63] As the precipitating event was pushed further into the past, its explanatory power diminished.[64] A third interpretation was that Song had a crisis of faith because he was unable to integrate science and religion. A number of the hospital staff gravitated to this conclusion.[65] They believed that "Dr. Sung had been advancing in his grasp of the scientific problems involved in chemical research in rather an astonishing degree, but that he had not made any progress in re-shaping his religious or theological convictions accordingly."[66] They argued that the road to stability for Song lay in "cutting the Gordian knot of his religious-social-vocational complex by making a clean break and going to work in a hospital in China as a consulting or research chemist."[67]

---

[61] Staff Conference Minutes, April 28, 1927, Staff Records (Cases), vol. 5, Bloomingdale Hospital, 1926–1936, Medical Center Archives of New York-Presbyterian/Weill Cornell.

[62] William M. Alderton to Charles I. Lambert, February 17, 1927, UTS2.

[63] William M. Alderton to Rev. Charles G. Webber, July 6, 1927, UTS2.

[64] Although Alderton left the explanation of a broken heart behind, it still persists in the literature about Song. Leslie Lyall, for example, sees Song's failed romance as a reason for why he sank into depression and a contributing factor to his hospitalization. Leslie T. Lyall, *A Biography of John Sung* (Singapore: Genesis Books, 2004), 40.

[65] This explanation also has lived on in more recent literature. See, for example, Daniel H. Bays, "The Growth of Independent Christianity in China, 1900–1937," in *Christianity in China: From the Eighteenth Century to the Present*, ed. Daniel H. Bays (Stanford: Stanford University Press, 1996), 315.

[66] William M. Alderton to Rev. Charles G. Webber, July 6, 1927, UTS2.

[67] William M. Alderton to Rev. Charles G. Webber, July 6, 1927, UTS2.

Whatever the diagnosis or the precipitating event, the entire staff recognized that Song was very troubled internally as well as a trouble to others. The medical team had to ban him from the basket-weaving class because he disturbed other patients. The frenetic pace at which he wove and periodically tore apart baskets upset those seeking repose.[68] Song was also belligerent with the nurses, battling with them to stay up late or rise early. Repeated conflicts with the staff eventually inspired Song to call them all devils, and he finally tried to escape their imprisoning hell. Song failed to get far on June 23, 1927; dogs tracked him down. The event, however, was pivotal. Ruminating on his capture, Song concluded he needed to change tactics: "The more we are patient, the more we love the people with our sincerity and kindness . . . the more we will win the final success. We must be cheerful and happy. . . . We must play on them instead of being played by them."[69]

Whether the strategy to reform his behavior worked or not, two months after his attempted escape Song was released from the hospital. On August 30, 1927, the note in the discharge book confirmed Song's success in modifying his attitude: "This patient has been much more cheerful, cooperative, and reasonable during the last several weeks."[70] But more than good behavior was at work. For one thing, Song had taken to writing in Chinese as a way to prevent the doctors from glimpsing what was going on in his mind. The decision was calculated and cunning, effectively masking from the doctors his magical thinking and the fact that he was still very much enamored with *shenmu*, the Queen Mother.[71] More important still, Song had become a financial drain on the hospital. President Coffin had reached a gentlemen's agreement with the asylum back in May. Coffin gave Bloomingdale Rollin Walker's one hundred dollars and the final one hundred dollars from UTS' emergency fund. That would cover one more month of residency. If Song needed additional care after that, then the asylum would assume the costs.[72] By the end of August 1927, Bloomingdale had, in fact, borne the costs of Song's medical care for three months. Hospital administrators, therefore, must have viewed the visit of the Reverend Wilbur Fowler as propitious.

[68] Song Shangjie Diary, March 5, 1927, YDS.

[69] Song Shangjie Diary, June 23, 1927, YDS.

[70] Discharge Book, vol. 2, Bloomingdale Hospital, 1921–1933, Medical Center Archives of New York-Presbyterian/Weill Cornell.

[71] Song Shangjie Diary, August 22, 1927, YDS.

[72] Mortimer W. Raynor to Henry Sloane Coffin, May 3, 1927, UTS2.

The pastor for Methodist students at OSU was passing through New York in late August 1927 and paid a visit to one of his distributed flock. Fowler discovered that the hospital was not only willing but even eager to release the young man to his care. Thus, the hospital righted its financial ledger, and Song achieved what he hoped for: unfettered freedom to pursue his mystical studies.

Immediately upon his release, Song sent jubilant word to UTS and announced his intention to resume his education when the semester began in a few weeks. "President Coffin has promised me to return to seminary for pursuing my theological study as soon as I am well. Now I am in perfect good health and decide to take up my study again next fall. Will you kindly reserve a room for me!"[73] When the academic dean notified the president of Song's plans, Coffin distanced himself from his earlier letter that had invited Song to return. "Last winter he became oppressed with the idea that we wanted to be rid of him. So at the suggestion of his physicians I wrote him a cheering letter from which he doubtless has derived the idea that we want him back."[74] Coffin instructed the dean to deny Song readmittance, stating, "We have put out enough money on Song, and we do not want to risk another breakdown."[75] The dean dutifully notified the enthusiastic student that he could not return to UTS.

Writing on Song's behalf, Fowler notified the seminary that because of its decision Song would soon have to return to China. He complained that Song was in fact "quite well and normal" and was "trying to believe in the sincerity and the Christianity of his friends who sent him to the Hospital." He appealed to UTS to give "Dr. Sung a great deal of thought and consideration to make up for what he has suffered." Fowler added that Song could not locate several valuable items, specifically two silk scarves and two Greek letter keys—the latter being symbols of his academic achievements. He insisted that the Phi Beta Kappa and Sigma Xi keys be recovered and sent to Song, or "duplicates of the same."[76] In Fowler's mind, it was a meager settlement for the egregious treatment Song had suffered at the seminary's hands.

In response, Henry Sloane Coffin sent a personal check for fifteen dollars to have the keys replaced, but his tone was not conciliatory.

---

[73] S. C. Sung to Dean of Union Theological Seminary, [received] September 1, 1927, UTS2.

[74] Henry Sloane Coffin to Dr. Gillet, September 4, 1927, UTS2.

[75] Henry Sloane Coffin to Dr. Gillet, September 4, 1927, UTS2.

[76] Wilbur H. Fowler to Henry Sloane Coffin, September 24, 1927, UTS2.

He chastised Fowler for inferring that Union had acted unfairly toward Song, explained the thoroughness by which UTS had him diagnosed, and reminded him of the cost for treatment assumed by the seminary.[77] In his mind, Union was the victim, not the victimizer, having absorbed the heavy cost of Song's mental care.

Thus ended Song's time in America. He made his way to Seattle, boarded a ship, and returned to China as a refugee fleeing the chaos of his dissolution in New York. The shameful experience was hardly the material for a revivalist's origin story, unless, of course, what happened in New York was a description of how far Song had fallen, a story of God's ability to restore someone so completely broken. Yet Song never described it that way. He would build his career on something grander, and certainly much bolder. He did not know it at the time, but Song sailed back to China poised to announce that what happened at Union and the 193 days he spent in the hospital were not the destruction of his life, but precisely what made him New.

---

[77] Henry Sloane Coffin to Wilbur H. Fowler, September 28, 1927, UTS2.

2

A New Man

The man who returned to China was a different person. When Song Shangjie stepped off the ship in November 1927, he was not wearing the traditional Chinese gown that he had set off in; he was now bedecked in a Western suit and tie. On the instruction of the Mother, his glasses were gone and never reappeared in his life.[1] He had also aged significantly. Two unsuccessful surgeries in the United States on an anal fistula had depleted the returning scholar; he was weaker now, even if that was masked by the ten pounds he had put on his slender 5'4" frame.[2] Song came back to China a changed man, if not yet a modern New Man.

Upon arrival he faced an immediate challenge. His family believed him unwell. Henry Sloane Coffin had sent a letter to his father explaining that his son "had a mental disturbance" and that he had "various delusions, taking the form of visions and the like, and we feel he needs complete mental rest."[3] The account was not detailed, but supplied

[1] Without his glasses Song's eyes struggled to focus. Throughout his subsequent career, he was repeatedly told that his eyes looked strange and that they frightened people. Song Shangjie, April 18, 1934, Song Shangjie Diaries, Trinity Theological College, Singapore. Henceforth this location will be referred to as SSD, TTC. See also Ka-tong Lim, "The Life and Ministry of John Sung: Sowing Seeds of Vibrant Christianity in Asian Soil" (Ph.D. diss., Asbury Theological Seminary, 2009), 234.

[2] "Siong-Ceh Sang," 1926, National Archives Arrival Investigation Case Files, 1884–1944, San Francisco Records, Records of the Immigration and Naturalization Service, record group 85, San Francisco, Calif.

[3] Henry Sloane Coffin to H. L. Sung, March 15, 1927, administrative file for Sung Siong Ceh, [aka] John Sung, UTS STM incomplete, 1926, 1926–2003, series 10A, box 4, folder 9, UTS2 Union Records, Burke Library, Union Theological Seminary, New York. Hereafter, this file will be referred to as UTS2.

enough information to raise concerns. Song complained that his family scrutinized his speech and behavior for any signs of derangement. They also forced him to wed Yu Jinhua immediately, perhaps anxious he consummate the arranged marriage before rumors reached the bride's family.[4]

Word had already reached the missionary community. Although Song possessed a Ph.D. in chemistry from an American university, a diploma highly prized in a nation where intellectuals and politicians were promoting that Western science would be the source of China's salvation, the disgrace of hospitalization ran so deep he could not secure a job. Even the Methodist High School rebuffed him, leaving Song a disappointment and burden to his family when he failed to assume the expenses of his brother's education as planned.[5]

Discouraged and confused, Song sought out a local temple to cast lots and seek divine direction. Fittingly, among the twelve hundred deities honored in Xinghua [Hinghwa], he selected a temple dedicated to Guanyin, a popular bodhisattva who perfectly fused his eclectic religious beliefs.[6] Guanyin was sometimes conflated with *shenmu*, the Buddhist Queen Mother of the West; hence she could go by the same name that Song used to address the Mother when he wrote in Chinese. Guanyin also had a history of being merged with the mother of Jesus and thereby could preserve his devotion to Mary.[7] Guanyin harmonized multiple symbolic systems for Song, but she failed to provide any resolution to his underlying conundrum: How was he to escape the stigma of his hospitalization and the assumption that he was crazy?

REVERSAL

Song never revealed how it happened. Despite meticulous, even obsessive journaling, he never narrated, reflected upon, or interpreted any event in China as a kind of breakthrough, a turnaround, or the start of

---

[4] Song Shangjie, *Wode jianzheng* [*My Testimony*] (1933; repr., Hong Kong: Bellman House, 1991), 94; Song Shangjie, November 14, 1927, SSD, TTC.

[5] Song, *Wode jianzheng*, 94.

[6] Kenneth Dean and Zheng Zhenman, *Ritual Alliances of the Putian Plain*, vol. 1, *Historical Introduction to the Return of the Gods* (Leiden: Brill, 2010).

[7] Yu Chun-fang, *Kuan-yin: The Transformation of Avalokitesvara* (New York: Columbia University Press, 2001), 41; Eriberto Lozada, *God Aboveground: Catholic Church, Postsocialist State, and Transnational Processes in a Chinese Village* (Stanford: Stanford University Press, 2001), 32.

something new. The most dramatic change in his life went uncommented upon, maybe even unnoticed. It requires other clues to put together how the chaos of Song's insanity was turned into a compelling story of conversion.

To begin, China was polarized in 1927. The country was divided both by recent political clashes and theological controversies. In 1926 Jiang Jieshi [Chiang Kai-shek] had launched the Northern Expedition, a military effort to reunite the country which had been fragmented by battling warlords. As the Generalissimo's soldiers entered Nanjing in March 1927, some looted foreign properties and, in their excess, killed seven foreigners. Jiang attempted to mollify the outcry of foreign governments and the conservative members of his own party by blaming the events on radicals. He even went so far as to dissolve his political coalition with the Communists, hunt down leftists, and violently purge them from the ranks. Still, anxiety about a new wave of anti-foreign sentiment swept through China, and most mission executives followed consular advice to evacuate their missionaries from the Chinese interior in the spring of 1927. At that point about 5,000 of the roughly 8,300 missionaries serving in China returned to the United States or Europe.[8] Almost all who remained in China huddled together in the foreign enclaves of a few treaty port cities, eyeing one another suspiciously, aggrieved as they were by the modernist-fundamentalist controversy that had just split Western missions. The China Inland Mission (CIM)—the largest mission organization in the country with close to 1,000 missionaries—had withdrawn from the National Christian Council (NCC) in 1926. Although a charter member, the CIM had become increasingly uncomfortable as the NCC printed literature sympathetic to liberal theology and invited social gospel spokesmen to make evangelistic tours through China. Fearing that people might interpret membership as endorsement of the NCC's modernist streak, mission executives ordered the CIM to withdraw from the council. The fallout was extensive. Other mission boards, which were likewise conservative, were suddenly vulnerable. How could they stay in the NCC after the largest conservative mission body had gone? Rancorously and with animosity on both sides, one conservative group after

---

[8]   William Hockman, "Missionary Department," *Moody Bible Institute Monthly* 28 (November 1927): 110. Hockman explains that 5,000 missionaries returned to the United States or Europe, 300 went to Japan, 2,500 sought safety in foreign enclaves in port cities, while 500 missionaries remained at their posts.

another withdrew from the NCC in 1926 and 1927, undermining the purpose of the organization and visibly leaving Protestant Christianity in China freshly and deeply divided.[9]

In that polarized and overheated environment a new explanation of Song's expulsion from Union materialized. It was a collaborative work, forged between two people whose separate goals and desires interacted to construct a complementary, though not necessarily identical, account of reality.[10] Song and the Methodist Episcopal missionary W. B. Cole developed a mutually useful depiction of what happened at UTS. Cole was a missionary in the Xinghua Conference, where Song's father ministered. When most of his missionary co-workers withdrew to a treaty port or returned home in 1927, Cole remained ensconced at a Methodist school for boys, wielding influence over the Methodist education system in which Song still hoped to gain employment.[11] By virtue of Cole's position, Song was inevitably drawn into contact with the missionary—and more importantly—with his fundamentalism, which at that time was in the ascendancy in conference politics due to the absence of Cole's modernist missionary colleagues.[12] Between them

[9] For a full exploration of the controversy, see Kevin Xiyi Yao, *The Fundamentalist Movement among Protestant Missionaries in China, 1920–1937* (Lanham, Md.: University Press of America, 2003), 183–230.

[10] Michael E. Harkin, introduction to *Reassessing Revitalization Movements: Perspectives from North America and the Pacific Islands*, ed. Michael E. Harkin (Lincoln: University of Nebraska Press, 2004), xxvi.

[11] F. Stanley Carson to Dr. Gamewell, September 27, 1927, in United Methodist Church (U.S.), *Missionary Files: Methodist Church, 1912–1949* (Wilmington, Del.: Scholarly Resources), roll 74. Hereafter, this location will be referred to as UMC. See also Song, *Wode jianzheng*, 94–95.

[12] See for example Elizabeth F. Brewster to Dr. Cartwright, April 30, 1929, roll 7, UMC; W. B. Cole to Frank T. Cartwright, April 19, 1929, roll 75, UMC; Student Club in Foochow, "A Bird's Eye View on the Religious Condition in Sienyu Religious Region," unpublished report, roll 74, UMC. Once the modernist missionaries had evacuated the Xinghua Conference, they found it very difficult to return. Apparently under the influence of Cole, a member of the fundamentalist Bible Union, Xinghua churches were reluctant to have them back. George Hollister, for instance, who had to stay at OWU, was not welcomed back to China for quite some time. His desire to return to the Xinghua Conference may have been hindered, in part, because the book he published in Chinese just before his evacuation used the historical-critical method to interpret the Hexateuch: "[T]he first six books of the Old Testament . . . which disturb faith, which create doubt, [and] which cause most difficulty in preventing non-Christians from understanding the purpose of the Church." Although Hollister intended to help answer some

a symbiotic narrative evolved that was narrowed by their separate, but nevertheless compatible, aims. The first report of Song Shangjie in China sent to the United States was penned by the hand of W. B. Cole, but the voice was no less Song's:

> [Song] decided to go to Union Theological Seminary, New York and study theology. . . . While at Union during private Bible Study and prayer the Spirit flooded his soul with a new light. The Bible became a new book. He spent hours reading it. . . .
>
> His experience turned him back from modernistic paths to a renewed faith in the Bible and its message. He threw aside all of his science as a help to his faith and turned to his new and recent experiences. Soon it was whispered around in the school that he claimed to have had a vision. . . . Union decided he was insane so they got him to a hospital on the pretext that he was going there sight seeing. . . . He decided that his prison was meant by the Lord to be "Paul's Arabia." So he settled down to Bible Study and prayer going carefully thru the Bible three times.
>
> Rescued by some friends he returned to Hinghwa. . . . Some of us in our talking with him and in our listening to his preaching have tried in vain to detect anything that borders on insanity. If this remarkable young man is insane then may more of our preachers here get it![13]

When the events were thus recorded, Cole and Song both gained. W. B. Cole could use Song's experience at UTS to lampoon his modernist enemies. Song could capitalize on Cole's fundamentalism to speak freely about supernatural experiences in New York, though now denuded of the miraculous secrets in the *New York Times*, the heavenly radio messages, his marriage to the Mother, or the like. Song understood that with Cole such things could not be the focal point of his transformation. In his present context a different explanation was required: Song had encountered the God made known in Jesus Christ at Union Theological Seminary, and he was rejected because of it.

When framed that way, Song's expulsion from Union became part of the same conflict that divided Protestants in China, exploiting prejudices

---

of the difficult questions posed by anti-Christian propaganda, his confession in the preface that "[t]ruth has more than one facet" and that "the viewpoint of the ancient writers differed from ours, [and] certain phases of truth which appeared important to them, may seem to differ radically from views we hold and consider important" would have made him a suspect character in the midst of the fundamentalist-modernist debate. George Hollister, "Translation of Preface," roll 76, UMC.

[13] W. B. Cole to the Berwyn M. E. Church, February 10, 1928, UTS2.

that lingered after the breakup of the NCC. Song was just another victim of theological liberals running roughshod over fundamentalists. The story was powerful because, in the contentious context of China, Union—the flagship seminary of theological modernism—could be drawn into binary opposition to Song (UTS/modernism/bad—Song/fundamentalism/good). Such a mythic narrative framework easily emerged from a divided Christian community and allowed Song to reverse the polarities of suspicion about his mental state. Among fundamentalists at least, if any party in this new story was deluded, it was Union.

Embraced for and empowered by this strategically worded testimony of theological conflict, Song became a schoolteacher for the Xinghua Methodist Church in the spring of 1928. By that fall, the conference hired him as a full-time evangelist. Unemployment was no longer a problem. Song's newly constructed testimony had integrated him into a new Christian community that was beginning to take shape in China. He now had an open door among fundamentalists.

REBUTTAL

News that Song was saying he had a life-changing, life-enhancing experience at UTS initially bemused the seminary. When a concerned friend forwarded a copy of W. B. Cole's letter to Harry F. Ward, Ward was dismissive. The seminary needed no defense: "I do not know personally the last chapter in Song's experience here, but I do know that 'Union never decided he was insane.' Expert medical opinion advised that he go to Bloomingdale for treatment."[14] From Ward's perspective, what more could a person want? Religion had properly deferred to science's domain.

Some in the faculty may have recognized that Ward's response only antagonized fundamentalists. It would stir up those already arguing that modernists had fled from the battlefield like cowards; it would stoke their rage over religious leaders abandoning facts to scientists alone. Professor A. L. Swift Jr. sent Ward a memo detailing how he himself observed Song having a hallucination. In Swift's presence, Song had declared himself a prophet of a new dispensation and insisted that "he was 'clothed in all white with a great girdle about my waist'—'a cross always in my right hand and a Bible in my left. No one else can see them,

---

[14] W. B. Cole to the Berwyn M. E. Church, February 10, 1928, UTS2.

but I can!'"[15] Walker Alderton also tracked down his colleague and gave him a firsthand account of Song's bizarre behavior on the day of his hospitalization. Despite the biting cold of February, Song had stood in the seminary quadrangle for the entire afternoon. Sometimes he stared "straight ahead into space, and later in the afternoon [watched] the children play. . . . He was there until almost supper time when he joined some passing students and went off with them for supper."[16] Armed with these new details, Ward sent a letter about Song's mental breakdown to all of the churches on Cole's mailing list. Everyone, professors and medical professionals alike, had seen that Song was sick.[17]

Such a patchwork response failed to quell the questions and complaints Union continued to receive, particularly from its large alumni base serving in China.[18] So in 1931 Dean Gaylord White stepped in and produced a standardized rebuttal of the charges that UTS mistreated Song back in 1927. Consulting Song's file, he argued that "Dr. Sung's mental condition was serious and . . . that the steps which the Seminary took for his recovery were dictated not only by professional advice and common sense but also by Christian sympathy and a genuine interest in the young man's welfare." Song, he argued, was sick before he ever arrived at Union. "In his correspondence with regard to entering the Seminary there are evidences of a mind under tension. There was a mystical quality about his state of mind bordering almost on the fantastic which might have forewarned us that Dr. Sung was not by any means an ordinary type." In White's account of the events, the interview between the psychiatrist and Song disappeared. In its place stood Song in a catatonic state. "Dr. Sung . . . seemed a little queer. This became accentuated and finally when he remained in the quadrangle one cold day for, as I recall it, several hours without moving and without speaking even when he was addressed, it was evident that he was in an abnormal condition."[19] In this rendition, the psychiatrist had no choice but to rescue Song, who

[15] A. L. Swift Jr. to Harry F. Ward, May 10, 1928, UTS2.
[16] Walker M. Alderton to Harry F. Ward, May 17, 1928, UTS2.
[17] Harry F. Ward to Rev. John Richards, May 21, 1928, UTS2.
[18] Between 1911 and 1949, 196 Union alumni went to China, an average of 5 students from each graduating class. Christopher David Sneller, "Let the World Come to Union and Union Go into the World: Union Theological Seminary in the City of New York and the Quest for Indigenous Christianity in Twentieth Century China" (Ph.D. diss., University of London, 2015).
[19] Gaylord S. White to Paul G. Hays, May 12, 1931, UTS2.

had become incapacitated, and take him to the hospital. Union found satisfaction in White's narrative and henceforth had all professors insert his two-page justification into the letters that they wrote in response to queries about John Song. Union had created a codified account.

EXPANSION

Whereas Union's different descriptions of what happened were streamlined over time, missionary versions of what Song experienced proliferated. Missionaries interacted with Song, who was a peripatetic preacher. It turned out that his story, like his body, was in perpetual motion. Song had studied in Ivy League schools (not Ohio); Song had entered Union to study philosophy (not theology); Song first heard the pure gospel at the well-known fundamentalist Dr. I. M. Haldeman's First Baptist Church; etc.[20] While particulars fluctuated, the core story coalesced.

The attacks on Union and modernism, in particular, intensified. Shortly after Song's arrival in New York, for instance, one missionary charged that "Union took his Bible from him," and another used his story to accuse UTS professors of being hypocrites.[21] Song was depicted as jubilantly breaking with "nominal Christianity," but his classmates and professors were vilified because they "objected to their [spiritual] slumber being disturbed."[22] "What a terrible indictment of the Professors at Union," one missionary letter opined, "that they did not recognize the workings of the Spirit of God. Blind leaders of the blind taken up with their own wisdom, setting their own theories in the place of the Word of God. They did not know when the Spirit of God was working

[20] See, for example, Ruth M. Bayliss to Daniel J. Fleming, January 21, 1932, UTS2; Anne E. Foster, "Dr. John Song at Kaying, Kwantung Province, China," unpublished paper, 1932, UTS2. The issue of where Song heard the gospel in New York is complicated. Later in his life, he attributed his conversion to Uldine Utley, the child preacher. (See Chen Renbing, "Shisui zhengshi kaishi chuandaode meiguo Wu Delei [American Uldine Utley Really Began Preaching at Ten Years Old]," *Budao zazhi* [*Evangelism*] 7, no. 1 [January–February 1934], 35.) It is true that Utley was in New York the same time as Song was in school, and there is little doubt he went to one of her meetings. But did one of those meetings open him to new and greater life? If anything, the evidence suggests his life shrank in New York as he became obsessed with little more than the Mother.

[21] Ruth M. Bayliss to Daniel J. Fleming, January 21, 1932, UTS2; Anne E. Foster, "Dr. John Sung at Kaying, Kwantung Province, China," unpublished paper, 1932, UTS2.

[22] Anne E. Foster, "Dr. John Sung at Kaying, Kwantung Province, China," unpublished paper, 1932, UTS2; Ruth M. Bayliss to Daniel J. Fleming, January 21, 1932, UTS2.

in their midst, but said, 'He is crazy.'"[23] Union, standing in for theological modernism, was pitifully lost.

This polemicized version of Song's experience at Union flourished in the acidic fundamentalist-modernist soil in which Song and Cole had first planted it. Their interpretation of the events not only justified the withdrawal of conservative mission organizations from the liberal—and therefore spiritually blind—NCC, but it also mirrored fundamentalists' perception of their own recent history in the United States. Song, just like fundamentalists in American denominations, was briefly an embattled minority in an institution hostile to his spirituality until, ultimately, the so-called "experts" forced him out.[24] Song's experience at UTS could be depicted, and therefore explained, as a microcosm of fundamentalism's process of marginalization in the late 1920s.[25]

Yet missionaries did not continually repeat his story simply because of the twinning of their experiences, but as a way to revitalize fundamentalism's identity. Told from their position as recently alienated outsiders anxious to avoid falling further and eager to regain cultural significance, at least two features of Song's life were accentuated. First, his education was a prominent part of every fundamentalist missionary account. Song's academic pedigree was precious at a time when the movement's popular appeal and populist proclivities in America had been eclipsed by the rising esteem for science and university-trained "experts."[26] Therefore, fundamentalist missionary versions of the pertinent events in Song's life invariably highlighted his Ph.D. in chemistry and often remarked on the incredible speed at which he attained it. In their attempt to depict him (and, by association, themselves) as intellectual, scientific, and modern, his achievements were occasionally embellished. His promotion to an Ivy League school, for instance, was presumably done in order to impress a more respectable identity upon an insecure fundamentalism. Second, conservative missionaries also focused on Song's revival ministry as the glorious outcome of his struggle with UTS. Although driven from the institution, so their stories went, Song was never defeated. In

[23] Ruth M. Bayliss to Daniel J. Fleming, January 21, 1932, UTS2.

[24] See for example the parallel stories of Northern Baptist and Northern Presbyterian Churches in George M. Marsden, *Fundamentalism and American Culture: The Shaping of Twentieth-Century Evangelicalism: 1870–1925* (New York: Oxford University Press, 1980), 171–72, 191–93.

[25] Joel A. Carpenter, *Revive Us Again: The Reawakening of American Fundamentalism* (New York: Oxford University Press, 1997), 35.

[26] Carpenter, *Revive Us Again*, 36.

fact, his expulsion was more properly a liberation that inaugurated his dramatic rise in influence and power. Before American fundamentalism retreated into prophetic pessimism—in which fundamentalists narrated their alienation as a sign of the ruin of the church, and the precursor to Christ's return—this version of Song's experience at UTS offered the beleaguered movement hope and promised renewal.[27] The popularized story of Song having an unwelcome spiritual awakening while attending UTS was created, in part, by the anxieties and aspirations of American fundamentalism.

On the other hand, Song's story was also created in and for China. In the wake of the May Fourth Movement, many elites had turned to scientism, the conviction that every aspect of the universe was knowable by science. Although not scientists themselves nor trained in the philosophy of science, these reformers believed science could transform the nation. It was the tool China needed if it was going to strip itself from all that inhibited its modernization. Science could separate truth from error, fact from opinion, religion from superstition.[28]

Zhao Zichen [T. C. Chao], a leader in the progressive NCC and eventual dean of the Yanjing [Yenching] School of Religion, wrote his first of several autobiographies in those terms. In 1923, he described how his spiritual experiences had been upended:

> My life has gone through a big change. I used to live in a mystical way, now in a purely ethical way; I used to live in a realm of empty speculations, now in the realm of scientific studies. As a result, my thinking is not abstract and obscure as it was, but clear and concise based on empirically researched evidence. . . . I have switched from an individualistic religion to a social religion, from an otherworldly religion to a religion of this world, down to earth.[29]

Here was a religious life that could build a modern nation. And by 1928, the Nationalist government wanted more of them. It launched the Smashing Superstition Movement to purify religion, to make it look more like Zhao's. The goal was to eradicate everything that might prevent the kind of spiritual life necessary for New China to

---

[27] Carpenter, *Revive Us Again*, 38.

[28] D. W. Y. Kwok, *Scientism in Chinese Thought, 1900–1950* (New Haven: Yale University Press, 1965), 3.

[29] Zhao Zichen, "Wode zongjiao jingyan," *Shengming* 4, no. 3 (November 1923): 16, quoted in Xing Fuzeng, "Zhao Zichende zongjiao jingyan," 12, accessed October 26, 2019, http://www.csccrc.org/files/c%204.4%20passage.pdf.

flourish. It therefore attacked esoteric doctrines, withdrawal from the world, and the pursuit of supernatural experiences in favor of creating an activist religiosity that was committed to social—i.e., national—welfare.

The state's insistence that science was the final arbiter in this process of religious reevaluation encouraged Song and missionaries to capitalize on his scientific credentials. His career as a traveling evangelist for the MEC coincided with the beginning of the Smashing Superstition Movement, so it was no accident that Song declared from the start, "[R]eligious truth is to be tested by spiritual life and science."[30] He had the rare academic degree to judge what was scientifically sound. Thus, Song constantly promoted his Ph.D. in chemistry. It certified that everything he said must be safely within the state's canon for a modern religiosity.

Yet even as he grandstanded on his education, Song's actual testimony undermined the government's goals. Although the Smashing Superstition Movement condemned such things as prognostications, dreams, visions, theophanies, and the like, Song's narrative of what transpired at Union increasingly emphasized those very elements. Unlike Zhao Zichen's life story, which chronicled his deliverance from such otherworldly phenomena, Song's tale reveled in them. And it did so safely, because his Ph.D. in science provided the necessary authorization for him to sanction large swaths of popular Chinese religiosity. His revivals, therefore, acted as points of resistance to the despised Smashing Superstition Movement. They became safe places to celebrate what was condemned elsewhere.

The Chinese context, as much as the anxieties and aspirations of American fundamentalists, encouraged the evolution of a double-voiced narrative. Whenever Song spoke of his personal transformation, he was preoccupied with his scientific credentials and ecstatic experiences.

SOLIDIFICATION

For several years Song's story of what happened at Union and the Bloomingdale Hospital was an oral performance. He shared it over dinner with a missionary or he retold it behind a pulpit. The multiple tellings account for the differing details, but with the publication of *My*

---

[30] Chin Cheak Yu, "Uncovering Seeds for Awakening and Living in the Spirit: A Cross Cultural Study of John Sung and John Wesley" (Ph.D. diss., Claremont School of Theology, 2001), 31.

Testimony in 1933 Song's narrative coalesced into a stable form. There, he reimagined not only the events in New York, as he had done with W. B. Cole in 1928, but now he made his entire life conform to the narrative structure of an evangelical conversion testimony.[31] That meant he simplified, suppressed, or changed many details, but his revisions made the point clear: Song progressed from being an Old Man, to meeting Jesus in New York and being turned into a New Man.

The first step in his tale of transformation required readers to grasp the corruption of the Old Man. Thus, Song spent the majority of his book vilifying his past. He portrayed himself as a child that was little more than a cauldron of anger, obstinacy, filial impiety, and pride. His college years were even worse. His moral compass wavered. He cheated on an exam, took shortcuts in his laboratory research, and fibbed about his work hours.[32] But the most pointed attacks on his past were always associated with his religious activity. Recognizing that this was where his claim to be New was most vulnerable, Song heaped scorn on his previous Christian work. Whatever he appeared to do for God as a child in China was a sham. "I was just a crafty cunning fox," Song explained.[33] During college his error was compounded. In the gospel team, the YMCA, the ISF, and his own church, Song was a hypocrite, a "lifeless disciple," who turned the Truth into a lie.[34] Song bemoaned how at ISF meetings he talked about Jesus as nothing more than a moral teacher, the equivalent of Confucius, Mencius, Laozi, and Zhuangzi. Of course such a claim contradicted the fact that the ISF removed Song from office for making the organization too Christian, but in *My Testimony* that fact disappeared.[35] What was essential to communicate was that Song, despite outward appearances, had been spiritually dead.

[31] D. Bruce Hindmarsh, *The Evangelical Conversion Narrative: Spiritual Autobiography in Early Modern England* (New York: Oxford University Press, 2005), 344. The expansion of Song's testimony to cover his entire life brought his story into alignment with the genre of evangelical conversion narratives established in the eighteenth century.

[32] Song, *Wode jianzheng*, 48, 64, 49.

[33] Song, *Wode jianzheng*, 19.

[34] Song, *Wode jianzheng*, 65.

[35] The veracity of Song's claim is contradicted not only by the ISF's actions, but by the testimony of his contemporary Lin Yutang. Lin grew up in a pastor's home and attended Christian schools. Circumscribed by the church, Lin—probably like Song—learned nothing about China's sages. It is difficult to imagine, therefore, Song comparing Jesus with people he knew virtually nothing about. See Lin Yutang, *From Pagan to Christian* (Cleveland: World Publishing, 1959), 34.

As a subset of this first point, while Song was purposeful about disparaging his youthful piety, he always drew back from depicting himself as utterly despicable. A key object of an evangelical testimony is evangelism, to invite other people to experience the same change as the testifier. That means the audience must be able to sympathize with the story at some level. If Song became grotesque it would defeat his purpose. Thus, even as he exaggerated his sinful condition, he carefully groomed his desirable image as an intellectual. Song, so his story went, had what everyone else wanted. The book cover itself made that plain. Emblazoned on the card stock was the author's name and his Ph.D. credential. Inside, the book was crammed with stories of Song's academic achievements. Many chapters were used to describe how he completed his bachelor's degree at Ohio Wesleyan University (OWU) in just three years, despite the president telling him it would take five. Not only did he finish a year earlier than anyone else, but Song claimed (incorrectly) that he graduated at the highest rank.[36] He told readers that newspapers from around the country and Europe picked up the story of the Chinese genius and turned him into a celebrity (though in reality, coverage spread no wider than the OWU student newspaper).[37] At the Ohio State University, Song's star only rose higher, at least in his telling. After studying German briefly, he managed (impossibly) to translate an entire thick German chemistry textbook into English in one afternoon.[38] By working all day, and sometimes through the night, Song was able to earn his degrees quickly. He added an M.A. in nine months, and then

[36] Song, *Wode jianzheng*, 50. Song did indeed graduate cum laude, but this would not be the "highest rank." Eight students graduated magna cum laude. Nonetheless, his achievements were impressive. Phi Beta Kappa recognized Song for his academic excellence and 2.70 grade point average by electing him and only sixteen others from his class to the society. Still, this did not put him among the "top four students" as he claimed elsewhere. See "Honors and Awards Given Mon. Morn. During Final Chapel," *Ohio Wesleyan Transcript*, June 12, 1923; "17 Seniors Make Phi Beta Kappa in Spring Elections," *Ohio Wesleyan Transcript*, March 28, 1923; Song Shangjie, "Song Shangjie boshi geren jianzheng [The Testimony of Dr. Song Shangjie]," as recorded by Liao Guotian, afternoon, April 2, 1931, *Shengjie zhinan yuekan* [*Guide to Holiness*] 3, no. 6 (June 1931): 28.

[37] "17 Seniors Make Phi Beta Kappa in Spring Elections," *Ohio Wesleyan Transcript*, March 28, 1923. Absence of evidence is never conclusive. However, major newspapers from Europe and the United States were consulted to see if Song appeared around the time of his graduation. Nothing was found. Ohio newspapers were likewise silent. Even the local newspaper carried nothing about Song. The only article found that talks about his academic record is the one named above.

[38] Song, *Wode jianzheng*, 61–62.

went so far as to assert that he obtained his doctoral degree in chemistry in just six months![39] *My Testimony* made it clear that Song had reached the pinnacle of human learning. By inflating his academic success, Chinese readers, who valued education, could respect and at least identify in an aspirational way with the Old Man of Song Shangjie.

As the book drew near its climax, Song brilliantly synthesized his need to lionize his achievements and demonize his past. UTS was America's most admired seminary, and Song wanted to drink every last drop from its fountain of learning. With bravado and inaccuracy, he made readers believe that he arranged with the seminary to take all "the valuable courses" at the school within one year and thereby complete the three-year program in just two semesters.[40] Not long into his study, though, Song reported he had absorbed all that Union could possibly teach him, so he withdrew to the library where he could advance farther on his own.[41] He claimed his independent activities were devoted to exploring other religions, writing several books (the most important being a translation of Laozi's *Daodejing* into English), and chanting Buddhist sutras. It was the ideal picture. Simultaneously one saw Song the cosmopolitan intellectual *and* his darkened spiritual condition.[42]

That image of Song set up the second and most condensed move in the conversion narrative: his encounter with Jesus. With Song uncertain about which religion was right, he had become "like a small leaking ship in the deep sea, with no captain and not knowing where it was going."[43] He drifted toward depression, until "I got to the point where I simply

---

[39] Song Siong Chiat, *My Testimony: Being the Autobiography of Dr. John Sung (Song Siong Chiat) the Chinese Evangelist*, trans. E. Tipson (Kuala Lumpur: Caxton Press, 1936), 68. I should point out that Song did graduate quickly. He completed his Ph.D. in two academic years. However, that is considerably longer than his half-year claim. Granted, current Chinese manuscripts (printed in 1995) accurately state Song graduated after a year and a half. The earliest extant manuscript (although in English) translated the section in question by saying Song graduated in half a year. I find the exaggeration consonant with Song's general pattern of inflating his academic successes, and I am convinced that his unbelievable claim to complete a Ph.D. in six months is something that is more likely to be corrected later rather than mistranslated earlier. Therefore, I follow Tipson's English translation on this point.

[40] Song, *Wode jianzheng*, 71. Song was part of a one-year, non-degree-seeking program, not a condensed bachelor of divinity course of study.

[41] Song, *Wode jianzheng*, 74.

[42] Song, *Wode jianzheng*, 74–75, 79.

[43] Song, *Wode jianzheng*, 75.

had no desire to live."[44] Then, on the evening of February 10, 1927, his sins appeared to him one by one in his dorm room. Their collective weight was crushing. In a panic that he would not escape the torments of hell, Song frantically dug in his trunk and pulled out his neglected Bible. When it fell open to Luke 23, he was pulled into the narrative of Jesus' crucifixion. Song felt as if he were truly following the Messiah to Golgotha. In the vision he suddenly saw "Jesus already hung up high on the cross. His head hung to one side, his two hands dripped blood."[45] The power of the image tormented Song's soul, convulsing him with tears until at midnight his pleas for mercy were answered by a voice, declaring, "Son, your sins are forgiven." It was, in Song's words, "my spiritual birthday."[46]

Although he claimed it was the night in his life that he remembered best, his recollections were characteristically incomplete, faulty, or invented. For instance, Song recorded in *My Testimony* that on the night of his new birth God gave him the name "John." Readers were informed that God commissioned Song to be a new John the Baptist. Just as the Baptizer was the forerunner of the Lord, so at this late hour Song was chosen to be a forerunner of the returning Christ.[47] In his book, "John" had a clear theological meaning, befitting Song's career in 1933 as a popular evangelist. What the book failed to mention were any of the other names that were also bestowed upon him that night, like "Love," "Riter," or "Ring." Song could justifiably leave them out of his memoir because they were superfluous, confusing, or forgotten details. Such a decision was emblematic of how Song constructed his entire narrative. He simplified events in order to make it a clear-cut Christian conversion.

In the third and final step of the conversion narrative, Song needed to prove that he was indeed a New Man, that his faith in Jesus Christ had fundamentally changed him. He first provided rather conventional evidence. Instead of feeling lost and depressed, he now felt joyous and bold. His inward transformation was confirmed by people who "could not but admit that I had passed through a wonderful change."[48] But

---

[44] Song, *Wode jianzheng*, 79.

[45] Song, *Wode jianzheng*, 81.

[46] Song, *Wode jianzheng*, 81. Whereas missionary documents had been reticent to define his experience in New York as a conversion, preferring to label it as a renewal of faith or a break with nominal Christianity, *My Testimony* insisted it was the moment Song was "born again."

[47] Song, *Wode jianzheng*, 81–82.

[48] Song, *Wode jianzheng*, 82.

grander evidence was at hand. Before his encounter with Jesus, Song had been at home at UTS. In fact, *My Testimony* painted it as the exact reflection of his own soul. On the one hand, UTS was portrayed as the most academically sophisticated seminary in the country.[49] On the other hand, its spirituality was totally corrupt. "The highest religion really was not Christianity," but secular science, Song confided to his audience, to the point that students wondered why Song even bothered to move to New York since he already had a degree in something better.[50] That attitude permeated the entire atmosphere of the school, withering all spiritual life and corrupting every so-called Christian act. In other words, UTS combined the highest academic honors with the lowest spirituality. The school looked exactly like Song, until it didn't.

After Song met Jesus, things changed. According to *My Testimony*, one week after his new birth a globe he was looking at morphed into the shape of Jesus Christ, with the continents and countries each finding a place on the Lord's body. Surrounding the figure of Jesus were monsters, and when he looked closer, Song discovered that the ghouls had the faces of his seminary professors. That very afternoon, he informed readers, the seminary acted monstrously and had him barred from the premises. After returning from a walk, the president blocked the seminary entrance. Henry Sloane Coffin told Song he needed to go to the countryside for a break, never informing him that he would be staying in a psychiatric ward. That was not true, of course. Records from 1927 make it clear that Song was interviewed inside the seminary and signed his own self-admittance form for hospitalization, and that Coffin only learned about the situation through a series of memos. But like the other alterations in *My Testimony*, these were strategic. They were proof that Song was categorically different; he no longer fit at Union.

The hospital, likewise, became an alien place. Song liked to tell audiences that he tried to meet with the staff, doctor-to-doctor. His mind was fine, he politely informed the clinicians. His prodigious memory, his unique achievements, his terminal degree all testified to that. Dr. Song was one of them, he practically shouted.[51] Yet his words always fell on deaf ears. He was so changed, he winked at readers, that even doctors could no longer recognize him as one of their own.

[49] Song, *Wode jianzheng*, 69.

[50] Song, *Wode jianzheng*, 75, 71.

[51] Song Shangjie, "Song Shangjie boshi geren jianzheng [The Testimony of Dr. Song Shangjie]," as recorded by Liao Guotian, afternoon, April 2, 1931, *Shengjie zhinan yuekan* [*Guide to Holiness*] 3, no. 6 (June 1931): 30.

Song was describing a total transformation, a complete reversal. Observe how he perfectly inverted the twin thrusts of his story. First, until his meeting with Jesus Christ, Song relentlessly described himself as spiritually dead; now, he was very much alive. Second, whereas Song had devoted many pages to his intellectual successes, at the end, they turned out to be null and void. Not only did all his degrees fail to get him a fair audience with his colleagues at the hospital, but his education turned out to be entirely unnecessary for being born again. His expertise in astronomy, geology, zoology, biology, chemistry, history, politics, economics, and "every kind of science," was empty.[52] To the relief of audiences who could only wish for such an education, Song absolved them of the necessity. Education did not matter. In fact, in one of the most beloved additions to his testimony, Song told audiences that he tossed his diplomas along with his Phi Beta Kappa and Sigma Xi keys into the ocean on his way back to China.[53] The first in education had

[52] Song Shangjie, *Fenxingji* [*Revival Messages*], 6th ed. (1935; repr., Hong Kong: Bellman House, 1989), 8. Compared to many people in his audience, he probably was better informed on most subjects. Nonetheless, it probably did not warrant calling himself a "Doctor of Everything." Song, *Wode jianzheng*, 67.

[53] The tossing of Song's emblems of worldly success into the ocean became a central story in his legacy. Over time, in fact, that vignette may have superseded the significance of the conversion story. In the Song Shangjie Memorial Hall in Putian, China, for instance, an enormous painting hangs that depicts Song throwing the symbols of his academic success into the ocean, rather than his encounter with Jesus at Union. However, like the conversion account, it is difficult to discern precisely what happened. The painting, for instance, shows Song tossing his diplomas and not the keys into the water. Apparently in 1932 he told the story that way. In 1931 a missionary reported that Song took "his six diplomas and three 'keys'" and threw them all into the Pacific Ocean—grossly overstating the number of diplomas Song would have had as well as inflating the number of keys he had earned. Later, William Schubert wrote that Song took all his diplomas and honors and threw them out a porthole. Leslie Lyall said that Song threw his diplomas, medals, and keys overboard except for his doctoral degree to satisfy his father. It is impossible to know what happened on the boat. One wonders, though, if Song simply kept the money that Coffin sent him to replace the keys and used it to help with expenses during his return trip. In that case nothing was thrown overboard, but the absence of the keys would be given spiritual significance. See Anna Hockelman, "The Story of a Thirty-Nine Day Revival," *Latter Rain Evangel* 26, no. 10 (July 1935): 19–20; Jennie Hughes, ed., *Bethel Heart Throbs of Revival* (Shanghai: Bethel Mission, 1931), 24; Song Shangjie, "Yongyuan shifang [Eternally Set Free]," as recorded by Zhao Aiguang, *Budao zazhi* [*Evangelism*] 7, no. 3 (May–June 1934): 17; William E. Schubert, *I Remember John Sung* (Singapore: Armour Publishing, 2005), 259; Leslie T. Lyall, *A Biography of John Sung* (Singapore: Genesis Books, 2004), 45.

become the last. Everything in his life had been flipped. Song was truly a New Man.[54]

CHINA'S NEW MAN

My Testimony was emphatic: Song declared himself a New Man. But was he? The testimony changed so often and so much; was Song a liar? Was his conversion just a scam? Without a doubt facts were slippery in Song's mouth. He spit them out in abbreviated, touched-up, or invented forms, according to convenience. Even after the publication of his testimony, Song continued to alter the events of his conversion right up to the very end of his life. Shortly before his career ended, Song was in the Dutch East Indies, the nation with the largest Muslim population in the world. There he adjusted his story to say that at Union he had not been translating Chinese religious classics or chanting Buddhist sutras, but had immersed himself in the Quran.[55] It was not true, of course, but neither do such habitual alterations indicate he was lying for lying's sake. Song regularly reimagined his past, but his historical inventions were never random. He always made them submit to an unbendable rule. Exaggerations were wrong, he confided to his diary, but he told tall tales only because he hoped "people would be saved" through them.[56] On that matter, the facts bear him out.

The more damning charge may be that Song was a charlatan. The man was desperate to escape the label of being crazy when he returned to China, and he needed a job to support his brother, his parents, and his new wife. One could argue that just as he had modified his behavior and changed his tactics in the hospital to engineer a premature release, so Song said and did whatever was needed to gain W. B. Cole's trust. That is indeed likely. Song probably did change his story to win Cole over, but in the end, the story won him.

The testimony, which Cole and Song first outlined in 1928, turned out to reconfigure Song's life indelibly. Once Song dropped references to the Mother in favor of his new story of transformation through Jesus Christ, his relationships with other Christians began to flourish. His

---

[54] For more on how Song changed, modified, amplified, and revised his testimony, as well as how others later did the same, see Daryl R. Ireland, "John Sung's Malleable Conversion Narrative," *Fides et Historia* 45, no. 1 (2013): 48–75.

[55] Cornelie Baarbé, *Dr. Song, een Reveil op Java: Over de Evangelist Dr. Song en zijn preken* (Den Haag, Netherlands: Voorhoeve, 1960), 4.

[56] Song Shangjie, February 12, 1940, SSD, TTC.

marginalization ended. His new story created an intimate bond with the fundamentalist missionary community, it reestablished trust with his family, and it eventually won over the youth at the Methodist schools who had first mocked his insanity.[57] In this way Song experienced what one theorist of religious conversion has called integration into a new social reference group.[58] Regardless of his initial motivation, Song's reinvention of what happened in New York proved to be transformative, because he did not merely claim to be a changed man; new relationships made him so.

But more can still be said. After Jesus became the focal point of his story, Song's life really did change. And, if Jesus was the quickening presence who was providing him work, family, and friends back in his homeland, then Song had to reconsider in whose presence he had been in New York. That meant Song could discard everything from Union and the hospital that was crude, awkward, or unintelligible. Without comment or maybe even reflection, the Mother disappeared. On the other hand, whatever he found enlightening from his supernatural encounters in New York, he now attributed to Jesus, the real, if at the time unrecognized, companion in his suffering. So thoroughly did his testimony help him reconceptualize what happened in the asylum, he would have lied if he had gone on insisting that he had met the Mother. In China he came to know it was not her, but Jesus Christ. To say otherwise would have been a greater error than the first.

Song was thus not lying about becoming a New Man through the power of God. It may not have happened in New York as he claimed, but the transformation of his life was no less real for having occurred back in China. Jesus did become the integrating presence and force in his life. Near the end, when he knew he was mortally ill and his career as an evangelist was over, Song did not waver from that conviction. In fact, as he prepared to die he admitted many shortcomings in his personal journal: cruelty, vanity, pride, greed, even deception.[59] But his conversion

[57] W. B. Cole to the Berwyn M. E. Church, February 10, 1928, UTS2; Frank T. Cartwright to Early R. Hibbard, August 7, 1935, roll 70, UMC; Song Shangjie Diary, November 19, 1927, John Song Papers, record group 263, Yale Divinity School, New Haven, Conn. Hereafter referred to as YDS.

[58] Robert Hefner, *Conversion to Christianity: Historical and Anthropological Perspectives on a Great Transformation* (Berkeley: University of California Press, 1993), 25.

[59] Song Shangjie, February 12, 1940, SSD, TTC.

was not the fraud. If it had been, then why was he making his private deathbed confession to Jesus Christ?[60] The best answer is that Song truly became a New Man in China, even if the change was not as smooth or instantaneous as he led people to believe.

New Beginnings

The multiple and even contradictory accounts of his transformation illuminate something important about Song's rebirth. They show how Song was reconceptualizing his life in the form of the quintessential genre of the May Fourth Movement: the autobiography.[61] Crowding the literary landscape for the two decades following World War I, Chinese autobiographies were the site for the making and remaking of China's New Man. It seemed that everyone who picked up a pen took the opportunity to explain their life as an emancipation. The narrative arc moved from captivity to awakening to escape and extolled the freedom one experienced when unfettered from tradition or the past.[62]

Such stories were always very personal, but at the same time they were thin allegories for the nation. Whether one reads the autobiography of Yu Dafu, an ardent advocate for modern literature, or the life story of Beijing's most popular independent preacher, Wang Mingdao, one notices that both give obsessive attention to their own bodies in their autobiographies—its dirtiness, weaknesses, illnesses, and impotence. But even as they spoke of their personal failings, they were but an instantiation of the filthy, feeble, sick, and powerless nation of China.[63]

Yet autobiographies never ended there. They could explore personal failings unabashedly because the author no longer identified with that Old Man. Something new now existed. Leo Ou-fan Lee has argued that the foundation of Chinese modernity was the way it made the present normative.[64] Autobiographies certainly adopted that division of time.

---

[60] Song did not die right after penning his confession, as he assumed. Surgeries and prayer sustained him four more years, though he never preached again in public.

[61] Janet Ng, *The Experience of Modernity: Chinese Autobiography of the Early Twentieth Century* (Ann Arbor: University of Michigan Press, 2003), 145.

[62] John Fitzgerald, *Awakening China: Politics, Culture, and Class in the Nationalist Revolution* (Stanford: Stanford University Press, 1996), 98.

[63] Ng, *Experience of Modernity*, 149.

[64] Leo Ou-fan Lee, *Shanghai Modern: The Flowering of a New Urban Culture in China, 1930–1945* (Cambridge, Mass.: Harvard University Press, 1999); Leo Ou-fan Lee, "In Search of Modernity: Some Reflections on a New Mode of

Authors always described their former ways of life as something flawed, incomplete, or obsolete, whereas the present was unencumbered and packed with promise. A New Man made a self-conscious break with the past because, according to Janet Ng, that is precisely "what creates the experience of the modern."[65]

China's New Man thought of himself as standing on the peak of history. From there he could see and narrate everything that had come before as a series of "less-than" moments. Yu Dafu could cringe at his sexual inadequacy, Wang Mingdao could acknowledge his poor grasp of the Second Coming, and Song Shangjie could describe his years of church activities as nothing but hypocrisy. From wherever a person stood now, the past always looked bad. The only problem with that outlook was that when a person turned around, time had moved on and the peak of history had suddenly gotten even higher, because the present never stood still. Hence, modern subjects like Song had to hike higher and higher, and renew themselves by breaking with the past again and again, so that *now* they could freely live.[66]

Song's testimony is a particularly potent expression of this point. His explanations of what occurred in New York proliferated because time never stood still. He had to keep updating his message to fit the current situation. That meant his testimony took one form when he first returned to China, then another when his career started during the Smashing Superstition Movement, and yet morphed again when he spoke to Muslims at the end of his twelve years of preaching. In truth Song's testimony never stopped evolving. He took the need to stay in the present so seriously that when the events in New York, the very cocoon of his new life, threatened to harden into a historical relic, he even dared to tear free from his own conversion. After telling people for years that he had become a New Man in the United States, Song updated his testimony in the early 1930s by introducing a more recent rupture. He declared that until a few weeks prior, all his ministry in China had been "haphazard and aimless. I was struggling in the tide of modernism,

---

Consciousness in Twentieth-Century Chinese History and Literature," in *Ideas across Cultures*, ed. Paul Cohen and Merle Goldman (Cambridge, Mass.: Harvard University Press, 1990), 108–35. See also Jürgen Habermas, *The Philosophical Discourse of Modernity* (Cambridge, Mass.: MIT Press, 1987), 1–22.

[65] Ng, *Experience of Modernity*, 9.

[66] Lee, *Shanghai Modern*; Lee, "In Search of Modernity," 108–35. See also Habermas, *Philosophical Discourse of Modernity*, 1–22.

being knocked about here and there, and did not know how to get out."[67] Such a statement sat incomprehensibly next to everything else he said and wrote about escaping modernism in 1927 and the beginning of his new life in New York, but that did not matter. Song's conversion was not only to Jesus, but also to a modern temporality. That forced him to make repeated revisions. To remain a New Man, Song always had to seek new breaks with the ever-lengthening past.

What Song was doing was not entirely unique. Other autobiographers found themselves pulled in similar directions. Yu Dafu ended up writing multiple and different autobiographical essays; he also published twenty-four different collections of diaries between 1921 and 1937; and he still managed to rework all those materials for yet another autobiography. Wang Mingdao originally slow-dripped his life story into the pages of his magazine *Spiritual Life Quarterly* before he reimagined it all in a full-length autobiography several years later. China's New Man had to make and then remake himself because that is how the modern self operates: it must reestablish itself in the ever-dawning present.

Still, Song's testimony can be differentiated from what others produced. His secular peers, like Yu Dafu, assumed they could create a coherent story out of the disparate and seemingly pointless collection of their life experiences. With hard work they could choose the meaning of their own lives. Song, and Christians in general, shied away from such an outlook. For them identity was not only constructed—though they did a fair share of that—but also bestowed. Even the liberal theologian Zhao Zichen, who in the early part of his career worked to exorcise transcendence, explained at the end of his first autobiography that he did not invent himself—he discovered himself.[68] Song concurred. His work was to find the story God was authoring in him.[69] It was a story riven by his encounters with God, but Song never thought those breaks in his life were self-selected. They were given, not created. The difference is significant and bears witness to what Bruce Hindmarsh has called "an important alternative version" of modern individuality.[70] Song's testimony generated the New Man just as surely as secular autobiography, but did so on its own terms.

---

[67] Song Shangjie, *Forty John Sung Revival Sermons*, vol. 1, trans. Timothy Tow (Singapore: Alice Doo, 1978), 110.

[68] Zhao Zichen, "Wode zongjiao jingyan," 16.

[69] Hindmarsh, *Evangelical Conversion Narrative*, 346.

[70] Hindmarsh, *Evangelical Conversion Narrative*, 344.

His autobiography can also be distinguished from what other Christians made public. The conversion narratives of Zhao Zichen and Wang Mingdao, for example, only reached a couple thousand readers.[71] Song, by contrast, shared his story of breaking with the past not only with thousands of readers, but also told it to more than a million listeners through his sermons. That meant Song's vision of becoming a New Man through Jesus Christ was able to reach more people than even Yu Dafu's *Nine Diaries* [*Riji jiuzhong*], the most popular secular autobiography on the market.[72] Due to its extraordinary circulation, Song's testimony modeled for China the Christian alternative to secular reinvention.

He popularized a way for people to update themselves and remain new through Jesus Christ. The fact that God was with them now made the present normative. The past became pliable. For Song, whenever history threatened to undo him, he need only turn to the Lord. Whether he then described Jesus as rescuing him from insanity, a divided heart, sin, or something else ultimately mattered very little. What was important was that he was free. Song's dynamic and adaptable testimony could generate a split with the past every time it threatened to catch up to him. Released from the grip of history, Song appeared triumphant, capable of overcoming any new obstacle or set of circumstances. His spiritual autobiography injected something fresh into China's modernization. The power of Jesus to separate him from the past allowed Song, and all who dared follow his example, to proclaim: Behold! *I* am China's New Man!

---

[71] Wang Mingdao's *Spiritual Food Quarterly* was one of the more popular Christian periodicals, but its circulation barely exceeded two thousand. Lian Xi, *Redeemed by Fire: The Rise of Popular Christianity in Modern China* (New Haven: Yale University Press, 2010), 129.

[72] Ling Shiao, "Culture, Commerce, and Connections: The Inner Dynamics of New Culture Publishing in the Post-May Fourth Period," in *From Woodblocks to the Internet: Chinese Publishing and Print Culture in Transition, circa 1800 to 2008*, ed. Cynthia Brokaw and Christopher A. Reed (Leiden: Brill, 2010), 213–48.

3

A New Means

Individual awakenings were the focus of post–May Fourth autobiographies, but Chinese authors and Christian testifiers did not become totally self-absorbed. Alert, now, to the dire circumstances from which they had escaped, they believed it was their moral responsibility to wake those who still slumbered. The political activist Luo Jialun spoke for a generation when he wrote, "The glory of the May Fourth movement lies precisely in getting China to move."[1]

Nothing seemed more important to Song Shangjie. From the moment he returned home, he was determined to remake the nation. With characteristic energy and persistence, he set about to mobilize people. In the mythology of May Fourth, to move China was to modernize China because it suggested "an irrevocable and total break with the past."[2] Song spared no effort as he sought ways to communicate the urgent need for people to change. He learned how to make his transformative experience with Jesus transferrable. He also discovered means to radicalize those who listened to him. Song proved to be very effective at mobilizing the masses, but it took time. His first efforts to move China floundered as he initially struggled to connect with the people.

---

[1] Vera Schwarcz, *The Chinese Enlightenment: Intellectuals and the Legacy of the May Fourth Movement of 1919* (Berkeley: University of California Press, 1986), 7.
[2] Schwarcz, *Chinese Enlightenment*, 7.

Infatuation with Ideology

The noise and smoke of firecrackers masked the ambivalence of the villagers of Huangshi. The return of Song Shangjie from the United States should have been a moment of communal pride and joy. In centuries past Huangshi had produced more graduates of the imperial exam system than any surrounding town or city in Fujian Province. During the Qing dynasty, however, those numbers had dwindled and then dried up entirely.[3] Song's return to the village on horseback in November 1927 was an opportunity to reclaim that past, to look forward to a renaissance of Huangshi's intellectual status. Men, women, and children dutifully lined the dirt road to welcome the homecoming of the region's first Ph.D., and the young people ignited honorific firecrackers. Yet no one was certain what to make of their long-absent son, nephew, and neighbor. Song Shangjie had not chosen to come home after he completed his degree; he was forced home after being exiled from the United States for insanity.

The small hometown crowd politely listened to his impromptu speech that winter afternoon. They would have to endure several more over the coming weeks. Song had quite a bit to say about the state of his village and of China in general. He spoke with shame and disgust about Chinese habits of hygiene.[4] He tried to inspire his countrymen to new heights by speaking in the idiom of the age. He invented ideologies for Huangshi, convinced, like other reformers, that adding "-ism [*zhuyi*]" to a word made it sound modern. The social critic Hu Shi had been alarmed by the superficiality of the multiplying neologisms in China and urged his fellow intellectuals to cease speaking about ideology altogether. "Improving one kind of bean, one strain of cotton, or one breed of silk worms," he pleaded, "is better than a million tons of essays talking about 'isms.'"[5] Few listened, however, and Song tried to prod his sleepy hamlet to action by calling for its total transformation through an

---

[3] "Ming Entry Exams (Persons)" and "Qing Entry Exams (Persons)," China's History in Maps, Harvard University, accessed November 21, 2019, https://worldmap.harvard.edu/maps/china-history.

[4] Song Shangjie, November 6, 1927, Song Shangjie Diaries, Trinity Theological College, Singapore. Henceforth, this location will be known as SSD, TTC. Song Shangjie, November 9, 1927, SSD, TTC.

[5] Charles W. Hayford, *To the People: James Yen and Village China* (New York: Columbia University Press, 1990), 64.

ill-defined program of humble-ism, love of God-ism, sacrifice-ism, and forget yourself-ism.[6]

When that failed, Song tried piggybacking on the Guomindang's (GMD) political rhetoric that permeated Fujian in the wake of the Nationalist army's recent victory in the region. For students at the Methodist school where he got a job in early 1928, Song altered Sun Zhongshan [Sun Yat-sen's] "Three Principles of the People [*sanmin zhuyi*]," which promoted nationalism, democracy, and people's livelihood, and offered them his own concoction: "Christ's Three Principles of the People [*jidu sanmin zhuyi*]."[7] He never reported how hijacking the sacrosanct language of the GMD for his own purposes went over, but he did quickly run afoul of the Nationalist government. It is unclear what prompted the party to notice him. Song circulated at least two explanations. Sometimes he said that his messages appeared to transplant the official ideology of the state and therefore raised opposition. Other times he indicated that he drew the GMD's ire because he condemned the party's requirement that students bow to the portrait of Sun Zhongshan.[8] Quite possibly both happened, though a third possibility, less framed as a form of religious persecution and more in terms of the political realities of the day, may explain the GMD's interest in Song. After the GMD did an about-face and purged the Communists from its ranks in April of 1927, the party was especially vigilant to root out the Communists' influence. Local GMD officials carefully monitored schools since Communists had been the most effective in recruiting members and organizing protests among students. Song may have become a person of interest because the GMD suspected intellectuals working in rural China to be Communists.[9] Song, with his Ph.D. in chemistry from an American university but working at a small high school in China's hinterland, would certainly fit the vague profile of someone suspicious. Regardless of the reasons, the state's intrusion into his classroom pushed Song out the

---

[6] Song Shangjie, November 8, 1927, SSD, TTC.

[7] Song Shangjie, November 17, 1927, SSD, TTC.

[8] Song Tianzhen, ed., *Shi'er fude de riji* [*The Journal Once Lost*] (Kowloon, Hong Kong: China Alliance Press, 2006), 47.

[9] Chiang Kai-Shek, "A Message to the Students of China," *China Christian Advocate* 18, no. 1 (January 1931): 3–4; Ka-che Yip, *Religion, Nationalism, and Chinese Students: The Anti-Christian Movement of 1922–1927* (Bellingham: Western Washington University, 1980), 84.

door. He henceforth took his message of China's crisis and its need for reform on the road.

The results were dispiriting. "People know what is happening by ear, but they do nothing about it," Song confided to his journal.[10] No matter how he poked or prodded, scolded or wooed an audience, he discovered that people were apathetic. China's biggest problem, as the leftist politician Wang Jingwei put it in the late 1920s, was not imperialism or warlords, but the masses' maddening inability to change.[11] "What can I do to deal with people like that?" Song asked.[12] Like so many other dreamy reformers, Song found himself at a loss when faced with simple human inertia.

CURATOR OF DIVINE MYSTERIES

Song was learning what other reformers were discovering at the same time. Those who acted as "self-styled mentors of the ignorant commoners" did not get very far.[13] Inevitably, listeners became defensive when attempts to awaken them sounded like thinly veiled attacks upon them. Neither top-down orders to shape up nor scorn of a person's way of life won the hearts of the masses. Frustrated, some elites gave up in self-righteous exasperation. Others, however, were chastened by their experiences and began exploring alternatives. Instead of speaking to the masses, they tried to talk with them.[14] For Chinese political parties, that meant opening conversations about such things as labor conditions and mercantile concerns.[15] For Song, it meant being attentive to the spiritual interests of his rural Fujian audiences.

When the Xinghua [Hinghwa] Methodist Episcopal Conference commissioned Song to be an evangelist in the fall of 1928, he traveled from village to village. Everywhere he went he encountered a distinctive religious syntax. People were not primarily interested in the latest ideology or an explanation of Christian doctrine. What fascinated them were stories in which the supernatural world penetrated the natural world.

[10] Song Shangjie, November 6, 1927, SSD, TTC.

[11] Joseph Fewsmith, *Party, State, and Local Elites in Republican China: Merchant Organizations and Politics in Shanghai, 1890–1930* (Honolulu: University of Hawaii, 1985), 103.

[12] Song Shangjie, November 6, 1927, SSD, TTC.

[13] Schwarcz, *Chinese Enlightenment*, 55.

[14] Schwarcz, *Chinese Enlightenment*, 9.

[15] Fewsmith, *Party, State, and Local Elite in Republican China*, 109.

He jotted down people's dreams that acted as heavenly messages. Evil spirits were noted as regular afflicters of the sick, and ghosts and angels appeared in a variety of contexts. Healings, visits to heaven, and an audible voice giving divine direction were standard Chinese religious fare. In fact, Song's eyes were opened to the fact that the presence of extraordinary events in someone's religious experience is what lent the story credence. Increasingly, therefore, he turned his attention to such supernatural activities in his own life.

In 1930, for instance, Song was given the honor of representing the Xinghua Conference at the National Christian Council's (NCC) Christian Home Forward Movement, which was meeting in Huzhou, Zhejiang Province, five hundred miles away. All the new methodologies that were promoted and various ideas that were shared garnered little of Song's attention. What he reported as significant was his failure to introduce himself properly. When one of the leaders asked Song to make his own introduction, he recorded, "I only gave my name, nothing else. For suddenly I felt my head was as big as the whole world and my teeth weighed a ton, so it was extremely difficult to speak. This kind of spirit-world [*lingjie*] experience is truly precious."[16]

Nowhere else in Song's life were those kinds of experiences more intense or condensed than when he was in the Bloomingdale Hospital, the insane asylum. For it was there, he began to explain to those who heard him preach, that he penetrated the veil of this world and the mysteries of God were given to him. "These are not my words," Song insisted. "When I was locked in the mental asylum God's Spirit personally led me."[17] Far from covering up or shying away from talking about his hospitalization, he started to use his experience in the mental asylum to draw everyone's attention. In his first transcribed sermons, Song validated his messages by pointing out the circumstances under which he received them: "This teaching was given to me when I was in the wilderness, the asylum."[18] He was so certain of the appeal of such a special revelation that he suggested "many people wish they could live

[16] Song Shangjie, December 7, 1930, SSD, TTC.

[17] Song Shangjie, "Gelinduo qianshu dishisanzhang [First Corinthians Chapter Thirteen]," as recorded by Liao Guotian, morning, March 30, 1931, *Shengjie zhinan yuekan* [*Guide to Holiness*] 3, no. 6 (June 1931): 6.

[18] Song Shangjie, "Chuangshiji yu yuehan fuyin [Genesis and the Gospel of John]," as recorded by Chen Qiujin, April 1, 1931, *Shengjie zhinan yuekan* [*Guide to Holiness*] 3, no. 6 (June 1931): 19.

in the asylum with me, because they dearly long for this kind of teaching."[19] Song turned his diagnosis of mental illness into his greatest draw.

His story reenacted a popular trope in Chinese fiction. In book after book, readers learned to expect that a spiritual genius would reject the normal world because he understands higher things, while the normal world, alas, would reject him because it does not.[20] Song used his hospitalization as the ultimate evidence that he had special powers to "see/break through [*kanpo*]" the world.[21] Ordinary people, including his learned professors of religion and the hospital doctors, lacked Song's spiritual vision. Blinded by their materialism, they inevitably assumed he was crazy. They lacked the ability to penetrate reality the way he did. Song's listeners had the opportunity to do better. Just like the readers of popular fiction, if they accepted the hero and his message then they were proving that they could recognize the deepest truths of the universe; they were spiritual geniuses too.

It was a flattering thought, but Song's esoteric sermons put his listeners to the test. When he spoke at the second meeting of the NCC's Five Year Movement in Shanghai, March 30–April 3, 1931, Song had to rely on an interpreter to communicate his extraordinary messages to the assembly.[22] Lu Zu, someone noted, not only had to help make Song's Xinghua dialect understandable to the audience, but sometimes she also had the challenge of explaining the meaning behind his idiosyncratic biblical expositions.[23]

---

[19] Song, "Chuangshiji yu yuehan fuyin [Genesis and the Gospel of John]," 19. For a similar sentiment see Song Shangjie, "Chuangshiji yu shizijia [Genesis and the Cross]," as recorded by Chen Qiujin, April 3, 1931, *Shengjie zhinan yuekan [Guide to Holiness]* 3, no. 6 (June 1931): 32.

[20] E. Perry Link Jr., *Mandarin Ducks and Butterflies: Popular Fiction in Early Twentieth-Century Chinese Cities* (Berkeley: University of California Press, 1981), 65–75.

[21] Song Shangjie, "Matai fuyin di liu zhang [Matthew Chapter Six]," as recorded by Chen Zhenfan, March 31, 1931, *Shengjie zhinan yuekan [Guide to Holiness]* 3, no. 6 (June 1931): 9–13. This verb entered Song's vocabulary as a common way to express his ability to penetrate beyond the world as it is presented and see the spiritual reality beneath it.

[22] Note how Song's involvement with the NCC belies, again, the stereotypical image of him returning to China as a belligerent fundamentalist. At this point in his career, at least, Song felt comfortable working with and even for people assumed to be his theological opponents.

[23] "Wuyun lingxiu fenxing budao [Five Year Movement: Devotion, Revival, Evangelism]," *Zhenguang [True Light]* 30, no. 5 (May 1931): 80–82.

When his first of six sermons on Genesis 1 opened with, "This after-noon's theme is something I don't even know, because it is very mysteri-ous," the audience could be assured of a good hour or more of cocked heads and furrowed brows.[24] Song's early messages were filled with unique allegories. In this particular case, he drew parallels between each day of creation and the seven children of the kingdom of God, who appeared in the rest of the book of Genesis. For instance, on the first day of creation God created light and separated it from the darkness (Gen 1:3-5). Song explained that those verses referred to the first child in God's kingdom: Abel. Abel represented light and humility, whereas Cain was full of dark-ness and pride. The two were literally separated from one another (Gen 4). In a similar way the fifth day of creation, which described the creation of fish and birds (Gen 1:20-23), corresponded to Isaac's experience in life. Isaac, the fifth child of the kingdom, plunged to the depths like a fish when he was bound and about to be sacrificed by his father (Gen 22), but he also soared to the heights like a bird when he received God's promise that a savior would come through his descendants.

Subsequent sermons added more and more layers to the first chapter of Genesis. The next day, for example, Song pushed the parallels further. Genesis 1 was also a template for the first seven chapters of the Gospel of John: the first day God created light, which summoned images of light and darkness, Cain and Abel. But it also signified how the true light entered the world and was rejected by it (John 1). On the fifth day God created fish and birds, which were symbols of Isaac's life experiences and also indications of how the crippled man in John 5 felt as he moved from a lower existence to a higher one when Jesus healed him.[25] By the end of the series, the sermons were getting both more convoluted and yet easier to follow. The methodology was consistent. The seven days of creation described at the beginning of the Genesis were the "key" to the mysteries of the whole Bible.[26] In his series of sermons, Song used those seven days to explain many things: the creation story was a shorthand account of

---

[24] Song Shangjie, "Chuangshijide qi xiaohai [The Seven Children of Genesis]," as recorded by Chen Zhenfan, March 31, 1931, Shengjie zhinan yuekan [Guide to Holiness] 3, no. 6 (June 1931): 13.

[25] Song, "Chuangshiji you yuehan fuyin [Genesis and the Gospel of John]," 18–23.

[26] Song Shangjie, "Matai fuyin di wu zhang [Matthew Chapter Five]," as recorded by Chen Zhenfan, March 30, 1931, Shengjie zhinan yuekan [Guide to Holiness] 3, no. 6 (June 1931): 6.

the lives of the seven main characters who appeared in Genesis; it clarified the meaning of the first seven chapters of John; the seven days of creation acted as a concise summary of the seven narrative blocks Song identified as comprising the Old and New Testaments; they forecast all of church history; and, in his final presentation, Genesis 1 prefigured his own spiritual narrative, which moved incrementally from darkness to rest.[27] Amazed by the comprehensiveness of the first chapter of the Bible, Song voiced his awe: "This chapter is extremely mysterious. Too bad so many people today look down on this chapter. They have eyes corrupted by secular ways. Thank God, when I was in the desert (the insane asylum), he gave me this kind of revelation, and allowed me to see things clearly."[28]

Such messages did little to move people, but they worked marvelously to intensify their sense of wonder. The Bible was a mysterious and awesome book. What appeared so straightforward in the text was, in fact, imbued with layer upon layer of meaning. Song repeatedly emphasized that each stroke in the text had significance, and as those meanings were brought to the surface the listeners were expected to marvel at how God had buried such treasures in plain sight.[29] Thus, the creation account in Genesis, which functioned as a lightning rod in the fundamentalist-modernist conflict, played a different role in Song's sermonic repertoire. He did not try to prove that the biblical story of creation was consonant with modern science, like so many fundamentalists.[30] His attention fell elsewhere. Every sermon certainly implied that Genesis 1 was divinely inspired, for no other explanation could account for the surprising parallels or precise forecasts

---

[27] Song, "Chuangshijide qi xiaohai [The Seven Children of Genesis]," 13–15; Song Shangjie, "Chuangshiji yu xinjiuyue [Genesis and the New and Old Testaments]," as recorded by Chen Quijin, April 1, 1931, *Shengjie zhinan yuekan* [*Guide to Holiness*] 3, no. 6 (June 1931): 15–18; Song, "Chuangshiji yu yuehan fuyin [Genesis and the Gospel of John]," 18–23; Song Shangjie, "Chuangshiji yu jiaohui lishi [Genesis and Church History]," as recorded by Chen Zhenfan, April 2, 1931, *Shengjie zhinan yuekan* [*Guide to Holiness*] 3, no. 6 (June 1931): 23–26; Song Shangjie, "Song Shangjie boshi geren jianzheng [The Testimony of Dr. Song Shangjie]," as recorded by Liao Guotian, afternoon, April 2, 1931, *Shengjie zhinan yuekan* [*Guide to Holiness*] 3, no. 6 (June 1931): 26–31; Song, "Chuangshiji yu shizijia [Genesis and the Cross]," 31–36.

[28] Song, "Chuangshijide qi xiaohai [The Seven Children of Genesis]," 15.

[29] Song Shangjie. "Song Shangjie boshi jiejing [Dr. Song Shangjie's Explanation of Scripture]," as recorded by Liao Guotian, *Shengjie zhinan yuekan* [*Guide to Holiness*] 3, no. 4 (May 1931): 2.

[30] George M. Marsden, *Understanding Fundamentalism and Evangelicalism* (Grand Rapids: Eerdmans, 1991), 173–79.

of the future that he uncovered for his audiences, but Song's more explicit agenda was to usher those in attendance into reverent awe.

For that purpose he did draw on his scientific education. Chemistry could illustrate the profundity of the biblical mysteries. For example, Song helped explain the connection between the second day of creation and Jesus changing water into wine in John 2 via a chemical formula. On the second day of creation, God separated the waters—waters below and waters above—and named the vault between them "sky," or in Chinese, "heaven [*tian*]." Song explained, "Water is H_2O. If you want it to become wine, you need to add carbon, so wine is $C_6H_{12}O_6$. Water originally belongs to the earth [i.e., water below]. Carbon is found in the heavens [*tiankong*]. Now when they are brought together wine is made. This is the meaning of the Word made flesh."[31] Whether or not his audience found his illustration of the incarnation enlightening, Song made his greater point: the Bible was filled with amazing facts if one but knew how to look.

Certainly not everyone was impressed with his arcane explication of Scripture. One listener to his sermons on Genesis sent Song a note complaining, "During these days of Bible exposition you have offered far-fetched interpretations, and misunderstood the Bible at many points."[32] It was not the first negative evaluation he received. Soon after his return to China, Song's father gave a withering evaluation of one of his son's enigmatic messages.[33] Some of the missionaries in Xinghua, too, noted that his sermons were clumsy and believed other ministers in the conference were more gifted preachers and held greater promise.[34] Francis Jones, former principal of the Methodist high school, saw Song as "theologically immature, delighting in torturous allegorical exegesis, and constantly inclined to go off on tangents."[35] Even those who were more appreciative of Song's sincere efforts to hold an audience's attention

[31] Song, "Chuangshiji yu yuehan fuyin [Genesis and the Gospel of John]," 20. The translation of *tiankong* as "heavens" is admittedly loose, as it is normally rendered "air," but I chose to translate it this way in order to capture the connection Song observed and the thrust of his argument.

[32] Song Tianzhen (Levi), ed., *Shi'er fude de riji* [*The Journal Once Lost*] (Kowloon, Hong Kong: China Alliance Press, 2006), 103.

[33] Song Shangjie, November 13, 1927, SSD, TTC.

[34] F. Stanley Carson to Dr. Frank Cartwright, May 27, 1929, United Methodist Church (U.S.), *Missionary Files: Methodist Church, 1912–1949* (Wilmington, Del.: Scholarly Resources), roll 74. Hereafter, this location will be referred to as UMC.

[35] Francis P. Jones, "John Sung," *China Bulletin* 5, no. 4 (February 1955): 2.

were wont to comment on the oddity of his sermons. "Mr. Song has great spiritual power and a cordial attitude. His themes are not according to current practices, but he brings novelty into full play."[36]

Song had ceased to insist on his own ideologies, but he had not yet discovered how to mobilize a crowd. Until 1931 he held his audience's attention primarily by mirroring their own spiritual proclivities, speaking with them as a wandering curator of divine mysteries.

THE BETHEL MISSION

During Song's sermons on Genesis, which he preached in April 1931, he looked up from his archaeological dig through the various layers of heavenly secrets long enough to tell people that for the last three years in Xinghua, "God's Spirit was with me. I knew something about the Three Principles of the People, socialism, and science—they were all empty. Only the cross of Jesus had the power to save a person's soul."[37] Yet when he returned to Shanghai three months later and spoke in the same auditorium, he was dismissive of all that work: "The three years I spent working in Xinghua are a warning. At that time, I spent day and night busily applying learning to instruct people . . . but in the end it had no effect. But now I am careful. I do not know anything else, but Jesus and him crucified on the cross."[38] Song perceived that something critical had changed in his preaching over the summer. In fact, the difference was so stark he dismissed his previous three years of ministry as rubbish.[39] That made it difficult to reconcile all the positive things he said earlier about his work in China, but he risked the contradiction. Something extraordinary had to be said to express the magnitude of the change that had come to pass.

What caused the seismic shift? What happened between April and July of 1931 that so radically altered Song's view of his ministry? The answer lies in the Bethel Mission, the organization that hosted the Five Year Movement's assembly in Shanghai, where Song spoke about the

---

[36] Jing Wu, "Wuhu erjie jiaoqu fenxinghui [Wuhu Second Street District Revival Meeting]," *Xinghua bao* 28, no. 13 (April 8, 1931): 28–29.

[37] Song, "Song Shangjie boshi geren jianzheng [The Testimony of Dr. Song Shangjie]," 31.

[38] Song Shangjie, "Make di'erzhang [Mark Chapter Two]," as recorded by Chen Zhenfan, *Shengjie zhinan yeukan [Guide to Holiness]* 3, no. 9 (September 1931): 19.

[39] Song Shangjie, *Forty John Sung Revival Sermons*, vol. 1, trans. Timothy Tow (Singapore: Alice Doo, 1978), 110.

mysteries of Genesis in April and where he preached again in July. In between those two visits Shi Meiyu [Mary Stone] and Jennie Hughes, the co-directors of Bethel, had integrated Song into their vibrant Holiness-revival ministry.

Shi Meiyu was something of a celebrity as she and Kang Cheng [Ida Kahn] were the first two Chinese women to earn medical degrees from a Western university (Michigan, 1896). Shi returned to China as a crown jewel for the Women's Foreign Missionary Society (WFMS) of the Methodist Episcopal Church (MEC). While working in the Elizabeth Skelton Danforth Memorial Hospital in the Jiangxi Province, Shi became close friends with Jennie Hughes. Hughes was the daughter of George Hughes, the editor of the influential American Holiness periodical *Guide to Holiness*.[40] Their decision to leave the MEC together in 1920 over its perceived theological modernism and inattentiveness to the message of entire sanctification was a public affair. To fund their new venture, Shi and Hughes mailed out letters, magazines, and booklets to Holiness groups and individuals, even managing to siphon off financial support from the WFMS.[41] Their well-known names, their decision to locate their self-governed work in the cosmopolitan space of Shanghai, and their thick support network made Bethel a crucial node in the international Holiness-revival network.

For example, between 1925 and 1928, Bethel was at the center of four major revivals. The first and most famous happened just shortly after the May Thirtieth Incident in 1925. A. Paget Wilkes, a member of the Church of England who founded the Japan Evangelistic Band, dared to visit Shanghai despite the fury over British policemen gunning down Chinese protesters. Inspired by the Holiness movement, his sermons ignited something like Pentecostal fire in the charged atmosphere of the city and convinced Shi Meiyu to begin leading her own revival services.[42] The Quaker-turned-Nazarene-turned-Pilgrim Holiness preacher Seth Cook Rees held revival meetings at Bethel during his worldwide preaching tour of 1926, where he not only excited spiritual fervor but also

[40] "Personals," *Christian Advocate* 91 (July 6, 1916): 897.

[41] Rev. Thomas S. Brock to Miss Lewis, May 31, 1921, Biographical Files, "Jennie Hughes," General Commission on Archives and History, United Methodist Church, Madison, N.J. (hereafter referred to as UMC); Clotilda L. McDowell and Evelyn Riley Nicholson to Dear Secretary, June 24, 1921, Biographical Files, "Jennie Hughes," UMC.

[42] "Shi Meiyu yisheng," in *Jiushizhounian ganen tekan* [*90th Anniversary Thanksgiving Publication*] (Hong Kong: Bethel, 2011), 9.

stirred up controversy by ordaining Shi and Hughes as ministers of the gospel.[43] In 1927 Bethel rallied around the Holiness Church of India's African American missionary Edward Carter when his son's typhoid fever forced him to disembark in Shanghai. Bethel helped promote Carter's impromptu revivals which, by their successes, led to the establishment of several new Holiness churches in China.[44] Then, in 1928, Bethel welcomed the Methodist George Whitefield Ridout of Asbury Theological Seminary to reawaken people from their spiritual slumbers through his preaching.[45] Such high-profile services were indicative of the fact that Shi and Hughes had become prominent figures in a multiethnic, interdenominational, and international network of Holiness revivalism.

Precisely what these two leading Holiness women saw or heard when Song preached at Bethel in April 1931 is unclear. It may have been his charisma on stage, or maybe the fact that at twenty-nine years old he would add some maturity—a kind of ballast—to their youthful organization. Just as likely, Shi and Hughes heard something important in his sermons on biblical mysteries. For although Song's early esoteric sermons were not traditional fare for revivalism, that did not mean they were insipid or without effect. Their obscurity seldom deterred people. On the contrary Song found audiences were eager, like their Buddhist and Daoist neighbors, to penetrate to deeper layers of meaning embedded in a holy text.[46] Students especially appreciated Song's handling of biblical material. His methodology showed them that Scripture was coherent even if it sometimes appeared contradictory. The implication was that all the questions which troubled them had a solution. The idiosyncrasies and inconsistencies of the Bible, with which many students were familiar and, in some cases, well versed through anti-Christian literature, probably had an explanation. A person only needed the right key to unlock

---

[43] *Bethel Newsletter*, 1951, Biographical Files, "Jennie Hughes," UMC; Paul S. Rees, *Seth Cook Rees: The Warrior-Saint* (Indianapolis: Pilgrim Book Room, 1934); Floyd Cunningham, ed., *Our Watchword and Song: The Centennial History of the Church of the Nazarene* (Kansas City, Mo.: Beacon Hill Press, 2009), 204–13.

[44] Frank Rawlinson, ed., *China Christian Year Book, 1928* (Shanghai: Christian Literature Society, 1928), 92–93; Allene G. Carter and Robert L. Allen, *Honoring Sergeant Carter: A Family's Journey to Uncover the Truth about an American Hero* (New York: Amistad, 2004), 51–78.

[45] "Buoteli jiaohui lishi [The History of the Bethel Church]," in *Jiushizhounian ganen tekan [90th Anniversary Thanksgiving Publication]* (Hong Kong: Bethel, 2011), 19.

[46] Holmes Welch, *The Practice of Chinese Buddhism, 1900–1950* (Cambridge, Mass.: Harvard University Press, 1967), 376.

the apparent contradictions.[47] Song's focus on uncovering hidden secrets made the Bible highly desirable. His ability to offer at least twelve different spiritual truths from such innocuous texts as, "When he returned to Capernaum after some days, it was reported that he was at home" (Mark 2:1), implicitly promised audiences that God's Word always had something more for those who were still hungry and thirsty.[48] If other biblical expositors could not satisfy, then Song's ability to part the veil of a text to reveal innumerable delicacies could awaken a profound spiritual hunger—an insatiable appetite for more.[49] No wonder observers noted that wherever he traveled Bible sales soared.[50] Whether for those reasons or some other, Shi and Hughes compiled Song's talks and, for only the second time, published an entire issue of the *Shengjie zhinan yuekan* [*Guide to Holiness*] on one subject, namely Song's sermons on the mysteries of Genesis.[51]

The first special issue had appeared only two months earlier and announced the formation of the Bethel Worldwide Evangelistic Band (BWEB).[52] It contained the testimonies of Ji Zhiwen [Andrew Gih], Li Daorong [Philip Lee], Nie Ziying [Lincoln Nieh], and Lin Jinkang [Frank

[47] Song Shangjie, March 2–3, 1931, SSD, TTC; William E. Schubert, *I Remember John Sung* (Singapore: Armour Publishing, 2005), 270; Yip, *Religion, Nationalism, and Chinese Students.*

[48] Song, "Make di'erzhang [Mark Chapter Two]," 18.

[49] Song saw his task as making the gospel digestible. He suggested, for instance, that people often looked at the words in the Bible and saw nothing appetizing; it was like gazing at the shell of a peanut. Only those like Song who knew something delicious was inside the shell could peel the rough exterior, get to the delicacy inside, and share the bounty. See Song Shangjie, "Make disizhang [Mark Chapter Four]," as recorded by Chen Zhenfan, July 7, 1931, *Shengjie zhinan yuekan* [*Guide to Holiness*] 3, no. 11 (November 1931): 13.

[50] Hinghwa Annual Conference, *Official Minutes of the 25th Session of the Hinghwa Annual Conference of the Methodist Episcopal Church* (Shanghai: Methodist Publishing House, 1929), 142, Records of the General Conference, United Methodist Church Archives—GCAH, Madison, N.J., remarked on how Song's work signaled numerous purchases of the Bible, as did H. R. Williamson in "Evangelistic Work in China To-day," *Christian Recorder* 69 (September 1938): 449. More famously, Francis P. Jones, "John Sung," in *Encyclopedia of World Methodism, L–Z*, ed. Harmon B. Nolan (Nashville: United Methodist Publishing House), 2283, recalled, "The Bible Societies had no difficulty in following his trail, for the sale of Bibles and Testaments always doubled and tripled wherever he went."

[51] *Shengjie zhinan yuekan* [*Guide to Holiness*] 3, no. 6 (June 1931).

[52] The Chinese word "band" should not be associated with a musical group or a Wesleyan small group for intensive discipleship. A band referred to a team of evangelists.

Ling] and how they were inspired by a visit of evangelists from Asbury College in Wilmore, Kentucky. In conscious reproduction of what they saw in their American guests, these young men formed the BWEB to "work in China for two years, and then follow the Lord's leading as to where to minister, possibly making a trip around Asia, and then afterwards to every country in the world."[53]

The issue was filled with fanfare and described in copious detail how the evangelistic team was commissioned. The Bethel church had been covered in various scriptural texts and references like, "Ask and you will receive," "Get up and cross the Jordan!" and "I am with you always, to the end of the Age." To symbolize the larger support of the Christian community, dignitaries from various Christian organizations joined the team on the platform. The dedication ceremony was strategically held on the tenth anniversary of Bethel's formation. Dr. Shi Meiyu and Jennie Hughes had organized Bethel in 1921 after they resigned from the MEC.[54] Not wanting external interference in their plans, the two women started their own church, school, and hospital. Over the following decade they added a Bible school, a nurses training college, and an orphanage. All of it was located in the commercial center of China, in Shanghai. However, when they dedicated the evangelistic team in 1931, Shi and Hughes definitively shifted the identity of their work. It would no longer be exclusively tied to the city. Bethel would become a traveling mission available to all. The ceremony described that transition by likening the mission's ten-year anniversary to the ten-day period between Christ's ascension and Pentecost. At the commissioning service it was as if the time was fulfilled.

---

[53] "Bentuan xuanyan," *Shengjie zhinan yuekan* [*Guide to Holiness*] 3, no. 4 (April 1931): 10.

[54] Evelyn Nicholson and Susan Townley to Miss Hughes, May 14, 1920, Biographical Files, "Jennie Hughes," UMC; Ellin J. Knowles to [no name], June 24, 1920, Biographical Files, "Jennie Hughes," UMC; "A Statement from New York Branch," n.d., Biographical Files, "Jennie Hughes," UMC. Lurking beneath the criticism of the church's handling of schools was a theological argument. Christian schools were supposed to register in China and adopt standardized curricula, but Jennie Hughes and Shi Meiyu felt that government regulations would prohibit the proclamation of the gospel. To compromise on the issue was to compromise the gospel. After they left the Methodist Church, the two women steadfastly refused to register any of the educational institutions that they began in Shanghai. See Lu Ming, "Boteli mingmingde youlai [The Origin of Bethel's Name]," in *Jiushizhounian ganen tekan* [*90th Anniversary Thanksgiving Publication*] (Hong Kong: Bethel, 2011).

Prayer and preparation were over. The gift of the Holy Spirit would now be offered to all through revivals conducted by the BWEB.[55]

The exceptional publication of Song's arcane sermons just two months later appeared anticlimactic in light of the momentous changes Bethel had just undergone. Why elevate the sermons of one of the many preachers that traveled through the Bethel chapel to the same level as the commissioning of the Worldwide Band? Apparently, the editors of the *Guide to Holiness* sensed the incongruity and promised that special issues were indeed reserved for special occasions and that this phrase would not be overused.[56] But something wonderful was happening again! After Song preached at Bethel in April 1931, he had agreed to travel with the BWEB, so the second special issue was but an extension of the introduction of the team made earlier. Song was now touring with the Bethel Band as it traveled through Jiangsu and Shandong provinces and, the publication announced, would return with them to Shanghai in July and be the featured speaker of the Bethel Summer Conference.[57] So what had happened between April and July 1931 that so profoundly changed Song's preaching? He had been inducted into the pulsating heart of Holiness revivalism in China.

Song took to Bethel's revivalism immediately. It provided a way for him to reproduce his experience of becoming a New Man for large audiences. As he mastered the techniques of revivalism, his rise through the organization was meteoric. In November 1931 the *Guide to Holiness* announced that Song had become a permanent member of the BWEB. He was listed second, just after the Rev. Ji Zhiwen, who was a longtime member of the Bethel Mission, close associate of Jennie Hughes and Dr. Shi Meiyu, and the appointed leader of the group. Song's presence, however, shifted the dynamics of the team. He was the oldest of the small group, having turned thirty by that time, and he had several years of ministerial experience.[58] Li Darong, who was not yet twenty, believed

[55] "Boteli huanyou budaotuan fengxian dianli dahui ji," *Shengjie zhinan yuekan* [*Guide to Holiness*] 3, no. 4 (April 1931): 33–35.

[56] "Juantou yu," *Shenghie zhinan yuekan* [*Guide to Holiness*] 3, no. 4 (April 1931): 1.

[57] Back cover of *Shengjie zhinan yuekan* [*Guide to Holiness*] 3, no. 4 (April 1931).

[58] Jennie Hughes, ed., *Bethel Heart Throbs of Revival* (Shanghai: Bethel Mission, 1931). The youthfulness of the group reflects how it was part of the May Fourth era, when youth was privileged over age and experience. See Rana Mitter, *A Bitter Revolution: China's Struggle with the Modern World* (New York: Oxford University Press, 2004), 112.

it was important that he do many of the difficult or thankless tasks in a service, feeling it was better to "spoil a young preacher rather than an important old one."[59] Song's influence within the team, over audiences, and at Bethel grew rapidly. Within a few months, his name was listed first in reports about the band in the Christian press.[60] Ultimately, he also became preeminent within Bethel itself. In January 1932, only two months after officially joining the team, he was named editor in chief of the *Guide to Holiness*, and by the end of that year Bethel, which had always faithfully referred to its trusted associate Ji Zhiwen as the captain of the team, capitulated to the new reality and named Song as the first evangelist on staff.[61]

Jennie Hughes gushed about Song. She even rushed to the printer in December of 1932 to get one more story into her annual *Heart Throbs* publication. It appeared that through Song's work, "The great World Revival that you and we are praying for these days may be on its way by way of Peiping [Beijing]."[62] Song had finally found a way to make an audience New.

REVIVALISM

Revivalism recreated the pattern of Song's own experience of transformation and did so in a highly condensed form. It did not require months in a hospital, a period of confusion, and then a slow reconstruction and reinterpretation of events. A revival squeezed the conversion experience into a church service. Within an hour, or maybe three, a person could discover he was an Old Man, encounter the transforming presence of Jesus Christ, and walk away a New Man.[63] Revivals had that kind of power.

[59] Hughes, *Bethel Heart Throbs of Revival*, 21.

[60] "Wuzhou kongqiande fenxing budao dahui [Wuzhou's Unprecedented Revival Evangelistic Meetings]," *Zhenguang* [*True Light*] 31, no. 7 (July 1932): 85.

[61] Jennie Hughes, ed., *Bethel Heart Throbs of Surprises* (Shanghai: Bethel Mission, 1932).

[62] Hughes, *Bethel Heart Throbs of Surprises*, 67. After the Nationalists took power in 1927, they moved the capitol to Nanjing, which literally means "Southern Capitol." They renamed Beijing [Northern Capitol] to Beiping [Northern Peace]. That was the convention for most of the years of Song's ministry, but for the sake of recognizability, I have taken the liberty of transcribing Beiping as Beijing.

[63] A careful reading detects one slight modification in Song's recreation of the conversion experience for audience members. Whereas Jesus came to him, Song invited listeners—in the second move—to go to Jesus. In other words, they could

Revivalism turned Song's sermons from expositions and explanations into events and experiences. The change began with publicity. Whereas he previously hurried from village to village, covering as much ground as he could in a single day, Bethel taught Song to move deliberately. Thoughtful planning allowed the BWEB to circulate announcements about their itinerary in advance. Numerous Christian papers and periodicals reported the team's schedule, building a sense of anticipation. "The Shanghai Bethel Worldwide Evangelistic Band will be in Tingxian, Shandong from April 19–29 at the Presbyterian Church."[64] The printed program would include a report informing readers that a special work of the Holy Spirit had been accompanying Bethel's labors. Acting as a subtle script of how people were to act, these notices explained that everywhere the team went sinners were being converted through tears and that the rumbles of group confessions were rattling buildings as people collectively sobbed.[65] The mighty wind of Pentecost was again shaking the church's foundations. No one should miss it!

As the date of the Bethel Band's arrival drew closer, their destination city was flooded with further advertisements. Newspapers would sometimes report the upcoming services. Flyers were printed and distributed on the streets. Banners were painted and hung above the church door where the young men would soon enter to preach. Bethel borrowed every technique that department stores were pioneering in China.[66] They did what it took to bring people in.

If one stepped inside, or curiously cracked the door to peek at what all the fuss was about, one would hear music. Songs were an extremely important feature of everything Bethel did. The younger team members warmed audiences up with peppy songs and zippy lyrics, as one of them energetically pounded out notes on the piano while another amused the audience with

---

choose to be saved. No one needed to wait passively to be rescued. In the midst of China's national crisis to say otherwise would have sounded despairing. China could not wait for others to decide if the nation would modernize or not; Chinese people had to will it.

[64] Zhang Jing, "Fuxingdahui shengkuang [Highlights of the Big Revival Meeting]," *Xinghua bao* 28, no. 14 (April 15, 1931): 31–32.

[65] "Wuzhou kongqiande fenxing budao dahui [Wuzhou's Unprecedented Revival Evangelistic Meetings]," 86; Anna Hockelman, "The Story of a Thirty-Nine Day Revival," *Latter Rain Evangel* 26, no. 10 (July 1935): 19–21.

[66] Sherman Cochran, ed., *Inventing Nanjing Road: Commercial Culture in Shanghai, 1900–1945*, Cornell East Asia Series (Ithaca, N.Y.: Cornell University, 1999).

exaggerated slides on his freshly burnished trombone. Church decorum prevented attendees from gliding or hopping about the sanctuary, so they channeled the energy of China's urban dance halls into clapping and singing the uncomplicated, contagious tunes with simple lyrics.

By the time Song strode to the center of the platform in his long traditional gown, an effervescent atmosphere had been created, and a sense of anticipation hung in the air. He immediately captivated audiences with the look, techniques, and mannerisms of traditional Chinese storytellers. Whenever he preached he dressed like a storyteller, eschewing the Western cut suits of his Bethel teammates. He entertained crowds with props, exaggerated gestures, and mime. He delighted them with his ability to change the pitch or quality of his voice as he mimicked characters in his sermons. And just like a paid storyteller, he would periodically interrupt his speaking with a song. His simple choruses were the storyteller's way of reinforcing a point and reengaging any drifting attentions. Song looked and sounded just like any other traditional storyteller, except that his tales followed a different narrative arc.[67]

People may not have realized where Song's stories were going at first. They probably just enjoyed how he could dramatically produce a pen out of his wide sleeves and then use it to sketch a caricature—a cartoon similar to those beginning to appear in Chinese magazines.[68] He could rapidly draw, for instance, a hypocrite on poster-size paper. Exaggerating a person's features by giving him bulging eyes, flapping ears, a big mouth, and a round belly, Song offered his audience a memorable depiction of those who only see what is wrong with others, listen to flattery, speak critically, and gorge themselves on the mistakes of others. The addition of tiny arms and shrunken legs drove home the point.

---

[67] For a description of Chinese storytelling, see Vibeke Børdahl, "The Storyteller's Manner in Chinese Storytelling," *Asian Folklore Studies* 62, no. 1 (2003): 65–112; Vibeke Børdahl, "Professional Storytelling in Modern China: A Case Study of the 'Yangzhou Pinghua' Tradition," *Asian Folklore Studies* 56, no. 1 (1997): 7–32. It is also important to note that the Suzhou storytelling style that Song employed had taken over radio. Almost 45 percent of radio shows in Shanghai were *tanci*, storytelling and the storytellers' songs. Carlton Benson, "The Manipulation of *Tanci* in Radio Shanghai during the 1930s," *Republican China* 20, no. 2 (1995): 117–46.

[68] Martina Caschera, "Chinese Cartoon in Transition: Animal Symbolism and Allegory from the 'Modern Magazine' to the 'Online Carnival,' *Studies in Visual Arts and Communication: An International Journal* 4, no. 1 (2017): 2.

Hypocrites can do nothing.[69] If the picture on the easel was not clear enough, Song acted it out. He pulled his hands into his chest and waddled about the stage ineffectively. Audiences laughed appreciatively as Song mocked hypocrisy, but then he moved to buckle their knees.

The transition could happen suddenly. In the middle of a sermon on Jesus raising Lazarus from the dead, Song unexpectedly pulled out a small casket—a ritually unclean object—and waived it about with impunity.[70] He taunted his audience that their hearts were like tombs, filled with the stink of rotten sin. "No! Don't open it!" he parodied those obviously aghast by his frank disregard of propriety. "It will smell!" But open it he did. Sinking his hand into the casket, he pulled forth a strip of cloth and dramatized his disgust as he dangled it before everyone's eyes: "Oh! The first stink . . . *hatred.*" He warned the audience about the seductive power of hatred and explained how such sins bound Lazarus and held him in his grave. Then he leveled his heavy stare on the crowd. "Who has committed this sin?" Eyes dropped down, hoping to avoid Song's notice, while a charged and uncomfortable silence filled the hall. Song pressed on determinedly: "Do you hate? Father, mother, brother, sister, teachers, grandmother, daughter-in-law, husband, wife, friend, children, fellow workers, students? Do you hate in your heart? Do you hate to the very bone?"[71] He paused, waiting, waiting, until finally someone indicated she knew the burning power of hatred. Then another and another raised her hand in confession. On and on it went, women and men weeping with remorse, until Song was satisfied that hatred had been fully disgorged. Then he thrust his hand back into the box and drew out another stinking cloth: "Visiting brothels! Who has committed this sin?"[72]

---

[69] Song Shangjie, *Fenxingji* [*Revival Messages*], 6th ed. (1935; repr., Hong Kong: Bellman House, 1989), 38ff.

[70] Death was considered to be powerfully polluting. Those touched by it were not allowed to worship traditional Chinese deities. To bring death into the place of worship, even symbolically as Song did, was provocative and upsetting. See Emily M. Ahern, "The Power and Pollution of Chinese Women," in *Women in Chinese Society*, ed. Margery Wolf and Roxane Witke (Stanford: Stanford University Press, 1975).

[71] Schubert, *I Remember John Sung*, 288.

[72] Song, *Fenxingji* [*Revival Messages*], 76; and Song Shangjie, "Xiangwo chuilingqi [May the Spirit Breathe on Me]," as recorded by Zhao Aiguang, *Budao zazhi* [*Evangelism*] 8, no. 3 (May–June 1935): 10–14.

Song might go on to pull thirty to forty more sins from the casket that evening. Variations of each sin were elucidated carefully, trampling social taboos. It was awkward enough when Song asked if anyone had fornicated, but then he made everyone squirm by asking, "Did you almost? Mentally? With people in your own family, sister, brother, man and man, woman and woman, with animals?"[73] Time and again, Song left no stone unturned as he doggedly hunted his quarry. No one could walk away from one of his sermons guilt free. He wanted everyone to acknowledge the grip sin had on them, recognize the shame of their behavior, and admit that they were still very much the Old Man, the kind of degenerate person China had to escape from.

The good news was that Jesus offered an exit. After the ruthless unmasking of the Old Man, the second move in Song's revivalism invited people to turn to Jesus to be saved. That required each person in the audience to make a decision. In fact, everything hung on that. Salvation required a choice. Everyone had to choose his or her own religious identity. No one could rely on family or clan.[74] You would be a fool to act like Lot, who assumed that being connected to Abraham was sufficient for salvation. You cannot borrow your spiritual identity, Song warned.[75] That is something you have to decide yourself. *You* choose to be different by choosing a new life in Jesus Christ.

Individual choice was what created a new beginning. Song amplified that point to the extent that he even reimagined biblical texts to make them align with his preaching. In his telling of the lost sheep, for instance, the story no longer turned on the shepherd leaving the ninety-nine in search of the one who wandered off (Luke 15:3-7). Instead, Song told the parable so that the lost sheep itself decided to go home.

As the service neared its climax, Song prepared the audience to do the same. Choosing Jesus was a matter of urgency: "Today is the day of acceptance. Do not wait any longer!"[76] He enhanced the crisis by making life hang in the balance at the moment of decision. Something needed to be

[73] Schubert, *I Remember John Sung*, 289.

[74] Song Shangjie, "Shituxingzhuan disanzhang [Acts Chapter Three]," as recorded by Yang Zhicheng, *Shengjie zhinan yuekan* [*Guide to Holiness*] 3, no. 11 (November 1931): 10.

[75] Song, *Fenxingji* [*Revival Messages*], 165.

[76] Song Shangjie, "Shituxingzhuan diyizhang [Acts Chapter One]," as recorded by Chen Qiujin, *Shengjie zhinan yuekan* [*Guide to Holiness*] 3, no. 9 (September 1931): 33.

done immediately. If a person missed this opportunity, he or she faced dire consequences. Song provided an imaginary account of what happened in an Egyptian home before Passover. A young Egyptian boy, he informed the congregation, heard about the coming Passover from an Israelite child:

> The Egyptian boy said, "I am the eldest, but we don't have any blood!" So he left his friend, and returned home. He told his father, and pleaded with him to kill a lamb. His father answered: "Do not be troubled by them, Jews are the most superstitious people. Come and eat!" Poor little child, he could eat but not swallow. His mother took him to sleep, but the child did not dare. His mother said, "Do not worry! I will sleep with you." A little after ten the child woke up: "Mama! Quick, kill a lamb!" His mother once again patted him, and used comforting words until the boy once more fell asleep. All was quiet and still for an hour and a half, when suddenly the terrified boy once more woke up, yelling: "Mama! Hurry, kill a lamb!" His mother again comforted him, and his father said, "Son! Do not be afraid! If an angel really comes, your daddy will fight him off." The boy once again relaxed. . . . Time flew by, and it was already 11:50. The child woke for a last time, and pleaded—as his whole body was drenched with sweat—saying, "Mama! Hurry, kill a lamb. The angel is coming soon!" The mother saw how anxious her son was, and told him a little lie: "I already killed it." The child, who knew no better, fell back asleep, but soon thereafter his mother heard footsteps, [saw] a flash of light like the sun, and she heard her precious child's dying cry: "Mama!" That was his last sound. The mother hurriedly said, "Angel! Stop!" Unfortunately, it was too late! Dead![77]

Do not make the same mistake, he urged. To make excuses, to pretend Song's warnings were idle or superstitious, or to delay any longer was to invite an irreversible calamity. The time for decision was now. Come and meet Jesus.

After Song issued the climactic call for people to seek Jesus, the third phase of the revival commenced. The wall that separated the spectators from the performer collapsed. Every person in the audience was suddenly aware that he or she was part of the unfolding liturgical drama of salvation and was forced—willingly or unwillingly—to play a role with eternal consequences. Song conceded his lead role and prompted the audience to take center stage. He told all those who had recognized their sinfulness and their need for Jesus to separate themselves symbolically from their old, wretched lives by leaving their seats. Come to the

[77] Song Shangjie, *Lingcheng zhinan* [*A Guide for the Spiritual Journey*] (1932; repr., Hong Kong: Shengwen Publishing, 1969), 12.

front of the sanctuary, he implored. That simple invitation managed to erase familiar social categories and distinctions.[78] Penitents would gather on the platform with Song, or he would meet them at the altar, closing the distance between clergy and laity. More shocking still: men, women, and children would mix freely as equals beneath the cross. In the presence of one another, they articulated their failures clearly and out loud, neither boisterously shouting nor timidly mouthing them.[79] Repentance occurred in deep sorrow and with tears. Crying was a kind of baptism—tears helped cleanse the soul.[80]

In that socially porous moment, a New Man was born. The old was gone (one need only look around the auditorium to see how different things were); the new had come. The change was that quick. Song assured the emotionally wrung-out audience, which after a while would fall silent except for the occasional sniffle, that their past was obliterated. Like Zacchaeus in the Bible and Song Shangjie in New York, five minutes in the presence of Jesus was all it took to become a totally different person. For those who had come forward to receive the promise of a New Birth, their lives could now be separated into two categories: everything in life that was before Christ and now.[81] Having repented of the past, a person was free to live in the present. This completed the three-step process, whereby audiences reenacted Song Shangjie's own experience of transformation. They moved from acknowledging the Old Man to choosing Jesus Christ, embracing a new beginning unsoiled by the past.

---

[78] Dickson D. Bruce, *And They All Sang Hallelujah: Plain-Folk Camp-Meeting Religion, 1800–1845* (Knoxville: University of Tennessee Press, 1974), 87.

[79] Song, *Fenxingji* [*Revival Messages*], 110; Song Shangjie, "Yongyuan shifang [Eternally Set Free]," as recorded by Zhao Aiguang, *Budao zazhi* [*Evangelism*] 7, no. 3 (May–June 1934): 11.

[80] Song Shangjie, *Forty John Sung Revival Sermons*, vol. 2, trans. Timothy Tow (Singapore: Alice Doo, 1983), 51ff. Recent literature has suggested that tears in confession and repentance have been especially powerful in remaking masculine identities. Men trying to leave gangs are encouraged to cry. Tears are a graphic break with the hypermasculinity associated with their violent pasts. See Edward Orozco Flores and Pierrette Hondagneu-Sotelo, "Chicano Gang Members in Recovery: The Public Talk of Negotiating Chicano Masculinities," *Social Problems* 60, no. 4 (2013): 476–90. Perhaps something similar was happening among Chinese men as they confessed and renounced gender-related sins, such as being members of a gang, visiting brothels, or getting into fights. The details of the sins confessed during Song's revivals will be explored in more detail in chapter 3.

[81] Song, *Forty John Sung Revival Sermons*, 1:2.

Squeezed into one service, the revivals were quite an extraordinary event, and crowds flocked to the drama. When services would be suspended for an afternoon or even until the next morning, some dared not leave the building lest they forsake their seat.[82] For many the revival was too compelling an experience. It offered mysterious, fascinating, frightening, comic, and lurid displays. No one, it seems, could pull their eyes away. That was why Song could report that when he was in one city people from India—who could not understand a word of his preaching—were miraculously converted and physically healed. The apostle Paul wrote in Romans 10:17 that faith comes by hearing, but in Song's powerful performances, *seeing* a revival was sufficient unto salvation.

Mobilization

Song Shangjie perfected Chinese revivalism. His services were compact reproductions of the evangelical conversion narrative. They moved a person from being the Old Man to the New Man by way of Jesus Christ. The formula was so ironclad that Song could amaze audiences by tossing out the question, "What chapter in the Bible do you want me to preach from?"[83] In an incredible display of mental agility he would then concoct a sermon on the spot. In part that emerged from Song's genius, but it was also born of his firm grasp of revivalism's structure. Regardless of what chapter in the Bible he faced, Song knew he had to lead a crowd through three steps. He needed them to recognize their sin, choose Jesus Christ, and reconfigure their lives around the present instead of the errors of the past. To pull that off from a passage like Habakkuk 2 might not be easy, but Song always managed to make it work.[84] It sometimes required him to focus on the hidden meaning in a Chinese character, build off a reference to the human body embedded in the text, or jump

[82] Hockelmann, "Story of a Thirty-Nine Day Revival," 19–21; Bobby E. K. Sng, *In His Good Time: The Story of the Church in Singapore, 1819–1978* (Singapore: Graduates' Christian Fellowship, 1980), 176–82.

[83] W. B. Cole, "Sienyu Notes," *China Christian Advocate* (June 1929): 15; see also Schubert, *I Remember John Song*, 286.

[84] Song Shangjie, "Hagaishu <Part 2> [Haggai]," *Light in Darkness* 6, no. 11 (September–October 1935): 22–24.

to an illustration from his own life, but one way or another he would reach his goal.[85] His services were designed to produce New Creations.

However, they never settled there. A New Man or New Woman was not enough to change China, as radicals discovered. In the aftermath of May Fourth, the nation saw plenty of "awakened" individuals form study groups and discuss the challenges the country faced, but they did little to alter it.[86] That required more organization and radicalization. By the end of the 1920s, a person could not declare himself a New Man; he had to act like it. So instead of lamenting with colleagues about the immovable masses, revolutionaries started to work with them in rallies, parades, boycotts, and strikes. The aim was mass mobilization. Only such large-scale efforts could save the nation.[87]

Song agreed, and he used all his rhetorical skills to move the New Man out of the church and into the world. The time was short, he cautioned; the end of the world was at hand. Jesus Christ could return any moment. This was not the time for half-hearted commitment or a wait-and-see attitude. Everything was at stake. Song poured forth a litany of polarities. A person could choose either Jesus or Satan, the present or the past, life or death, light or darkness, to be hot or be cold.[88] Dualisms tumbled out of his mouth left and right. Some even contradicted one another, not because Song was a fool, but because he never stopped to work them out systematically. The important thing was not the precise content, but the creation of a polarized world. Song wanted to simplify life's options and reduce them to two: someone could decide to help or hurt. No other options existed.

---

[85] For more information about how Song filled his sermons, see Daryl R. Ireland, "John Sung: Revitalization in China and Southeast Asia" (Ph.D. diss., Boston University, 2015), 122–31.

[86] Hans J. van de Ven, *From Friend to Comrade: The Founding of the Chinese Communist Party, 1920–1927* (Berkeley: University of California Press, 1991), 38–39.

[87] John Fitzgerald, *Awakening China: Politics, Culture, and Class in the Nationalist Revolution* (Stanford: Stanford University Press, 1996), 276, 284.

[88] Song Shangjie, *Peilingji [Devotional Messages]* (1935; repr., Hong Kong: Bellman House, n.d.), 12; Song Shangjie, "Zuidan tuoluo: Yuehan fuyin di bazhang [Casting Off the Burden of Sin: John Chapter Eight]," as recorded by Zhao Aiguang, *Budao zazhi [Evangelism]* 7, no. 2 (March–April 1934): 9; Song Shangjie, "Dujing make diyizhang [Reading Mark Chapter One]," as recorded by Chen Zhenfan, *Shengjie zhinan yuekan [Guide to Holiness]* 3, no. 9 (September 1931): 16.

The way Song boiled every choice down to a binary option did not come strictly from revivalism; it also imitated the political language that surrounded him. Throughout his years working in China, politicians and activists were busily carving the world into opposite camps. Intellectuals mobilized the New Culture Movement of the 1910s and 1920s by juxtaposing their utopian vision of China to a past they described as subservient, hierarchical, patriarchal, and decadent.[89] A variety of "anti-" movements quickly flourished and then withered in the first third of the twentieth century. Their very titles—"Anti-Christian Movement," for example—categorized all people as belonging to either one of two groups.[90] Others, like the Nationalists (GMD) and Communists (CCP), turned to a polarized vocabulary to glorify nationalism and demonize imperialism. The state meanwhile came to define religion so that it, too, was understood by its opposite: superstition.[91] Bit by bit dichotomous thinking colonized virtually every aspect of life in China. Song's messages were but a part of the linguistic dualism that permeated the country in the 1930s. He, like his political counterparts, wanted to intensify and simplify the choice before people, hoping to make them act.

Studies on the rhetoric of political polarization have observed three things. First, despite the verbal pressure produced, most people are unchanged by it. Some remain oblivious to the dualistic language; others ignore it, resist it, or take it for granted. Second, although the majority of people are not mobilized by polarized terms, a minority is radicalized by the dichotomous language. Third, those who do intensify their commitment are almost always already engaged in the political process.[92] A close look at Song's ministry confirms the same dynamics at work in his revivals.

First, Song's messages never motivated the majority of the population to do anything. His incessant demands for people to save themselves and save China were a storm in a teacup. Even his largest revivals reached but a tiny proportion of the local population. In 1935 Song held a month-long

---

[89] Peter Gue Zarrow, *China in War and Revolution, 1895–1949* (New York: Routledge, 2005), 129.

[90] Yip, *Religion, Nationalism, and Chinese Students*, 32.

[91] Rebecca Nedostup, *Superstitious Regimes: Religion and the Politics of Chinese Modernity* (Cambridge, Mass.: Harvard University Press, 2009).

[92] Markus Prior, "Media and Political Polarization," *Annual Review of Political Science* 16 (2013): 101–27; Ryan L. Claassen and Benjamin Highton, "Policy Polarization among Political Elites and the Significance of Political Awareness in the Mass Public," *Political Research Quarterly* 62, no. 3 (September 2009): 538–51.

campaign in the treaty port of Xiamen [Amoy]. During that time he led a revival and, simultaneously, a course on the Bible. Delegates from all across China swelled the audience to 6,000 people, making it the largest group he ever addressed. Yet at that high-water mark, those in attendance barely represented 3 percent of the 177,000 people living in the city.[93]

Song not only failed to move the majority of Chinese people, he struggled to even inspire Christians. It is difficult to make a case from silence, but after reading extensively through correspondence written at the time of Song's revivals in numerous cities as well as the writings in the months following, one cannot help but notice the absence of references to his services. The overwhelming Christian response was silence. The exception, by its Spartan account, reinforces the rule. Jeanie McClure, an American Board of Commissioners for Foreign Missions (ABCFM) missionary in Fuzhou, wrote to her parents,

> We had a full day on Sunday. It began with 2-hour church. The first speaker was an army man who had just had a thrilling rescue from brigands, and told all about it. . . . Then we had communion, and then a member of the Bethel Band holding special meetings here for a couple of weeks talked till the 2 hours were up. He has a most dramatic way of preaching, much like the story-tellers on the street which the Chinese are so fond of listening to.[94]

That was it. She, along with most Chinese Christians, was simply not mobilized by Song's uncompromising dualisms.

Second, Song did succeed in radicalizing a minority of people. The exact numbers are elusive. During his life and afterward, friendly observers estimated that his ministry converted at least one hundred thousand people, or approximately 10 percent of the one million Chinese Protestants in the world.[95] The records he kept in his journal indicate that

---

[93] Jan Lahmeyer, "China: Historical Demographical Data of Urban Centers," accessed November 21, 2019, http://www.populstat.info/Asia/chinat.htm.

[94] Jeanie McClure to Folks, June 8, 1932, China Records Project Miscellaneous Personal Papers Collection, record group 8, box 122, Special Collections, Yale Divinity School Library, New Haven, Conn. Hereafter this will be referred to as YDSL.

[95] Song, *Forty John Sung Revival Sermons*, 2:79. Song declared that "[d]uring the last nine years of my travels I have seen several hundred thousand born again." Others have been slightly more conservative. Schubert, *I Remember John Sung*, 275, put the number at one hundred thousand, but he only spoke of the conversions during a three-year period, not all those converted during his entire ministry. Lian, *Redeemed by Fire*, 10, used one hundred thousand as an estimate for Song's whole career.

many more than one hundred thousand people physically responded to his invitation to accept Christ. Yet how many of those people actually converted—that is, moved from one religious tradition to another—is more difficult to tell. A number of the people responding to Song's invitation to choose Jesus and eternal life may have been responding for the second, seventh, or eighteenth time that week. Repeated walks to the front of the sanctuary were not uncommon.[96] In those cases the respondents would have already identified as Christians before Song came to town. After their latest trip to the altar, they may have said they were only *now* saved—which may have been true—but until Song helped them realize that their faith had been shallow or insufficient, they had counted themselves among the believers. For the others who only went forward once during his revival campaign, the evidence indicates that they, too, would have overwhelmingly identified themselves as Christians before Song arrived. Penitents in Song's revivals were not so much converted by his ministry as much as they were "radicalized." A significant minority, somewhere around 10 percent of all Chinese Protestants, were mobilized by Song's polarizing rhetoric.

Third, as suggested above, the vast majority of people who were energized by his messages were already engaged in the church. He did not convince them to change their religion so much as helped them intensify their commitment. This contravenes the popular image of Song, so it deserves closer attention. What evidence indicates that Song radicalized believers rather than converted unbelievers?

To begin, church reports speak univocally on the matter. In Henan, Ernest Weller reported to the China Inland Mission (CIM), "[T]he year has been one of unusual blessing, and yet of *no baptisms.*"[97] He went on to explain that Song's revival came among those already within the church. "Does it puzzle and shock you to hear of Church members being saved? It puzzled me," he confessed. Mary Crawford, who served in Shandong, likewise noted that "[Bethel's revival] messages were mostly given in circles where God's grace had been preached for years." Yet their services generated new energy because, until the revival, "most of the church members, more than a thousand, had only been converted to Christianity

---

[96] Song, *Forty John Sung Revival Sermons*, 2:30–31, 52.
[97] *China and the Gospel: The Glory of Thy Kingdom*, Report of the China Inland Mission (Edinburgh: R & R Clark, 1933), 15.

and not to Christ."[98] In Fujian, Wenona Jett wrote her friends that "[t]he majority of them [who came to Song's services] were those who had some contact with the church, students who had left school without making a decision for Christ, and backsliders of one sort and another."[99]

Other evidence can be found in the way Song spoke to audiences who gathered to hear him speak. For example, after he adopted revivalism he hardly ever addressed matters such as idol worship.[100] Instead, he explained forthrightly that his objective was "to make church members understand their own sin."[101] His sermons, therefore, presumed audiences were familiar with biblical characters and stories, and his words were chosen to lead "believers to recognize the sin in their hearts, and pray and repent with tears, asking God to save them."[102] After all, Song once told his listeners, "It is utterly necessary that a *Christian* be born again!"[103]

Chen Chonggui [Marcus Cheng], the editor of *Evangelism*, recognized Song's intended audience. In 1931 he promised to print in every issue one "article on the gospel designed for people who are outside the church, with the purpose of introducing them to Jesus, and drawing them to believe in the Lord," and one "article on revival designed for people who are inside the church, hoping that the revival will begin with us!"[104] Without fail Chen published Song's sermons second. They filled the slot intended for articles that would heighten the faith commitments of those inside the church.

Song's journals also confirm that the preponderance of listeners were choosing to be more committed to Jesus rather than choosing to follow Jesus for the first time. Records of those who came to the altar to receive God's transforming touch after Song preached were repeatedly

[98] Mary K. Crawford, *The Shantung Revival* (Shanghai: China Baptist Publication Society, 1933), 22.

[99] Wenona Jett to Friends, July 12, 1935, China Records Project Miscellaneous Personal Papers Collection, record group 8, box 104, folder 5, YDSL.

[100] In an analysis of the ninety-nine sermons preached between 1931 and 1939, Song only referred to idol worship three times.

[101] Song Shangjie, "Fujia yu ling'en [Carrying the Cross and Gifts of the Spirit]," as recorded by Chen Zhenfan, *Shengjie zhinan yuekan* [*Guide to Holiness*] 3, no. 12 (December 1931): 32.

[102] "Wuzhou kongqian weiyoude fenxing budaohui [Wuzhou's Unprecendented and Never-Seen-Before Revival Evangelistic Meetings]," *Zhenguang* [*True Light*] 32, no. 7 (July 1933): 69.

[103] Song, *Forty John Sung Revival Sermons*, 1:52 (italics mine).

[104] Chen Chonggui, "Budao zazhi lainiande jihua [*Evangelism* Magazine's Plan for the Coming Years]," *Budao zazhi* [*Evangelism*] 4, no. 6 (November–December 1931): 1.

phrased in terms like, "Men and women, about one hundred, came to the front and dedicated their lives to the Lord, confessing their sins, and being filled with the Holy Spirit. About four or five people were saved for the first time."[105] The intensification of his hearers' devotion, a kind of radicalization of those who already identified as Christians, was the overriding feature of his meetings.

In light of the evidence, it is prudent to conclude that Song's use of polarizing language produced predictable results. First, most people were unmoved by it as evidenced by church rolls. The number of Protestants in China remained virtually stagnant during Song's itinerant years. "Paper numerical gains have been small, if any," Charles Boynton reported in 1933 when he checked to see if the Five Year Movement's aim to double the number of Christians in China was successful.[106] Figures were not much higher a few years later either as Song reached the pinnacle of his career.[107] Revivalism, and its polarizing language, did not sweep much of China into the church. Second, a significant minority of people who heard Song speak, perhaps one hundred thousand listeners, believed that until Song came along they were spiritually asleep. His unsparing demand for people to decide for themselves, to choose their religious identity right now, bolted them awake. Third, the people he radicalized were already part of Protestant Chinese Christianity. Song did not add many new Christians to the Chinese church, but he did intensify the commitment of a minority who already belonged.

What did it mean to be radicalized by revivalism? For Song it meant to move people into action. That had two dimensions. Immediately, he expected people to go to the front of a sanctuary, confess their sins, and receive a new life through Jesus Christ. He wanted to see his audiences physically step forward and claim faith for themselves. Subsequently, in order to prove their new lives were different from their old, he charged those transformed in his revivals to leave the building and evangelize. They needed to go out and change China. Song took time to organize his followers into teams that were to go out and evangelize weekly. Witnessing was the litmus test of radicalization; it was the surest way to see

[105] Song Shangjie, April 15, 1934, SSD, TTC.

[106] Charles L. Boynton, "Five Year Movement," in *China Christian Year Book, 1932–1933*, ed. Frank Rawlinson (Shangai: Christian Literature Society, 1934), 210.

[107] Kenneth Scott Latourette, *A History of the Expansion of Christianity*, vol. 7, *Advance through Storm* (Grand Rapids: Zondervan, 1970), 346.

if someone was truly a New Man or New Woman. Would a person dare to tell others? Evangelism became the last and most important step in the order of salvation. At the front of a church sanctuary, sins could be confessed and a divided heart overcome, but Song insisted that until someone shared about Jesus his or her spiritual sickness was never completely healed.[108] For those whose faith had been intensified during his revivals, evangelism became the necessary means to complete salvation and deepen zeal. It was also the surest way to spread change across China.

Evangelism gave listeners a way to play a meaningful role here and now at the end of the age. Song vividly described China embroiled in a final conflict. He told his listeners that history entered into its final stage in 1927.[109] Things were now speeding toward an explosive end. Already the first four steps in the march to Christ's return had taken place. False Christs had appeared in the countryside, civil wars as well as conflict with Japan were devastating the Republic of China, famines were destroying the interior, and earthquakes were reported in various places. The end was coming. In the fast-approaching apocalyptic confrontation, on whose side would his audience be? Evangelizing became the decisive test for determining who among the people professing to be Christian would be saved.

Song pointed out that many of the Chinese people who attended church were neither hot nor cold, just as Scripture predicted. Their enthusiasm for Jesus had waned, and they no longer shared the good news with others. Gathered in opulent buildings built by Western missions, they were like the biblical church in Laodicea, saying, "I am rich; I have acquired wealth and do not need a thing," when in fact they were

[108] Song Shangjie, "Zhiyao yangwang yesu [Just Look to Jesus]," as recorded by Xiao Liangtong, November 8, 1933, in Changsha, *Budao zazhi* [*Evangelism*] 7, no. 1 (January–February 1934): 10.

[109] Song, *Peilingji* [*Devotional Messages*], 40–41. Song does not explain why he categorizes the sixth stage of Christian history running from 1517–1927 and the seventh and final stage starting in 1927. Clearly he saw 1927 as having momentous significance. Though Song was silent on the rationale of his periodization, one is tempted to speculate. The year 1927 had enormous political significance in China as it was the time when the Nationalists claimed to unify China. It was also was the launch of the Chinese Christian Church, the united denomination that absorbed about 25 percent of Protestants. Did Song see eschatological significance in either act? I doubt it. I believe that Song saw 1927 as a pivotal year because he was "converted" at that time. Since he came to see himself as a kind of John the Baptist, his transformation and vocation in February of that year acted as the inaugurator of the final age of humankind.

poor, blind, and naked.[110] Instead of focusing on personal evangelism, these so-called Christians had fallen into thinking that clothing, educating, and doctoring the masses could save the nation.[111] Foolishness, he raged! That was a mistake of eschatological proportions because it made the church a servant of the state rather than of Jesus Christ. To neglect personal evangelism was to fall into a semi-moribund state. The failure to share the gospel with neighbors was the single biggest proof that a person or a church had become tepid. It was damning evidence that they belonged to the world, and were citizens of the earthly kingdom, and Christ would cast them out upon his return. Being active in evangelism, on the other hand, preserved someone from the grim destiny that lukewarm Christians faced.

Evangelism was also what preserved someone from falling into heresy, the other danger Jesus predicted would surface at the end of history. Whereas Song warned that congregations founded by Western missions fulfilled Jesus' warning that the church would lose its zeal at the end of the age, he associated indigenous groups like the Little Flock, the Jesus Family, and the True Jesus Church with Christ's prophecy that before his return false prophets would appear and mislead some of God's chosen.[112] During the late 1920s and through the 1930s, these indigenous Christian movements flourished.[113] They rapidly grew throughout China, often by absorbing members from mission churches. Song believed those in the independent churches were liars. He even resurrected the politically charged language of China's imperial age and spoke of these sects

---

[110] Song, *Forty John Sung Revival Sermons*, 2:6.

[111] Song tended to link the mission churches to Judas Iscariot. Judas and the churches in China, he believed, became convinced that their purpose was to use money to save people. This outlook, of course, led Judas to betray Jesus. He was the first, but not the last, victim of the social gospel. See, for example, Song, "Chuangshiji yu jiaohui lishi [Genesis and Church History]"; Song, "Shituxingzhuan diyizhang [Acts Chapter One]."

[112] Much attention has been given to Song's attacks on mission Christianity, but he was equally vociferous in his denunciation of Chinese indigenous Christian movements. This fact has been muted in the scholarship on Song, presumably because Song and the independent movements were being tied together historiographically. See, for example, Daniel H. Bays, "The Growth of Independent Christianity in China, 1900–1937," in *Christianity in China: From the Eighteenth Century to the Present*, ed. Daniel H. Bays (Stanford: Stanford University Press, 1996); and Lian, *Redeemed by Fire*.

[113] For an introduction to these popular indigenous Christian movements, see Lian, *Redeemed by Fire*.

as dangerous *xiejiao*, crooked teachings that undermined the health of the nation.[114]

> Everywhere I go to lead meetings, I hear people say: if you observe the Sabbath you will be saved; if you are baptized by immersion you will be saved; if you speak in tongues you will be saved; if you leave the established churches you will be saved; if women cover their heads they will be saved; if you believe in the True Jesus you will be saved. However, don't believe them. None of them are saved.[115]

Their claims to having the baptism of the Holy Spirit were spurious. How could Song tell? "Witnessing," he explained to his audience, "is the necessary evidence of being baptized by the Holy Spirit."[116] Moving people out of their pews and into the world to evangelize was the one

[114] Song Shangjie, *Moshide jidutu dang zhuyide er da wenti* [*Two Important Issues End-Time Christians Should Be Aware of*] (1936; repr., Beijing: Endiantang, 1963), 41. For centuries the Chinese state regulated religion through the use of the terms *zhengjiao* and *xiejiao*. The former expressed the idea of orthodoxy and compatibility with the state; the latter was used to label subversive religious movements as dangerous sects. That language largely disappeared from Republican Chinese political discourse as modern officials preferred to speak in terms of licit religion and illicit superstition. Song's employment of the imperial language, therefore, was surprising. He reached back to an older vocabulary to accuse his opponents of being threats to the state. See Vincent Goossaert and David A. Palmer, *The Religious Question in Modern China* (Chicago: University of Chicago Press, 2011), 27.

[115] Song Shangjie, "Yesu zailai [Jesus' Return]," as recorded by Lü Daguang, Moore Memorial Church, 1936, *Lingsheng* 2, no. 5 (May 1936): 16. The list is a general description of practices associated with independent churches, not an attempt to isolate and condemn any specific one. Sabbath-keeping and head coverings, for instance, were associated with the Little Flock, whereas speaking in tongues and following the True Jesus were not. Those acts belonged to the True Jesus Church. Song returned multiple times in his sermons to condemn various independent Christian practices such as those named above. He also worked to undermine their teachings about the use of unleavened bread in the Eucharist or the place of dancing, visions, dreams, and the like in worship. In virtually every case, it is difficult to isolate any one indigenous church as the butt of his attacks, though he appeared to castigate the practices of the Little Flock more than any other. Lian Xi suggests Song may have been particularly antagonistic toward the followers of Ni Tuosheng [Watchman Nee] since they attended his meetings to "test" the spirit of Song and determine if his healings were really from God. Lian Xi, e-mail message to author, June 7, 2013. See also W. B. Cole, "Work of the Hinghwa Conference 1925," unpublished report, roll 75, UMC, for a description of how these independent movements looked and worked in Xinghwa, which was where Song first encountered them.

[116] Song, *Fenxingjji* [*Revival Messages*], 108.

way to roll back the advance of false teachers and the surest way to prove who were the sheep among all the wolves.

Mobilization was critical for Song. Becoming a New Man or a New Woman was never enough. He believed that sending Christians out to testify about Christ's transforming power had epoch-making significance. Their activism could halt the spread of the social gospel, which Song considered an export from the West, and their labors could even be the source of "a great revival that will travel from East to West."[117] The work of his converts, in other words, could transform the mission churches and also the churches in Europe and America from which the missionaries came. For, he grinned, "In this era something out of the ordinary happens."[118] Similarly, Song imagined that his mobilized minority could topple the false teachings of the various indigenous movements by evangelizing them. Using martial language, Song ordered his bands of devotees "to wipe out the false Christs."[119] In other words, if radicalized Christians were faithful in their witness, then Christ's opponents would be defeated and a worldwide revival would be ignited that would take the gospel to all people and precipitate Jesus' much-anticipated return. Song's revivalism mobilized some people with the promise that their witness could not only rescue China but also help save the entire world.

CONCLUSION

Over the first three years of Song's ministry in China, his work was totally overhauled. His message and methods were transformed. He began with ideological harangues, which were ill-fated attempts to fix his countrymen during his first months back in China. Within a year he moved from the position of speaking to them to speaking with them. Specifically, he started to talk with the religious vocabulary of his audience. He no longer focused on "-isms" or innovations, but on the supernatural experiences he had in the hospital and found reproduced in the Bible. The shift made Song popular, but left him rather ineffectual. He could entertain, but seldom move his listeners. It was the adoption of revivalism in 1931 that changed the trajectory of his ministry. Induction into the Bethel Mission did not force Song to abandon his love of

---

[117] Song, "Yesu zailai [Jesus' Return]," 21.
[118] Song, "Yesu zailai [Jesus' Return]," 21.
[119] Song, Fenxingji [Revival Messages], 183; Song, Moshide jidutu dang zhuyide er da wenti [Two Important Issues End-Time Christians Should Be Aware of], 24.

mysteries or supernatural events, but Bethel's revivalism gave them a purpose and direction. His idiosyncratic allegories and heavenly revelations became useful when Song deployed them to lead people through a three-step process of renewal, similar to his own conversion. Revivalism placed people in positions where they could see themselves as the problem, beset by sin, trapped in old ways and old habits. Song offered listeners a choice to move away from that and become new through Jesus Christ. When they accepted his offer, they not only experienced a symbolic rupture with the old and the past that seemed so unshakable, but they also received a mandate for their new lives. New Men and New Women were sent out to make other people new creations in Jesus Christ. Song's revivals, therefore, provided a structured way to transfer his own experience of being made new to the masses, and they moved those who participated in that three-act drama into action. Song had found a way to make the quest for a New Man, a New Woman, *and* a New China possible. He managed to turn revivalism into a modern means for mobilizing the masses.

4

A New Location

From the moment he joined the Bethel Mission in 1931, Song poured his volcanic energy into the Evangelistic Band's revivalism. He honed his skills as a preacher and performer and pushed the team to do more, say more, and travel farther. He hurried to trains and jumped on steamboats, trying to stay abreast of the deluge of invitations that pleaded with the band to come and help make them New Men and New Women. Song and his colleagues burned a trail of revivals across the country. In two years they covered more than 15,000 miles, held 1,199 revival services, collaborated with 13 different denominations, and spoke to 425,980 people, mostly in cities along the eastern seaboard.[1] It was an extraordinary achievement, and Song was rewarded by a rapid ascent through the Bethel Mission.

His climb did not stop at the ceiling, however. Song burst clean through. In November 1933, just thirty months after he first joined the team, he received a telegram from Jennie Hughes stating that she was dissolving the wildly successful Bethel Band. It would be reconstituted under the original leadership of Ji Zhiwen [Andrew Gih], and Song would not be included.[2]

The reasons for Song's dismissal were layered. In her telegram Hughes explained her decision as the logical outcome of Song's plan to

[1] Jennie Hughes, *Bethel Heart Throbs of Surprises* (Shanghai: Bethel Mission, 1932), 65; Andrew Gih, *Launch Out into the Deep! Tales of Revival through China's Famous Bethel Evangelistic Bands and Further Messages* (London: Marshall, Morgan & Scott, 1938), 69.

[2] Song Shangjie, November 20, 1933, Song Shangjie Diaries, Trinity Theological College, Singapore. Henceforth this location will be referred to as SSD, TTC.

assume a pastoral position in Beijing. Song countered that she misunderstood. True, some of the evangelistic teams which the Bethel Band had mobilized across the city had spoken together and were eager to receive Song as their pastor, but that did not mean he was plotting to depart.[3] Protestations aside, it was too late to make repairs. The relationship between Hughes and Song had already unraveled. For some time Hughes had been frustrated that Song was accepting personal gifts and even financial donations from enthusiastic converts. Those were all to be given to the Bethel Mission and used for the support of the entire band.[4] In addition the power struggles within the team could no longer be ignored. When the Bethel Band was at full capacity, it had been possible for Song and Ji, the two strongest leaders (and sometimes rivals), to separate. Song could take one of the younger members, and Ji two (or vice versa). In this way both men could lead separate revivals. It was a way for the popular band to cover more ground; it was also a way to defuse tension over who was in charge.[5] That, however, was no longer a tenable solution. Li Daorong and Nie Ziying, the two unmarried members of the team who had been the focus of young women's attention, had been removed earlier that year.[6] The remaining team of three could no longer be divided. That left Song and Ji in an unremitting struggle for dominance. Hughes' telegram signaled the resolution of the conflict. Ji was the anointed leader; Song had to go. Infuriated, Song accused Hughes of envy. She was like Saul who could not stand the success of his

[3]   Song Shangjie, November 20, 1933, SSD, TTC. Even after Song's protests to the contrary, Bethel still printed that Song planned to become a pastor. See *Shenjie zhinan yuekan* [*Guide to Holiness*] 6, no. 1 (January 1934): 64. It was virtually the only reference Bethel made to Song after he departed from the mission. In the first issue of the *Shengjie zhinan yuekan* that was printed after Song left the team, Jennie Hughes broke custom and wrote the editorial. She made enigmatic statements that in 1933 Bethel had been tested, but she also announced that God had been faithful to the organization. Whereas Bethel used to have only one evangelistic team, now it would send out more than ten. With that Song disappeared from the Bethel Mission records until decades later. Only under new leadership could the Bethel Mission celebrate what God had done through the first BWEB. See *Jiushizhounian ganen tekan* [*Special Ninetieth Anniversary Thanksgiving Publication*] (Hong Kong: 2011), 19.

[4]   Lian Xi, *Redeemed by Fire: The Rise of Popular Christianity in Modern China* (New Haven: Yale University Press, 2010), 150.

[5]   Ka-tong Lim, *The Life and Ministry of John Sung* (Singapore: Genesis Books, 2012), 156–62.

[6]   Lian, *Redeemed by Fire*, 150.

loyal subject David. Song denounced her decision as imperialistic and predicted that within two months the Bethel Mission would suffer the consequence of letting its finest preacher depart.[7]

As the Bethel Band collapsed in November 1933 under the combined weight of Hughes' autocratic authority and Song's unchecked ambition, the revivalist plummeted into unknown waters. He was on his own. When he had first started preaching in China, the Xinghua [Hinghwa] Methodist Episcopal Church (MEC) had given him considerable latitude to meander around his home district evangelizing villages, but the conference supplied him with money and direction.[8] Similarly, when Song joined the Bethel Band, he could focus on being an evangelist because the Bethel Mission managed the scheduling and financing of revival services.[9] Without that organizational support, Song temporarily floundered.

With the advantage of hindsight, Song publicized years later that this was a period of waiting on God. Did God want him to continue as an independent evangelist? If so, God would need to prompt people from five provinces to invite him to speak and provide 800 yuan for

[7] Song Shangjie, November 20, 1933, SSD, TTC; Song Shangjie, November 21, 1933, SSD, TTC.

[8] See the *Official Minutes* of the Hinghwa Annual Conference, 1928–1930 (Shanghai: Methodist Publishing House, 1928–1930). Song did not have a large salary as a "Conference Evangelist," but at least by the time he became a deacon in 1930, Song drew a salary of $15 a month ($9 for himself, $4 more because he was married, and an additional $2 since he was a graduate of Guthrie High School). When Song no longer collected a salary from the Xinghua Conference, he still remained affiliated. Upon joining the Bethel Mission, his home conference simply listed him as an "Evangelist-at-Large" and encouraged him to continue his course of study for ordination. For several years Song made no progress in his theological education, causing some consternation among church officials. Letters and visits from his father and bishop were meant to encourage him to complete the process, but they all failed. Song's success as a revivalist, however, motivated the conference to be creative. In 1937 they finally declared Song to be an "Elected and Ordained Elder under the Seminary Rule." He had not met the normal schooling requirements, but his ministry spoke for itself. Even so, Song did not return home for his ordination service. If it was ever more than a paper ordination, it must have been a ritual performed by a bishop who caught Song as he passed through Shanghai.

[9] "Bentuan xuanyan," *Shengjie zhinan yuekan [Guide to Holiness]* 3, no. 4 (April 1931): 10.

traveling expenses.[10] The image was entirely passive, making no mention of Song's energetic efforts to recruit new speaking engagements.

In fact, before he left Changsha, the city in which he first heard that his relationship with Bethel was being terminated, Song convinced Chen Chonggui [Marcus Ch'eng] of the Hunan Bible Institute to help. Chen had risen to national prominence as editor of the popular periodical *Evangelism*. The magazine had an impressive circulation of 4,500–5,000 subscribers, dwarfing the circulations of the majority of Chinese Christian periodicals, which ran 500–1,000 copies every month.[11] It was a great victory, therefore, when Chen announced in the next issue,

> This year *Evangelism* plans to print one of Dr. Song Shangjie's sermons in every issue. Dr. Song preached in Changsha for ten days. God greatly used him. The church was often far too small. In the last month or so, the results have still been visible; his services did not merely produce temporary emotions. While he was in Changsha he stayed below the dorm, so I had the opportunity to get to know him very well. Off the platform, I know his character to be even more likable and honorable.[12]

Chen did more than provide a character reference. He also added that Song would follow the Lord's leading in offering revival meetings and provided Song's address in Shanghai so interested readers could contact him.[13] Song placed a similar announcement in other Christian periodicals.[14] He purposely sought invitations to preach.

His persistence was rewarded. A few weeks after the publication of the periodicals, Song's call to independent itinerant evangelism was

[10] Song Shangjie, *Gongzuode huigu* [*Review of My Ministry*] (Singapore: Singapore Christian Evangelistic League, 1960), 20.

[11] Daniel H. Bays, *A New History of Christianity in China* (Malden, Mass.: Wiley-Blackwell, 2012), 139; Herbert Hoi-lap Ho, *Protestant Missionary Publications in Modern China, 1912–1949: A Study of Their Programs, Operations and Trends* (Hong Kong: Chinese Church Research Centre, 1988), 208.

[12] Chen Chonggui, "Bianji zhihou [Editor's Notes]," *Budao zazhi* [*Evangelism*] 7, no. 1 (January–February 1934), 110.

[13] Chen, "Bianji zhihou [Editor's Notes]," 110.

[14] Leslie T. Lyall, *A Biography of John Sung* (Singapore: Genesis Books, 2004), 139. In his biography Lyall mentioned that Song advertised in *Evangelism* and *Morning Star*. Little is known about the *Morning Star* except for what may be gleaned from the *Statistical Atlas of Christian Missions*, compiled by a subcommittee of Commission I of the World Missionary Conference (Edinburgh: World Missionary Conference, 1910), 47; and Charles Luther Boynton and Charles Dozier Boynton, eds., *1936 Handbook of the Christian Movement in China under Protestant Auspices* (Shanghai: Kwang Hsueh Publishing House, 1936), 214.

confirmed.[15] With multiple invitations and money in hand, Song started to make his way north from Shanghai in mid-January 1934, and he held revivals in Jiangsu and Anhui provinces. By early February he was in Shandong Province and spent the next two months there, largely revisiting the places where he had led revivals when he was with the Bethel Band. News of his activities spread, and messengers from Hebei Province traveled some three hundred miles to the southeast to call upon Song in Yantai [Chefoo]. They asked him to come back to Tianjin where, in 1932, he and the Bethel team had held an extraordinarily long twenty-day revival campaign.[16]

CIRCUMSCRIBED BY THE CITY

Song immediately agreed to speak in Tianjin. The urban setting suited him well. In fact, his career was built around cities. Revivalism grew alongside urbanization in China in the 1930s as it had in the United States a century before. Cities provided the combustible materials that seemed only to await a spark from a revivalist's tongue.[17] Whether it was Song Shangjie or other revivalists of the era, like Ding Limei, Wang Zai [Leland Wang], Wang Mingdao, or Chen Chonggui, all of them worked China's cities. First, urban areas had a critical mass of people. Since revival services were events, not beliefs, they required enough people who had free time to attend meetings and enough money to support them. Such an audience was almost exclusively available in China's cities. Second, revivalism's insistence that sinners needed to revive or recover something that was lost made sense to urban residents. Nowhere else in the nation had longstanding models of home and work been more disrupted than in its cities. Third, urban revivals spread from city to city through the infrastructure that tied China's urban areas together in the first half of the twentieth century.[18] The May Fourth Movement, which was also an urban phenomenon, demonstrated the point well. Events in Beijing triggered responses hundreds of miles away in Shanghai and

[15] Song, *Gongzuode huigu* [*Review of My Ministry*], 20.

[16] Song Shangjie, ed., *Quanguo jidutu budaotuan tuankan* [*National Christian Evangelistic League Publication*] (March 1936): 23.

[17] Richard Lee Rogers, "The Urban Threshold and the Second Great Awakening: Revivalism in New York State, 1825–1835," *Journal for the Scientific Study of Religion* 49, no. 4 (2010): 694–709. Rogers demonstrated that during the Second Great Awakening the factor that best predicted a religious revival was urbanization.

[18] David Strand, "'A High Place Is No Better Than a Low Place': The City in the Making of Modern China," in *Becoming Chinese: Passages to Modernity and Beyond*, ed. Wen-hsin Yeh (Berkeley: University of California Press, 2000), 98–136.

Guangzhou within hours, whereas it could take weeks to spread the news of China's awakening around Beijing's hinterlands, assuming someone even thought it important enough to try.[19] In similar ways revivals were both fueled and confined by the communication lines that linked cities together. They carried reports of revival out to other cities and carried invitations in for the revivalist to expand his work in new urban settings. The countryside was almost entirely omitted. For these reasons Chinese revivalism had a distinctly urban imprint.

At the time China had few cities. The population exceeded half a billion people, but only 193 places had crossed the urban threshold, that is, having a population that topped fifty thousand inhabitants.[20] The residents in China's cities accounted for but 8 percent of the national population.[21] No wonder missions had historically focused on the countryside.[22] Yet, despite the relatively small numbers, it was among the urban minority that Song learned his trade. When he joined the Bethel

[19] The most famous examples of how information traveled primarily among cities include the Revolution of 1911 and the May Fourth Movement in 1919. Incidents closer to the time of Song's services in Tianjin would have been the Anti-Christian Movement that exploded in response to a World Student Christian Federation meeting in Beijing in 1922 and organized boycotts after the May 30 Incident in 1925. See Yip Ka-che, *Religion, Nationalism, and Chinese Students: The Anti-Christian Movement of 1922–1927* (Bellingham: Western Washington University, 1980).

[20] Glenn T. Trewartha, "Chinese Cities: Numbers and Distribution," *Annals of the Association of American Geographers* 41, no. 4 (December 1951): 331–47.

[21] Population statistics for China in the 1930s are notoriously difficult. Trewartha, "Chinese Cities," helpfully collates the multiple and contradictory sources on China's urban population and provides the names of China's cities over fifty thousand. It proved to be extraordinarily valuable when trying to determine which places Song visited were urban centers and which were not. Other important demographic resources used in constructing information about the overlap between Song and China's urban centers include G. William Skinner, ed., *The City in Late Imperial China* (Stanford: Stanford University Press, 1977); Barbara Sands and Ramon H. Myers, "The Spatial Approach to Chinese History: A Test," *Journal of Asian Studies* 45, no. 4 (August 1986): 721–43; Peter Gue Zarrow, *China in War and Revolution, 1895–1949* (New York: Routledge, 2005), 9; and Jan Lahmeyer, "Population Statistics," accessed November 21, 2019, http://www.populstat.info/Asia/chinac.htm.

[22] Protestant missions in China had been overwhelmingly rural, but at the turn of the twentieth century a new wave of missionaries championed going to the cities. By 1920, two-thirds of missionaries had moved to urban areas. See William A. Brown, "The Protestant Rural Movement in China (1920–1937)," in *American Missionaries in China*, ed. Kwang-Ching Liu (Cambridge, Mass.: Harvard University Press, 1966), 220.

Worldwide Evangelistic Band (BWEB), he left behind the village evangelism he had performed in the Xinghua Conference. Bethel was located in
Shanghai and catered to urban audiences. Song had to learn to preach
for an organization that overwhelmingly held its services in China's cities. Three-quarters of the team's services were conducted in urban areas.

Little changed when Song launched out on his own. If anything, the
urbanization of his ministry intensified. When he left Bethel in 1933,
Song penned in his journal the idea, "Maybe God is going to use me to
go to big cities to evangelize first, and then there will be opportunities
to go to the United States of America."[23] Between Song's departure from
Bethel and the Marco Polo Bridge Incident, which marked the beginning
of the Sino-Japanese War in 1937, Song specifically targeted China's
urban areas. In the mainland he spoke in cities almost 85 percent of the
time.[24] More than half of his ninety-six revival campaigns were held in
just thirteen treaty port cities.[25] Song traveled much, but primarily kept
to a narrow circuit of foreign-influenced urban areas.

[23] Song Shangjie, November 21, 1933, SSD, TTC.

[24] The times Song did not speak in cities during this time period can be explained.
Most of those happened when he returned to his home district in Fujian and spoke
at some of the churches where his evangelistic ministry first began. The reasons
for visiting the other small venues may have been similar to why Song preached in
Daming, Hebei. Nazarene missionaries hosted Song in that town because, as relative latecomers to China, they were forced to work on the periphery of China's core
regions. The urban centers, Nazarenes discovered, had long been ceded to the older
denominations in comity agreements. Thus, the wave of new Holiness, Pentecostal,
and independent missions that flooded China after 1911 often moved into China's hinterlands. Although geographically isolated from Song's eastern seaboard
services, many embraced his message and revival tactics. The theological kinship
between Song and some of his hosts may explain his sporadic visits to towns. See
Peter Kiehn, "The Legacy of Peter and Anna Kiehn," unpublished manuscript,
biography, Kiehn Collection (file 192-61), Nazarene Archives, Kansas City, Mo.;
Peter Kiehn, "A Sketch of Our Work in China," *The Other Sheep* (October 1923):
16; H. A. Wiese, "China Crusaders," *The Other Sheep* (August 1935): 12; L. C.
Osborn, "God's Blessing at Fan Hsien," *The Other Sheep* (September 1935): 17;
H. A. Wiese, "Blind Receives Sight, Dumb Speaks," *The Other Sheep* (May 1936):
21–22; Katherine Wiese, "A Bible School Student," *The Other Sheep* (February
1942): 23; Daryl R. Ireland, "Unbound: The Creative Power of Scripture in the
Lives of Chinese Nazarene Women," *Wesleyan Theological Journal* 46, no. 2
(2011): 168–92; Daniel H. Bays, "The Growth of Independent Christianity in
China, 1900–1937," in *Christianity in China: From the Eighteenth Century to the
Present*, ed. Daniel H. Bays (Stanford: Stanford University Press, 1996), 307–16.

[25] The thirteen treaty port cities that Bethel visited between May 1931 and
December 1933 and the thirteen Song spoke in alone between January 1934 and

THE EXAMPLE OF TIANJIN

The transition of Song's services from the treaty port of Yantai to the treaty port of Tianjin in April 1934 conformed to his pattern of moving from one major city to another.[26] The only unusual feature was that when he showed up he had no place to preach. Publicly, Song smoothed things over by saying it was a matter of miscommunication. He thought the invitation to come to Tianjin was from a church, but it turned out that it was, in fact, just from "a group of people who loved the Lord."[27] Privately, however, he fumed. Song had wired the Wesley Methodist Church in Tianjin concerning the time and place of his arrival. They knew he was coming, but when he disembarked from that boat on April 10, 1934, he discovered that the circumstances had changed. A committee had voted eight to seven to bar him from holding services, explaining that the church did not want to overdo revivals. Song was outraged and assumed some of the committee members had been bribed.[28]

Unfortunately no other data exists about this incident, inviting one to speculate about Song's cool reception. It seems unlikely, for example, that the church was truly concerned about hosting "too many" revivals or that they feared revivals happened "too often."[29] As the city's flagship Protestant congregation, Wesley relished its place as "the center of many Christian activities in [Tianjin]" and boasted that with the South Suburb Church they had combined to hold five revivals in one year.[30]

July 1937 were not completely identical. They overlapped in eight cities: Fuzhou, Guangzhou, Hong Kong, Qingdao, Shanghai, Shantou, Tianjin, and Yantai.

[26] In 1935 Tianjin was China's third largest city and had been a treaty port for seventy-five years. Between the two World Wars, it always ranked second or third in direct foreign trade and therefore attracted a significant foreign presence. At various times, the city was divided into British, French, Japanese, German, Italian, Austro-Hungarian, Belgian, Russian, and American concessions. See Gail Hershatter, *The Workers of Tianjin, 1900–1949* (Stanford: Stanford University Press, 1986).

[27] Song, *Gongzuode huigu* [*Review of My Ministry*], 21; Song Shangjie, *Peilingji* [*Devotional Messages*] (1935; repr., Hong Kong: Bellman House, n.d.).

[28] Song Shangjie, April 10, 1934, SSD, TTC.

[29] Song Shangjie, April 10, 1934, SSD, TTC.

[30] North China Conference, *The Official Journal of the Forty-Second Session of the North China Annual Conference of the Methodist Episcopal Church Held at the South Gate Methodist Episcopal Church, Tientsin, Hopei, China, August 22–26, 1934* (Beijing: 1934), 334; North China Conference, *The Official Journal of the Forty-First Session of the North China Annual Conference of the Methodist Episcopal Church, August 23–27, 1933* (Beijing: 1933).

Multiple and extended revival campaigns in the same church were not that unusual.[31]

The deeper problem may have been that when Song departed from Bethel his name was tarnished. A number of Christians cast a wary eye on his newly independent ministry. For instance, the Presbyterian missionary Frank Millican praised the Bethel Band for reconstituting itself without Song. He expressed joy that team evangelism had superseded "'Lone wolfing' evangelism."[32] Never mind that in the same article Millican endorsed the solo evangelists Wang Zai, Chen Chonggui, and Zhao Junying [Calvin Chao]. Something about Song's departure from a team ministry set him apart, making him appear unreliable or dangerous. Perhaps that made some believers in Tianjin nervous to host him.

In addition Song may have been barred because of Methodist Church politics. During his career Song's revivals prompted Methodist bishops to circle their wagons on more than one occasion. It can hardly be coincidental that immediately after Song's revivals, Methodist leadership found it necessary to warn the faithful about outside evangelists: "[W]e urge pastors and local officials to give permission only to preachers who are personally known to them or who carry certificates from dependable leaders of the church."[33] Or, in another place,

> [P]astors invite evangelists without consulting the D.S. We should get together on this matter. The Discipline does not permit the pastors or church members to invite evangelists without consulting the District

[31] "Wuzhou kongqiande fenxing budao dahui [Wuzhou's Unprecedented Revival Evangelistic Meetings]," *Zhenguang* [*True Light*] 31, no. 7 (July 1932): 86; "Wuzhou kongqian weiyoude fenxing budaohui [Wuzhou's Unprecedented and Never-Seen-Before Revival Evangelistic Meetings]," *Zhenguang* [*True Light*] 32, no. 7 (July 1933): 69. These two sources hint at the frequency of revivals. Churches in Wuzhou, Guangxi, reported in *Zhenguang* an "unprecedented" revival led by the Bethel Band in 1932, but then had another "unprecedented" visitation of the Holy Spirit's reviving presence in 1933. Both happened during the planned annual revival meeting. In China, revivals were common, even formulaic events. Song's return to Tianjin just two years after holding services in the city with Bethel would not have been a problem for most churches.

[32] F. R. Millican, "Four Methods of Evangelism," *Chinese Recorder* 69 (May 1938): 246.

[33] Malay Conference, *Minutes of the Forty-Fourth Session of the Malaya Conference of the Methodist Episcopal Church Held in Wesley Church, Singapore, Straits Settlements, January 2–7, 1936* (Singapore: 1936), 74.

Superintendent. We need to get a list of the men within our own Conference who lead in evangelistic work.[34]

Even Song's most erstwhile supporter within the Methodist Church, Frank Cartwright, the Board of Foreign Missions' Secretary for China, Japan, Korea, and East Asia, developed doubts about Song. He expressed "personal regret" over the way Song's ministry evolved.[35] It is quite possible, therefore, that whispers about Song being an unapproved outsider preceded his arrival in Tianjin and thereby prevented him from securing the use of Wesley Church. No solid evidence from Tianjin exists, however, to confirm one way or another why Song was rebuffed.

Happily for the purposes of this chapter, why Song could not secure a church venue for his revivals is less relevant than how his supporters dealt with it. For the manner in which that "group of people who loved the Lord" handled the crisis allows one to piece together the social composition of Song's supporters. What otherwise might have remained hidden was briefly revealed in Tianjin.

Bourgeois Backers

The sting of rejection forced Song's supporters in Tianjin to fast, pray, cry, and within twenty-four hours successfully rent the Li Yuanhong Great Ceremonial Hall. They paid hundreds of yuan, several times more than the average worker's annual salary.[36] That fact suggests that those in the small group who invited Song to Tianjin were rich. They mobilized enough liquid capital in one day to rent a grand and impressive building in Tianjin's English Concession that could seat seven hundred to

---

[34] North China Policy Committee, Tientsin, April 15–16, 1935, United Methodist Church (U.S.), *Missionary Files: Methodist Church, 1912–1949*, N. China, Conference (continued) to Clay, E. H. (Wilmington, Del.: Scholarly Resources, 1999), roll 69. Hereafter, this location will be referred to as UMC.

[35] Frank T. Cartwright to Early R. Hibbard, August 7, 1935, N. China, Clay, E. H. (continued) to Wen Middle School, roll 70, UMC. Frank Cartwright had worked in the Xinghua Conference before assuming his denominational post. In his new position, he worried that he had not done enough to raise up new Chinese leaders for the church. News that the youthful Song had returned from the United States and was causing a stir gave Cartwright hope—perhaps his years had not been entirely wasted. See Frank Cartwright to Uncle John [Gowdy], December 22, 1931, Bishop Correspondence, United Methodist Archives and History Center, Madison, N.J.

[36] Song Shangjie, April 10, 1934, SSD, TTC.

eight hundred people.[37] The impressiveness of this feat becomes clearer when one recognizes the brutal economic circumstances that were choking the city. Tianjin was dying in 1934. The effects of the worldwide depression leeched virtually every bit of life from Tianjin's mills, while cannibalistic taxes devoured what remained of their industrial carcasses.[38] Unemployment that year soared to about 750,000 people, meaning almost two-thirds of the city's population had no work and virtually no money.[39] Even among families that still had at least one person gainfully employed, no margin existed for generosity. Food took almost all of a person's pay, leaving only tiny bits for rent, fuel, and clothing. Working families were happy if they had a surplus of three yuan at the end of a year.[40] Few could have mustered the resources to secure Song a place to speak so quickly. The backers had to be moneyed.

Song never wrote down who paid for the hall, but his journals confirm his connections to Tianjin's elites. Zhang Zhouxin started and owned the Northern China Trade Company. He had been energized by Song's preaching in 1932 when the Bethel Band held a revival in Tianjin. The entrepreneur Zhang and his wife Chen Sanli, an obstetrician who started and operated her own clinic, appear frequently in Song's journals in April 1934, and the local newspaper identified Zhang as the host of the revival.[41] In addition Song spent his two weeks in Tianjin at the home of Guan Songshen and his wife, Li Fenglin. Guan was a prominent figure in Republican China. After graduating from Tsinghua University,

[37] Song Shangjie, April 10–11, 1934, SSD, TTC; "Jidujiao budaotuan: qing Song Shangjie boshi jiangyan [Christian Evangelistic League Invites Dr. John Song to Speak]," *Tianjin dagong bao*, section 3 (April 15, 1934): 10. The price of the hall remains tantalizingly out of reach. The number Song recorded in his journal put the price in the hundreds. How many hundreds, however, is illegible.

[38] Hershatter, *Workers of Tianjin*, 32, 34.

[39] Hershatter, *Workers of Tianjin*, 45. Unemployment was endemic to Tianjin in 1934, though Hershatter notes that the rate is probably inflated. A number of the "unemployed" could get occasional work as "day-laborers," which provided some money, even if it was inconsistent. The larger point, however, holds true. The vast majority of people were in a financial crisis with little to nothing to give for renting a revival hall.

[40] Hershatter, *Workers of Tianjin*, 68. According to Brett Sheehan, *Trust in Troubled Times: Money, Banks, and State-Society Relations in Republican Tianjin* (Cambridge, Mass.: Harvard University Press, 2003), xiii, one yuan was equivalent to twenty-five U.S. cents.

[41] "Jidujiao budaotuan: qing Song Shangjie boshi jiangyan [Christian Evangelistc League Invites Dr. John Song to Speak]," 5.

he had studied architecture at the Massachusetts Institute of Technology and city planning at Harvard University. When he returned to China, he founded Kwan, Chu and Yang Architects and Engineers of Tianjin, the first Chinese owned and operated architectural and engineering firm in the nation.[42] Guan's Tianjin-based business built high-profile buildings that represented China's modernization. For instance, in 1931 his company erected the Central Hospital in the Nationalist capital, Nanjing. They also designed that city's athletic stadium, a project close to Guan's heart.[43] He was a firm believer in the value of sports and worked to overcome the stereotyped image of the "sick man of the East." Guan spent his own money and resources promoting China in the Asian and Olympic games as well as in his efforts to find talented Chinese athletes.[44] Guan Songsheng was not a Christian himself, but he was sympathetic to it insofar as he noted the improvements it made in his wife's behavior.[45] In terms of securing a place for Song to preach, the key was not Guan Songsheng's personal faith, but that his family, like Zhang Zhouxin's, had financial resources.

Importantly, these two families also had connections. The place they rented belonged to the former president of the Republic of China, Li Yuanhong. Like most politicians of his generation, Li had a colorful and convoluted career. He began his political ascendancy through the military. Stationed in Wuchang on October 10, 1911, Li found himself at the heart of the Xinhai Revolution that toppled the Qing dynasty. Though he was not inclined to join the uprising, the revolutionaries coveted his support and convinced the colonel to assume leadership of the revolution as the alternative to being shot. The first proclamations of the revolution, therefore, went out to the rest of the country in his name.[46] Yuan Shikai, the general who was dispatched by the Manchu Court to subdue the revolt, recognized Li's power. When Yuan chose to negotiate with the rebels rather than fight them, he accepted their offer to become

[42] Tsinghua University, "Peiyang rencai Guan Songsheng [Fostering Talent: Guan Songsheng]," accessed March 11, 2014, http://www.sports.tsinghua.edu.cn/three/?qhty=35 (link no longer active).

[43] Jianfei Zhu, *Architecture of Modern China: A Critique* (New York: Routledge, 2009), 58.

[44] Tsinghua University, "Peiyang rencai Guan Songsheng [Fostering Talent: Guan Songsheng]."

[45] Song Shangjie, April 11, 1934, SSD, TTC.

[46] James E. Sheridan, *China in Disintegration: The Republican Era in Chinese History, 1912–1949* (New York: Free Press, 1975), 41.

president of the republic and moved quickly thereafter to coopt Li Yuan-hong's authority. He wanted Li to make a display of his support and his subservience by becoming Yuan's vice president. Li, however, recognized the proposal for what it was and could muster no enthusiasm for the offer. He repeatedly postponed making a trip to Beijing. The standoff was only resolved when President Yuan had his minister of war enter Li's home by force, read him his summons to be vice president, and then escort him at gunpoint to the capital to receive his honor. Embittered by the experience, Li adopted a posture of passive noncooperation. Two years later, when Yuan Shikai died, Li Yuanhong became president for the first time.[47]

Li found that it was necessary and yet impossible to govern the new nation through regional warlords. During his brief presidency, he was the victim of the changing allegiances and aspirations of the military leaders who effectively controlled northern China and so resigned from office just thirteen months into his first term. His temporary withdrawal from politics, however, was not a withdrawal from public life.

Li built himself an impressive complex in the English Concession of Tianjin and did what other warlords and politicos did: he invested in a cotton mill. Of the twenty-five Chinese investors in Tianjin's cotton mills, all but two currently had, or in the past had held, high-ranking civil or military posts.[48] Li's stake in the Huaxin mill, one of the four Chinese-owned mills that dominated Tianjin's industry, kept him in the upper echelon of Chinese power brokers. It was also from there that he entered the presidency for a second time in 1922.[49]

Although Li Yuanhong died in 1928, the fact that Song's supporters had access to his family and estate spoke volumes about their social circle. They were not only able to secure the family hall, but they even convinced the deceased president's sister and daughter to attend some

---

[47] Yuan-Song Chen, *Return to the Middle Kingdom: One Family, Three Revolutionaries, and the Birth of Modern China* (New York: Union Square Press, 2008), 48.

[48] Marie-Claire Bergère, *The Golden Age of the Chinese Bourgeoisie, 1911–1937*, trans. Janet Lloyd (Cambridge: Cambridge University Press, 1989), 178–80, 185.

[49] James E. Sheridan, "The Warlord Era: Politics and Militarism under the Peking Government, 1916–1928," in *The Cambridge History of China*, vol. 12, part 1, ed. John K. Fairbank (Cambridge: Cambridge University Press, 1983), 313–14.

of Song's services.[50] The group of elite supporters was very small, but the fact that Song had any backing from the minuscule number of China's rich and well-connected bourgeoisie was significant. It indicated that his revivals were, in some measure, intertwined with China's urban elite.

THE POWER OF ASSOCIATION

Song capitalized on the prestige of Zhang Zhouxin and Li Fenglin. In a sense he borrowed it from them. While in Tianjin he stayed in the home of Guan Songsheng and Li Fenglin. There he enjoyed the service of their six or seven servants (they never appeared all at once, so he was unsure of the number).[51] He indulged in games of *yinqiu* in the midmorning and then rode in the Guan family automobile to the Li Yuanhong Hall to speak in the afternoon. Although cars were common enough in Tianjin, to actually ride in one was extraordinary. A taxi ride was beyond the experience and grasp of almost everyone in the city.[52] For Song to disembark from an automobile, therefore, indicated to his observers that he was enjoying certain privileges.

One of the keys to his success, however, was that Song was able to maintain that the wealth was not his own. True, his revivals generated substantial income. On his way to Tianjin, Song counted up the money he took in at Yantai from thank offerings, the sale of his books, and unsolicited gifts. It totaled 734 yuan. He would do even better in Tianjin, where in two and a half weeks people gave him somewhere between 768 yuan and 2,498 yuan.[53] Such an impressive influx of money would

[50] Song Shangjie, April 18, 1934, SSD, TTC. Mrs. Guan told Song that Li's daughter and sister attended and were moved by the service, but they were unwilling to confess their sins and thereby lose face.

[51] Song Shangjie, April 18, 1934, SSD, TTC.

[52] Hanchao Lu, *Beyond the Neon Lights: Everyday Shanghai in the Early Twentieth Century* (Berkeley: University of California Press, 1999), 14.

[53] Despite Song's meticulous bookkeeping in his journal, the amount of money that was given to him in Tianjin is unclear. The question surrounds 1,730.82 yuan that he recorded receiving on April 28, 1934. The money, he noted, was given in the afternoon. That was the same time that an offering was to be taken so his supporters could purchase their own church building. If that 1,700 yuan is added to the 6,000 yuan that was raised earlier for the building, then it would explain why Song—who was obviously relying on his own journals—claimed in his later memoir that the revival in Tianjin raised between 7,000–8,000 yuan for a new church building. See Song, *Gongzuode huigu* [*Review of My Ministry*], 21. On the other hand, the money may have been given to him for personal use. Every time Song

not put Song in the stratosphere with China's extremely wealthy, but it was certainly more than most people in Tianjin earned. Weavers and sock makers, for example, made 288 yuan in a whole year; mill hands, 261 yuan; and handicraft workers had an annual income of 177 yuan.[54] Song was very well off. He just seldom showed it.

He had little reason to display wealth. When he was in a city, those who invited him to preach took the responsibility of feeding him and providing him a place to stay. In extraordinary circumstances it was conceivable that he might pay for travel, but—as he learned from his time with the Bethel Mission—a faith ministry usually meant only foregoing a set fee for services. It did not mean that travel expenses fell on the evangelist.[55] The upshot was that by 1934 Song already had enough money to have a home in the French Concession of Shanghai, one of the most expensive districts in all of China.[56] Song certainly had his own money; his genius was not flaunting it.

---

received money that was not for his personal use, he wrote explicitly what it was to be used for. For instance, the 6,000 yuan that was given to him for the new church building was duly recorded as such. His silence in this case, therefore, suggests the 1,700 yuan might have been given to him personally. It is also worth considering that in her publication of her father's journals, Song Tianzhen does not mention the 1,730.82 yuan. That is consistent with her avoidance of mentioning any money that Song Shangjie ever earned, whereas she was comfortable reporting the 6,000 yuan raised for the church building. See Song Tianzhen, ed., *Shi'er fude de riji* [*The Journal Once Lost*] (Kowloon, Hong Kong: China Alliance Press, 2006), 213. Therefore, I am slightly inclined to believe the 1,730 yuan ledger entry was part of Song's income in Tianjin, making his earnings for half a month's work 2,498 yuan.

[54] Hershatter, *Workers of Tianjin*, 68.

[55] The Bethel Band's understanding of "faith ministry" seems to have shaped Song's own practice of it. In "Bentuan xuanyan," *Shengjie zhinan yuekan* [*Guide to Holiness*] 3, no. 4 (April 1931): 10, Bethel explained that the team would "rely on faith. They would not solicit funds where they go. They will follow Jesus' instructions from Matthew 10 on how to stay in a place [each city provides food and lodging]. If a church would like to have the team preach, they are very ready to agree. We only ask that you contact them before hand to negotiate the matter with them." This meant that "thank offerings" were always welcome and travel expenses usually underwritten by the host church or institution. See Jennie Hughes, ed., *Bethel Heart Throbs of Revival* (Shanghai: Bethel Mission, 1931), 62–63; Jennie Hughes, ed., *Bethel Heart Throbs of Surprises* (Shanghai: Bethel Mission, 1932), 66.

[56] Chen Chonggui, "Bianji zhihou [Editor's Notes]," *Budao zazhi* [*Evangelism*] 7, no. 1 (January–February 1934): 110; Song Shangjie, *Fenxingji* [*Revival Messages*], 6th ed. (1935; repr., Hong Kong: Bellman House, 1989), 153. Song and his family lived in a *shikumen* dwelling. These were not opulent, but neither were they

That strategy allowed Song to accomplish two things. First, his decision to operate his revivals by faith, that is, dependent upon the goodwill and donations of others, meant Song appeared to live day-to-day. Just as most workers in Tianjin's economy of 1934 could do no better than find day jobs as casual laborers, so Song could do nothing more than preach today and hope to find someone willing to pay for him to do it again tomorrow.[57] He famously wore "the common, blue cotton gown of the ordinary coolie," eschewing Western fashions and more sophisticated Chinese attire.[58] Time and again, the way he handled his money and presented his ministry allowed Song to identify with the precarious lives of the people in Tianjin.

However, and this is the second point, Song's own money and his intimate connection to the wealthy meant he was always more than just another person scraping by. Even such a simple act as getting out of the car with Li Fenglin allowed Song to appropriate the mantle of the Guan family's success. It communicated that he was hobnobbing with Tianjin's upper class, enjoying their friendships and, in the case of Mrs. Guan, basking in her reverence.[59] Song had made it. He embodied the dreams of many aspiring urbanites: he rode in cars, relaxed with the

---

associated with the homes of the working class. See Bergère, *Golden Age of the Chinese Bourgeoisie*, 102.

[57] Hershatter, *Workers of Tianjin*, 45; Song would sometimes insert into his sermons reminders that he had needs but that his audience could meet them. His comments never required people to support him, but they did hint that he was dependent on their support. He might explain, "I am a non-salaried preacher. What I need God sends." He would then proceed to explain, for example, how when he went to Manchuria he had no coat, but someone in a revival meeting gave him one for free. In Tianjin he received an influx of items from numerous people as an expression of love and gratitude right before he left, including silk handkerchiefs, shoes, socks, woolen goods, a new blue gown, stamps, a leather-bound Bible, pants, and—of course—money. See Song Shangjie, *Forty John Sung Revival Sermons*, vol. 2, trans. Timothy Tow (Singapore: Alice Doo, 1983), 50; Song Shangjie, April 27–28, 1934, SSD, TTC.

[58] Hughes, *Bethel Heart Throbs of Revival*, 24; Song, *Forty John Sung Revival Sermons*, 2:46. The blue gown, one should note, had taken on nationalistic tones in the 1930s. According to Wen-hsin Yeh, it was the "trademark item of machine-manufactured Chinese fabric" during that decade and therefore earned the nickname *guohuobu*, or "national products cloth." Wen-hsin Yeh, *Shanghai Splendor: Economic Sentiments and the Making of Modern China, 1843–1949* (Berkeley: University of California Press, 2007), 97.

[59] See, for example, Song Shangjie, April 10–13, 1934, SSD, TTC.

wealthy, and even enjoyed fame (a postcard of Song was available for purchase).[60] He looked to be the poor boy who made good.

This dual identity allowed Song's messages to cut two ways. At times he could sound like an angry populist. His sharp tongue would flay China's wealthy and powerful for their corrosive exploitation of the masses.[61] "[M]any capitalists there are," he spat bitterly, "who exploit and profiteer because they do not believe in heaven or hell."[62] He explained that they lived sumptuous lives, calloused to the suffering all around them—even just outside their own doors. The bourgeoisie were current incarnations of Dives, the rich landlord who despised the beggar Lazarus in Jesus' parable recorded in Luke 16:19-31.[63] Dives' eternal fate in hell was emblematic of the fate that awaited all of China's wealthy elites, for—as Song was inclined to point out—the more money you have the less faith you possess.[64] Whenever he referenced capitalists in his sermons, he always cast them in negative roles. For example, "Many church members today cringe before the rich and the capitalists."[65] Notice that church members are juxtaposed to the rich and the capitalists. There could be virtually no overlap in Song's thinking, because the capitalist was "a sinner through and through."[66]

That said, Song's own association with China's elite prompted him to rehabilitate their image through the logic of conversion. Revivals always presented the Chinese bourgeoisie as lost and spiritually dead, but their lives could be entirely changed if they turned to Jesus. In his sermons Song preached that even a capitalist could be saved if he would follow Jesus' instructions to the rich young ruler, selling all his possessions and giving the money to the poor.[67] In practice he never enforced such a costly repentance. Instead, he welcomed the addition of money, position, and power that China's elites brought to the church. Attention

---

[60] Hope College, "W88–0315, China Mission, Papers, 1888–1979. 1.50 linear ft.," 2012, Collection Registers and Abstracts, paper 204.

[61] Lu, *Beyond the Neon Lights*, 63. Lu estimated that Shanghai's bourgeoisie was but 1 percent of the population; Tianjin's proportion would have been smaller.

[62] Song Shangjie, *Forty John Sung Revival Sermons*, vol. 1, trans. Timothy Tow (Singapore: Alice Doo, 1978), 21.

[63] Song, *Forty John Sung Revival Sermons*, 1:20.

[64] Song, *Fenxingji* [*Revival Messages*], 152.

[65] Song, *Fenxingji* [*Revival Messages*], 63.

[66] Song, *Fenxingji* [*Revival Messages*], 27.

[67] Song Shangjie, *Peilingji* [*Devotional Messages*] (1935; repr., Hong Kong: Bellman House, n.d.), 17.

to his messages, in fact, reveals that Song elevated the conversions of the rich and powerful above all others. During one revival, for instance, "Hundreds of men and women confessed their sins and publicly took a stand for Jesus Christ."[68] Yet in subsequent reports, those hundreds of people were uniformly distilled to a rich official, a powerful military officer, and the influential chief of police.[69] In that way people of wealth, rank, and distinction became the exemplars of the revived Christian life.

CONVERGENCE WITH A BROADER DISCOURSE

Larger forces corroborated Song's attitude toward China's entrepreneurs. On the one hand, China's Communists had succeeded in pointing out the many faults of the bourgeoisie and the subtle measures they used to enrich themselves off the labor of the masses. Few could see them as national heroes, and Song's condemnations of China's capitalists reiterated popular opinion. On the other hand, the Nationalist government concluded—like Song—that bourgeois wealth and power were necessary to further its aims. When Jiang Jieshi [Chiang Kai-shek] attempted to unite the country in 1927, his military campaign stalled for lack of funding. He had to court the nation's elites to get a fresh infusion of money. In the end he made a pragmatic compromise. In order to keep his campaign going, Jiang agreed to purge the Communists from his party and enshrine the bourgeoisie's vision of how to strengthen the nation in his government's policies.[70]

Revolutionaries saw the move as an abandonment of the May Fourth spirit of radicalism, but radicalism—in fact—came in many forms. In the wake of May Fourth, Rana Mitter has observed, "One of the most potentially powerful new role models was the idea of the entrepreneur."[71] The bourgeoisie promoted new learning in China, drawing heavily on ideas from abroad to remake the nation. At the same time,

---

[68] James P. Leynse to Friends, Christmas 1932, China Records Project Miscellaneous Personal Papers Collection, record group 8, box 115, Special Collections, Yale Divinity School Library, New Haven, Conn.

[69] Hughes, *Bethel Heart Throbs of Surprises*, 69; Gih, *Launch Out into the Deep*, 34–35; Song Shangjie, "Zuidan tuoluo: Yuehan fuyin di bazhang [Casting Off the Burden of Sin: John Chapter Eight]," as recorded by Zhao Aiguang, *Budao zazhi* [*Evangelism*] 7, no. 2 (March–April 1934): 12.

[70] Bergère, *Golden Age of the Chinese Bourgeoisie*, 227–28.

[71] Rana Mitter, *A Bitter Revolution: China's Struggle with the Modern World* (New York: Oxford University Press, 2004), 90.

they were some of the country's most ardent nationalists. Entrepreneurs were at the vanguard of movements for buying only national products. With sincerity they believed that investing in the Chinese economy was the way to rebuild the nation and free it from foreign interference. Such purchases, of course, benefited their own local companies, but that did not make their pathway to a New China any less real. The country needed to strengthen itself by working hard and together to solidify the nation's fledgling economy. To overthrow it all in revolution, they warned, would only set China back by eliminating the primary beachhead of modernization.[72]

Jiang Jieshi formalized his alliance with this line of thinking by enshrining it in national policy. In February 1934 one hundred thousand people stood in drizzling rain to hear the Generalissimo call for a transformation of Chinese life through self-sacrifice and hard work. The country was in a state of acute crisis: "[O]rdinary processes of education and governance" were not enough to rescue China from foreign encroachment and internal dissension. The nation needed to see each citizen experience "regeneration."[73] It was time for a New Life Movement (NLM), lest the country succumb to the forces of chaos.

The NLM expressed the dominant Nationalist ideology of the mid-1930s. Offices were quickly opened at the provincial level to promote the government's chosen road to modernization. Within a month of Jiang's speech, Jiangxi Province had an NLM field office. By May, eight others would have their own.[74] Hebei Province, where Song was leading his meetings in April 1934, organized its branch during the first week of his revival. The announcement came on the same day that Song's services were first publicized in the city papers.[75] The newspaper article, which proclaimed the NLM office's opening, echoed the themes Jiang Jieshi had outlined in earlier speeches: in order to become a modern

---

[72] See Bergère, *Golden Age of the Chinese Bourgeoisie.*

[73] General Chiang Kai-Shek, *Outline of the New Life Movement,* trans. Madame Chiang Kai-Shek (Nanchang: Association for the Promotion of the New Life Movement, 1934), 3.

[74] Arif Dirlik, "The Ideological Foundations of the New Life Movement: A Study in Counterrevolution," *Journal of Asian Studies* 34, no. 4 (August 1975): 949.

[75] "Xinshenghuo yundong juxing daibiao dahui [New Life Movement Holds Representative Meeting]," *Tianjin dagong bao,* April 15, 1934; "Jidujiao budaotuan: qing Song Shangjie boshi jiangyan [Christian Evangelistic League Invites Dr. John Song to Speak]."

state, the "social customs and habits" of the Chinese people would need to be fundamentally changed.[76]

Which customs, though, and what habits? It did not take long for lists to appear: people should arrive to work on time, be physically fit, accept discipline, and be hardworking and eager to study when not on the job.[77] All worker protests over structural inequalities were deemed "selfish" because they elevated the welfare of a person, a family, or a work unit over the needs of the nation.[78] If this sounds like a wish list of the owners of the means of production, it was! Even those behaviors targeted by the NLM that seemed unrelated to workplace behavior often had their roots in bourgeois discontent. For instance, Tianjin cotton mill owners had been complaining for several years that their employees were inefficient because they visited brothels, gambled, and stole.[79] So, in 1934 the NLM named all those off-hour activities as unpatriotic vices that also needed reform.[80]

National progress, the NLM insisted, would come when city-dwellers in particular learned to conform to the aims of the elites. Song's revivals seemed to agree. He preached excoriating messages against the selfsame behaviors that the NLM was condemning. He not only rebuked audiences for visiting prostitutes, gambling, and stealing—rather stock descriptions of sin for Holiness preachers in the twentieth century—but also denounced breaking contracts, joining demonstrations, and being part of the *qingbang* or *hongbang*, gangs with the power to compromise a worker's loyalty to his or her company.[81]

The fact that Song maintained close friendships with people of the bourgeoisie and so clearly articulated their concerns raises the question of whether or not he was their stooge. It is a fair question and needs to be answered in context. In the mid-1930s, it is critical to remember

[76] Jay Taylor, *The Generalissimo: Chiang Kai-shek and the Struggle for Modern China* (Cambridge, Mass.: Belknap Press of Harvard University Press, 2009), 108; Dirlik, "Ideological Foundations of the New Life Movement," 947.

[77] "Xinshenghuo yundong juxing daibiao dahui [New Life Movement Holds Representative Meeting]."

[78] Dirlik, "Ideological Foundations of the New Life Movement," 958; Chiang, *Outline of the New Life Movement*, 1.

[79] Hershatter, *Workers of Tianjin*, 163.

[80] "Xinshenghuo yundong juxing daibiao dahui [New Life Movement Holds Representative Meeting]."

[81] Brian G. Martin, *The Shanghai Green Gang: Politics and Organized Crime, 1919–1937* (Berkeley: University of California Press, 1996).

that the bourgeoisie's description of the pathway to a New China was almost universally accepted in urban centers, and the alternatives were criminalized. The Chinese Communist Party was effectively outlawed in 1927, driven to the hinterlands of the country, and by 1934 the government was using military strikes to eliminate the last vestiges of the CCP that were holed up in rural areas.[82] In a less conspicuous manner, non-productivity—though not an ideology—was also prohibited in cities. Citizenship in China became coterminous with social productivity. Those who were not working were worse than useless: they were considered parasites on the nation. Thus, the government implemented a formal penal system around issues of indigence and unemployment and organized workhouses and poorhouses—homes that became "virtual prisons."[83] Viable alternatives to the emphases of the bourgeois NLM were almost impossible to find.

In that setting, were Song's frequent denunciations of gambling, drinking, smoking opium, and visiting prostitutes a thinly disguised mask for state or bourgeois propaganda? What about his instructions to obey authorities, serve others, and smile? Without a doubt Song's moral instructions overlapped with those of factory owners and the NLM, but that does not mean his revivals were part of a capitalist plot.[84] Instead, Song's sermons were clear-eyed instructions on how to navigate and succeed in Tianjin's arrangement of social, economic, and political power in 1934. Certainly Song's diaries made it clear that he found the bourgeois

---

[82] In 1934 the CCP had been almost entirely driven from China's cities. The remnants of the party lived in rural Jiangxi, surrounded by the Nationalist army. See Jerome Ch'en, "The Communist Movement 1927–1937," in *The Cambridge History of China*, vol. 13, ed. Denis Twitchett and John K. Fairbank (Cambridge: Cambridge University Press, 1986), 206–8.

[83] Janet Y. Chen, *Guilty of Indigence: The Urban Poor in China, 1900–1953* (Princeton, N.J.: Princeton University Press, 2012), 47.

[84] Paul E. Johnson, *A Shopkeeper's Millennium: Society and Revivals in Rochester, New York, 1815–1837* (New York: Hill and Wang, 1978), 141. After studying how the wealthy in upstate New York benefited from the meetings of Charles Finney, Johnson—despite his Marxist leanings—insisted the revival was not a guise for exploitation. William G. McLoughlin, *Modern Revivalism: Charles Grandison Finney to Billy Graham* (New York: Ronald Press, 1959), 181, had reached a similar conclusion in evaluating the work of Dwight L. Moody. McLoughlin readily admitted that Dwight Moody's revivals favored the "most conservative side in contemporary issues," but "this scarcely justified Engels in reducing revivalism to a bourgeois plot." Song's own revivalism should be interpreted in the same manner.

arrangement preferable to the Communist alternative.[85] Nonetheless, he never intended to be a front for his wealthy patrons or the state's NLM, even as their messages intertwined. Rather, the similarities of their messages were an example of how his revivals were embedded in the cities of China. In the mid-1930s, urbanites across the nation embraced and even sacralized one trajectory of the May Fourth Movement: the bourgeois conception of modern life. Like just about everyone else in the city, Song and his audiences found that life compelling and attractive, and his revivals became a way for people to reach for its respectability.[86]

---

[85] Song's political views have largely been hidden. One reason could be that his premillennial eschatology kept him from being too concerned or involved in China's political affairs. This world and its arrangements of power were soon to pass away. Another factor, though, is the systematic avoidance of the issue by Song Tianzhen, Song Shangjie's daughter. The excerpts of her father's journals, which she selected, have been careful to avoid any mention of Song's political outlook. An unfettered examination of the material, however, reveals that while Song did not dwell on politics, he clearly disliked the Communists. In his journal they always appeared in negative roles. For instance, on January 1, 1928, he wrote that the "Communist party is making a disturbance everywhere. At the end of the age, evildoers come forth in large number." On December 8, 1930, when he was visiting Hangzhou, he recorded a dream in his diary wherein Communists captured him and cut him with swords. His persecutors were people he knew from his hometown. Despite their efforts, he did not die. He was in great danger, though. Only the appearance of a heavenly army could finally rescue him. When he woke up, Song concluded that Communists were attacking his hometown and that was why God had brought him to Hangzhou. Communists did not fare better in his sermons. They were invariably against him and the gospel. He even took to referring to them in popular slang as *gongfei*, "communist bandits." Song's outlook was certainly not unique in the Christian community of the time. Only as fatigue set in over the interminable battles between the Nationalists and the Communists did a few Christians attempt a rapprochement with the "red bandits." The left-leaning Christian periodical *Chinese Recorder* tried to find some common ground between Christians and Communists in 1934. Most Christians, however, believed that no concord could exist between Christ and Belial, between Christianity and godless Communism. For more information on Song's opinion, or the perspective of other Christians toward Chinese Communists, see Song Shangjie, January 1, 1928, SSD, TTC; Song Shangjie, December 8, 1930, SSD, TTC; Song Shangjie, "Yesu zailai [Jesus' Return]," as recorded by Lü Daguang, Moore Memorial Church, 1936, *Lingsheng* 2, no. 5 (May 1936): 16; *Chinese Recorder* 64, no. 6 (1934); "Editorial Notes," *Bible for China* 70 (July–August 1934): 1–5; Fox Butterfield, "A Missionary View of the Chinese Communists (1936–1939)," in *American Missionaries in China*, ed. Kwang-Ching Liu (Cambridge, Mass.: Harvard University Press, 1966), 249–302.

[86] Yip, *Religion, Nationalism, and Chinese Students*, 87.

5

A New Audience

The New Man, which Song's revivals produced, was designed for the city. For people in the countryside, this new approach to life seemed irrelevant. Why should a farmer start to obey the clock instead of seasonal cycles? What use was it to tell someone to wash off dirt before going to work if he was about to sink his hands into the soil? The New Man that Song forged in his revivals attracted huge interest, but his popularity was centralized in China's cities.

There, crowds flocked to his meetings. If a sanctuary could seat five hundred, then a thousand people tried to mash together.[1] Photos show so many chairs added to the front of sanctuaries that those lucky enough to nab the first row of the overflow seating were actually pressed into Song's space, vying with him for a place to put their hands and feet.[2] Among those in attendance were a few of China's entrepreneurs, modern professionals, and cultural elites. That did not mean, however, that Song acted as a chaplain to the bourgeoisie. On the contrary, time and again he complained about the conspicuous absence of "merchants and tycoons" from his services. "Though the messages are good," he lamented, "to them wealth is of greater

---

[1] Leslie T. Lyall, *A Biography of John Sung* (Singapore: Genesis Books, 2004), 116.

[2] H. A. C. Hildering and J. A. Hildering, "Dr. John Sung Spreekt. In een stampvolle kerk," January 17, 1939, file 6212, Raad voor de zending (1102–2), Het Utrechts Archief, Utrecht, Netherlands.

importance."[3] Since no more than a handful of elites showed up at his services in Tianjin or anywhere else, the throngs that pushed to get through the doors to hear Song speak must have belonged to a different social segment. But who were they, and why did they come?

REVIVAL AND CLASS COMPOSITION

Class is a complicated subject in China. After the Communist victory in 1949, class stratifications had a particular Marxist axe to grind. Labels have been used to shoehorn people into predetermined categories so that the revolution was led by Karl Marx's chosen ones: a united proletariat revolting against their bourgeois masters. Such a description is politically convenient, but in no way reflects reality. For that reason language of the "proletariat" should be avoided. It is an unhelpful designation, murky, and does not clarify the kinds of people who attended Song's services.[4]

Instead, beneath the bourgeois stratum, three urban categories will be used: the *xiaoshimin* [petty urbanites], the working class, and the underclass.[5] It is important to avoid imagining all the groups as part of a linear social progression, somehow perfectly equidistant from one another. The gap between the underclass and the working class was large. The difference between the working class and the petty urbanites was minimal, if one looks at income. Other markers distinguished those two groups. Finally, to move from the working class or the petty urbanites to the bourgeoisie was an extraordinary leap.[6] Social differences were serious in China's urban centers. Tianjin, where Song held the two-week revival introduced in the last chapter, captures the dynamics well.[7]

To understand who was in Song's revivals, it is easiest to work backwards and eliminate the underclass. They were a rather amorphous social unit comprised of déclassé workers, immigrants or

---

[3] Song Shangjie, *Forty John Sung Revival Sermons*, vol. 2, trans. Timothy Tow (Singapore: Alice Doo, 1983), 41.

[4] Hanchao Lu, *Beyond the Neon Lights: Everyday Shanghai in the Early Twentieth Century* (Berkeley: University of California Press, 1999), 167.

[5] Lu, *Beyond the Neon Lights*, 63.

[6] Lu, *Beyond the Neon Lights*, 61.

[7] Although this chapter continues, like chapter 4, to be focused on Tianjin, the same general social composition of Song's audience played out over and over again across various cities.

refugees to the cities, vulnerable women, and people with physical disabilities. Making up 40 percent of the urban population of Tianjin in 1933, they could not be missed.[8] They were obvious, not so much because of what they had or did, but because of what they lacked. This was the class of the destitute.

People of the underclass were most easily recognized by their homes, or lack thereof. The urban underclass largely lived in *wopu*, improvised shelters built with scavenged wood and then filled in with mud and grass, or lean-tos made of reed mats. Even so, landlords collected rents from the squatters on their property.[9] Collectors came daily, not monthly, and evicted anyone who fell behind five days in their payments.[10]

Most people of the underclass had no regular work. Only a tiny portion found a way to earn a few coppers, possibly by making toilet paper out of grass, for instance. Many more, however, resorted to begging and scavenging. What elicited the most comment, though, "was that so many able-bodied people stayed home."[11] A newspaper reporter captured the hopelessness of the underclass in an article filed in 1935:

> In another small room, we found two strong young men lying on a special bed which had bricks spread on the four sides and straw spread out in the middle. One saw us and sat up, and looked at us with a glazed stare. We asked why he didn't go out to work, and he said, "Where is there work?" He sighed, then said, "We want to work but there isn't any. When we beg no one will give because we are young. There's no way out but to starve to death!" When he finished talking he lay down again.[12]

To slip into the city's underclass was to begin a slow slide toward death. In one of Tianjin's shantytowns, an investigator visited 1,400 *wopu* and found at least one sick person in each. No one could afford medical care.[13]

Despite their obvious needs, Song's revivals and healing services made no inroads among the class of the desperate. It is possible that a few of the city's poorest slipped into Tianjin's Li Yuanhong Hall or, more

[8] Gail Hershatter, *The Workers of Tianjin, 1900–1949* (Stanford: Stanford University Press, 1986), 76.

[9] Lu, *Beyond the Neon Lights*, 123.

[10] Hershatter, *Workers of Tianjin*, 79.

[11] Hershatter, *Workers of Tianjin*, 78.

[12] Hershatter, *Workers of Tianjin*, 78–79, quoted from *Yishi bao*, January 20, 1935, 9.

[13] Hershatter, *Workers of Tianjin*, 80.

likely, lingered by an open window to hear Song speak. But the reality was that the underclass was absent from his meetings. For one thing no one expected them to be there. Christian outreach to the destitute was not built around revivals. The Salvation Army, which arrived in China in 1916, established itself as the leading provider for the poor. The Salvationists introduced the "beggar colony," a place where the "flotsam and jetsam" could be turned into productive workers for the nation.[14] Other organizations adopted the Salvation Army's technique for ministering to the poor, so by 1934 outreach to Tianjin's underclass happened in relief or aid centers, such as those operated by the American Board of Commissioners for Foreign Missions (ABCFM), not in churches or great ceremonial halls.[15] In fact, Christian work among China's poorest was considered to be such a unique ministry that a survey entitled "Evangelistic Work in China To-day" declared, "The well known and important work of the Salvation Army is not included because it was not considered to come within the scope of the enquiry."[16] Evangelism aimed at China's underclass in the 1930s simply took a form other than Song's itinerant revival campaigns.

More pointedly, Song's sermons addressed a different audience. He warned his listeners to avoid going to movies, attending plays, reading novels, and visiting prostitutes. Yet as Gail Hershatter observed, no amusement halls or brothels existed in Tianjin's districts of the underclass. As one reporter had it, "[T]hese people have no money for bad habits."[17] The underclass, therefore, could not have been the ones Song wrote about in his journals—those who confessed that they smoked, purchased pornographic materials, went to shows, visited prostitutes, had a husband that kept a second wife, and the like.[18] Even the people who came to Song unemployed, like Zhao Guicui, who had recently lost

[14] Janet Y. Chen, *Guilty of Indigence: The Urban Poor in China, 1900–1953* (Princeton, N.J.: Princeton University Press, 2012), 71.

[15] Frederic Wakeman, *Policing Shanghai, 1927–1937* (Berkeley: University of California Press, 1995), 87; "North China Reports, 1930–1934," box 16.3.12, v. 54, American Board of Commissioners for Foreign Missions Archives, 1810–1961 (ABC 1–91), Houghton Library, Harvard University, Cambridge, Mass..

[16] H. R. Williamson, "Evangelistic Work in China To-day," *The Chinese Recorder* 69 (May 1938): 215.

[17] Hershatter, *Workers of Tianjin*, 80, quoted from *Tianjin shi zhoukan*, 1, no. 7, 13.

[18] Song Shangjie, April 11–27, 1934, Song Shangjie Diaries, Trinity Theological College, Singapore. Henceforth this location will be referred to as SSD, TTC.

his job, cannot be lumped with the underclass, because as Song noted in his diary, after Zhao lost his job at Butterfield and Swire he was able to secure a temporary loan from his cousin for twenty-five yuan.[19] It was not a fortune, but the money was more than the average monthly income of most working-class families.[20] The extra cash, along with the network his former job supplied, prevented Zhao from careening into Tianjin's underclass. He, along with the vast majority of Song's audience, was part of a different social stratum.

If the people who came to hear Song preach were by and large not the upper class nor the urban underclass, who were those in-between that flocked to his meetings? They could have been Tianjin's working class, laborers who congregated around jobs in industry, handicraft, and transport. They could also have been the *xiaoshimin*, the petty urbanites who gravitated toward commercial and clerical jobs in the emerging consumer sector. Or were Song's revivals a mix of both?

One would expect that Song had broad appeal. The sheer number of people who heard him speak over the years makes it easy to imagine working-class inquirers and curious petty urbanites sitting side by side, enjoying some of the city's rare free entertainment. Despite the appeal of such a picture, it is not borne out by the facts. The truth is social classes rarely mixed in Song's meetings. They were a remarkably homogenous gathering of petty urbanites.[21] The evidence indicates that his audiences hurried to the Li Yuanhong Hall from their jobs in department stores, factory offices, Western pharmacies, banks, foreign firms, or from their college classes.[22] As a social unit, they were distinguishable from the

[19] Song Shangjie, April 14, 1934, SSD, TTC.

[20] Brett Sheehan, *Trust in Troubled Times: Money, Banks, and State-Society Relations in Republican Tianjin* (Cambridge, Mass.: Harvard University Press), xiii.

[21] *Petty urbanites* is a literal translation of the Chinese term *xiaoshimin*. Hanchao Lu remarks that, "[a]lthough people who used the word—which was almost everyone—certainly knew what it meant, nowhere in Chinese sources is the term adequately analyzed." Because the petty urbanites were not the richest or the poorest in China, the temptation is to think of them as middle class. That would be an error, however, especially as it tends to import contemporary notions of the idea. Perhaps the closest current idea would be "lower middle class." Lu, *Beyond the Neon Lights*, 61–62.

[22] See, for example, Song Shangjie, *Forty John Sung Revival Sermons*, vol. 1, trans. Timothy Tow (Singapore: Alice Doo, 1978), 70; Cai Jianyuan, ed., *Zhonghua quanguo jidutu budaotuan huananqu chajingdahui baogaoshu* [*The National Evangelistic Association Southern Division Bible Study Meeting Report*] (Fuzhou,

working class not only by their professions but, importantly for Song, by their access to leisure and their ability to read.

One needs to remember that the working class congregated in small-scale operations where owners and employees spent all their days and nights together. They worked, ate, and slept as a unit with the singular aim of doing the same tomorrow. Petty urbanites, on the other hand, toiled in large factories, Western-owned companies, and schools where on-hours and off-hours were clearly delineated. Passing time, therefore, became an important element in their lives. The petty urbanites, not the working class, were the ones who had time built into their days to visit amusement halls, sit in tea houses, or go on a stroll along the streets lined with shops. Their schedules allowed them to while away time reading newspapers or to sit with friends listening to the radio.[23]

It was this literate and leisured group to whom Song primarily appealed. To move lower on the social scale was to preach to an illiterate class of laborers who would not be able to follow Song's instructions to read the Bible daily or could not enjoy the personal notes he scribbled on the photos, Bibles, and other memorabilia that people handed to him.[24] More importantly though, to go lower was to bump against the inflexible working-class schedule. Most of the working class had little freedom or time to attend Song's services, either in the morning, afternoon, or evening.[25] For all intents and purposes, his ministry was restricted to Tianjin's *xiaoshimin*, a relatively narrow slice of the population that

Fujian: Shiming Shuguan, 1937); Song Shangjie, ed., *Quanguo jidutu budaotuan tuankan* [*National Christian Evangelistic League Publication*] (March 1936); Song Shangjie, April 16–18, 1934, SSD, TTC. The snapshot of those who joined an evangelistic team is not necessarily identical to those who attended Song's services, but insofar as the two groups overlapped extensively, the occupations listed by people who joined teams provides the best data available on Song's audiences. In 1936, 40 percent of the team members were involved in education, either as teachers, administrators, or students. Thirty-one percent were involved in Christian ministry. Twelve percent of the evangelistic team members came from the medical profession. Eight percent were from business, 5 percent were homemakers, and 3 percent were government employees.

[23] Carlton Benson, "The Manipulation of *Tanci* in Radio Shanghai during the 1930s," *Republican China* 20, no. 2 (1995): 125.

[24] Song Shangjie, April 27, 1934, SSD, TTC; Timothy Tow, *John Sung My Teacher* (Singapore: Christian Life Publishers, 1985), 28.

[25] "Jidujiao budaotuan: qing Song Shangjie boshi jiangyan [Christian Evangelistic League Invites Dr. John Song to Speak]," *Tianjin dagong bao*, April 15, 1934. In some cities Song held morning and midmorning services as well. The same

differentiated itself from the working class less by income and more by education and set hours for recreation.

Even so, education and free time alone cannot explain Song's popularity among the petty urbanites. Such factors were just as likely to lead a person to the YMCA or YWCA, a coffee shop, a club, a sporting event, or the like. What was Song doing that appealed so powerfully to the lower-middle class? Among all the people in the city, why were his revivals so compelling to petty urbanites?

ANXIETY: A QUARTET OF FEARS

In the second quarter of the twentieth century, popular phrases extolled the virtues of the city. One saying had it that "having explored up to the edge of the world, one could not find a better place than the two sides of the Huangpu River [Shanghai]." Another line insisted that it was "a great fortune for a person to live in this colorful and dazzling world [of the city]."[26] Immigrants flocked to China's urban centers by the hundreds of thousands. Tianjin more than tripled in size from 320,000 inhabitants in 1900 to 1,385,137 by 1929.[27] Who could stay away? While China's northern interior was devastated by famine, flooding, banditry, warring generals, marauding soldiers, and rioting peasants, Tianjin offered people new jobs and opportunities as well as social advancement, all in the midst of tree-lined boulevards, public parks, neon lights, elegant shop windows, and lively entertainment quarters. Life in the city meant doctors, firefighters, welfare agencies, and policemen were all readily available.[28] No wonder people spoke so enthusiastically: the city seemed too good to be true.

For newly arriving peasants, the great disparity between urban and rural incomes meant that even doing menial work, such as pulling a rickshaw, for an inconsistent and absurdly low wage could still mean bettering their livelihood.[29] Even the most desperately poor praised China's

---

logic, however, still applies. For those without modern times of leisure, it would be almost impossible to attend his meetings.

[26] Lu, *Beyond the Neon Lights*, 48.

[27] Marie-Claire Bergère, "The Chinese Bourgeoisie, 1911–1937," in *The Cambridge History of China*, vol. 12, part 1, ed. John K. Fairbank (Cambridge: Cambridge University Press, 1983), 751; Hershatter, *Workers of Tianjin*, 50.

[28] Wen-hsin Yeh, *Shanghai Splendor: Economic Sentiments and the Making of Modern China, 1843–1949* (Berkeley: University of California Press, 2007), 119.

[29] David Strand, *Rickshaw Beijing: City, People and Politics in the 1920s* (Berkeley: University of California Press, 1989), 29.

modern cities, for if you "begged in the city you could get meat or fish soup. In the village all one could hope for was cornmeal."[30] The appeal of the city was powerful. It offered a new ladder for success, the promise of being the foundation for a New China, the glamor of a new and complex environment, and so on.[31] By all appearances, the petty urbanites were among the lucky ones who were able to live in a city.

But not everything was well in the nation's new capitals of commerce, wealth, and promise, and the petty urbanites knew it. For one thing poverty always seemed to be nipping at the heels of China's lower-middle class. Tianjin's economy was notoriously unstable; it went through nine financial crises between 1916 and 1937.[32] With each economic collapse some of the surplus workers would go back to their villages, but new faces replaced them quickly. The population would swell and contract, swell and contract, like a pulsating heart. Yet after each crisis it seemed the city swelled more and contracted less, creating an abundance of excess labor. New immigrants swamped the economy. The "massive reserve army of labor," as Gail Hershatter noted, "no doubt helped to keep wages low, and also to shape an occupational structure in which few people had steady jobs."[33] Job insecurity did not affect each profession evenly, and the petty urbanites, whose education made them less interchangeable than employees in some other lines of work, probably fared better than most. Nonetheless, their positions in large factories, banks, department stores, and the like were not immune from Tianjin's erratic economic fortunes. Indeed, having achieved a modicum of security, the *xiaoshimin* may have been especially anxious not to forfeit it. Perhaps for that reason they employed a variety of schemes to bilk money out of their employers.[34] The petty urbanites may have escaped

[30] Lao She, *Luotou Xiangzi* [*Camel Xiangzi*] (Hong Kong: Xuelin youxian gongsi, n.d.), quoted in Lu, *Beyond the Neon Lights*, 6.

[31] E. Perry Link Jr., *Mandarin Ducks and Butterflies: Popular Fiction in Early Twentieth-Century Chinese Cities* (Berkeley: University of California Press, 1981), 228.

[32] Sheehan, *Trust in Troubled Times*, 3.

[33] Hershatter, *Workers of Tianjin*, 76.

[34] See, for example, Song Shangjie, April 16–17, 1934, SSD, TTC. Many people who approached Song to make a private confession admitted to stealing money from their work, family, or friends. The offense should not blind us to two important realities. First, it is an important clue about class. The fact that these people stole money and not things is indicative of their lower–middle class status. To go much below the lower-middle class would be to interact with a class of people who

interminable poverty, but fears about their financial vulnerability never went away.

Another feature endemic to life in Tianjin was violence. Because jobs were tenuous, workers became extremely protective. Although the transport trade was characterized by more violence than most occupations, a closer look at this working-class profession puts in high relief the ferocity with which people commonly dealt with their rivals. Each transport worker's guild defined its boundaries by violence; if a guild member poached on another's territory he had to confess his mistake and have his boss apologize as well or bloodshed would begin.[35] Newspaper articles from the time indicate apologies were few because brutal fights were all too common. Headlines focused on the numerous battles in the streets with knives and axes between warring transport workers. Just as common, though, were stories of workers storming boats and thrashing captains for not knowing about or not paying the so-called "unloading fee." Other fairly common news items included reports of workers who raided factories, beat up employees, and smashed equipment when they became unhappy with the arrangement they had in moving the factory's goods.[36] Violence was so ubiquitous in China's cities that a survey of the nation's urban hospitals in 1933 discovered that it was the second most common cause for medical care.[37]

Violence could ensue unexpectedly. An employee might suddenly stab his boss for not paying fairly, or if someone was caught sneaking into a movie theater without a ticket, a fight was likely to follow.[38] It became an important survival strategy, therefore, to create associations of mutual protection. These were usually built around blood or native-place ties, though they were not limited to them. Those wanting more substantial protection affiliated with one of the gangs active in Tianjin, either the *qingbang* [Green Gang] or the *hongbang* [Red Gang]. Both

---

had a few things, but virtually no money. Second, those who attended Song's meetings apparently felt vulnerable, and many accessed cash in illicit ways. In this they were not alone. According to Wakeman, *Policing Shanghai*, 79, crime and theft became virtually synonymous in the 1930s. In Beijing, just a little north of Tianjin, 80 percent of felonies were theft related.

[35] Hershatter, *Workers of Tianjin*, 131.

[36] Hershatter, *Workers of Tianjin*, 132ff.

[37] J. A. Jewell, "The Development of Chinese Health Care, 1911–1949," in *Health Care and Traditional Medicine in China, 1800–1982*, ed. S. M. Hillier and J. A. Jewell (Boston: Routledge, 1983), 33.

[38] Hershatter, *Workers of Tianjin*, 131–35.

organizations provided vertical alliances that ran through every social stratum of the city.[39] Such connections did not guarantee safety, but they did provide a level of security. Song waged a verbal battle against fistfights and gangs. He denounced them as sin. But in a city that was ruled by violence, it was difficult for men in particular to heed his call for repentance.[40]

A third urban reality that belied the gilded image of life in the city was the prevalence of disease and sickness. Sanitation was a problem. The international concession areas, the parts of the city owned and operated by foreign governments, had running water and sewage, but the rest of Tianjin did not. This was a troublesome health issue as human and factory waste were dumped onto the street. In one neighborhood the refuse formed a "greenish current more than one foot deep."[41] Escaping the pollution was difficult. Whereas a few of the cotton mills provided bathhouses for their workers, most did not. That translated into Tianjin's higher paid workers visiting a public bathhouse two or three times in a month; those with lower wages did not bathe at all, but rinsed themselves in the river during the summer and with damp towels in the winter.[42] Inadequate facilities for public and personal hygiene ended up combining with the harsh climate and a generally poor urban diet to create a sick city.

Near the end of Song's Tianjin revival, women visited him at Zhang Zhouxin's home specifically for healing.[43] He dutifully recorded the name of each woman and her health complaint. Most asked to be healed of tuberculosis. Almost as many had issues with abdominal pain. Other

---

[39] Hershatter, *Workers of Tianjin*, 169–71.

[40] Hershatter, *Workers of Tianjin*, 181. In Song's sermons fighting and joining gangs are regularly named as sins. His journal from Tianjin, though, mentioned not one person who confessed to such sins.

[41] Hershatter, *Workers of Tianjin*, 74.

[42] Hershatter, *Workers of Tianjin*, 73.

[43] Interestingly, one of the seekers for divine healing was Mrs. Ding Limei. Ding Limei was one of the earliest Chinese Christian revivalists. He and his family were by education, reputation, and income squarely within the parameters of the *xiaoshimin*. For more information on Ding Limei and his family, see Daniel H. Bays, "Christian Revival in China, 1900–1937," in *Modern Christian Revivals*, ed. Edith L. Blumhofer and Randall Balmer (Urbana: Illinois University Press, 1993), 165–68; China Group, "Ding Limei," Biographical Dictionary of Chinese Christianity, accessed November 21, 2019, http://bdcconline.net/en/stories/ding-limei; and Wenzong Wang, "Yin Rexian," in *Salt and Light*, vol. 2, ed. Carol Lee Hamrin (Eugene, Ore.: Pickwick Publications, 2010), 123–42.

complaints included heart problems and strokes, headaches, inflamed kidneys, swollen hands and feet, and diseases of the eyes.[44] Clearly, to avoid urban poverty was not equivalent to escaping the city's most common illnesses.[45]

Fourth, and finally, something that constantly threatened to suck all savor out of urban life was boredom. Many *xiaoshimin* held enviable jobs as clerks in places like the Ministry of Communication (railroads), Maritime Customs Service, or banks. Popular slang reverenced such jobs for their relative security and wages, labeling them as an "iron rice bowl," "silver bowl," and "golden bowl," respectively.[46] Yet despite the popular image, many clerks bemoaned the tedium of their work. They were reduced to singular tasks repeated with mind-numbing regularity. In the Bank of China, leadership addressed an employee complaint about the boredom of dealing with telegrams for ten years by issuing a general announcement that workers should strive to be "anonymous heroes" and that the business was not so much a family as it was a piece of equipment. The clerk was admonished to be content in his role as "a cog in this complex machine."[47] Apparently the rebuttal did not suffice because management eventually added boredom as an issue to be addressed in the official training book of the bank. Boredom was a widespread personnel problem that was sabotaging morale. The "loss of control . . . and the diminishing relevance of individuals" drained work, and even life itself, of meaning.[48]

Financial insecurity, violence, sickness, and boredom were all intensified as the Tianjin economy bottomed out in 1934, the year Song arrived in town. The economic situation in the city was always volatile, but by 1930 analysts noted that the city had gone from a chronic to an acute crisis as the largest industry—cotton mills—began to lose twenty-seven yuan on every bale of yarn they sold.[49] The situation deteriorated over the following years as a series of global forces pounded the city. First, the worldwide depression shrank the demand for Chinese

[44] Song Shangjie, April 28, 1934, SSD, TTC.
[45] Hershatter, *Workers of Tianjin*, 74.
[46] Yeh, *Shanghai Splendor*, 93.
[47] Li Jilu, "Wo duiyu tongren," *Zhonghang shenghuo* [*Life in the Bank of China*] 1, no. 5 (September 15, 1932): 82, quoted in Yeh, *Shanghai Splendor*, 92.
[48] Yeh, *Shanghai Splendor*, 93–94.
[49] Hershatter, *Workers of Tianjin*, 35.

products.[50] Then in 1933, when the United States went off the gold standard, Tianjin experienced a bank run that marked the beginning of a three-year depression.[51] Shortly thereafter the Chinese government revised its tariffs in such a way that the duty on imported cotton was reduced, whereas taxes on domestic raw cotton and the textile machinery needed by Chinese manufacturers rose. Japanese mills exploited the situation and began to dump their goods in China, hoping to eliminate the homegrown competition.[52] All of these factors meant that "[b]y 1934 most of Tianjin mills were near collapse" and, by extension, the whole city was teetering uncertainly.[53]

The city's bourgeoisie took heavy losses for sure, but they were the few who could stand to lose something and still have a remainder. The underclass, somewhat counterintuitively, would have experienced the least change to their lives. Grinding poverty is terribly monotonous. It looks the same whether a city is thriving or imploding. The impact on the petty urbanites, though, was intense. They were the ones who felt like everything they had was threatened, as indeed it was. "In a country with no government support network, and where they might be separated from traditional family networks located back in the provinces, [the *xiaoshimin*] dreaded any sudden changes that might lead to them losing their jobs and falling into the awful commonality of the 'masses.'"[54] Trapped on a sinking ship over which they had no control, the lower-middle class could only dream of a way to escape.

SAFETY: WELCOME HOME

In the midst of this massive crisis, Song diverted petty urbanite anxiety about the city by reminding people of their rural homes. That message held visceral appeal in places like Tianjin, where something like four-fifths of the inhabitants had been born elsewhere.[55] Song's audience had memories of and connections to rural China.[56] He capitalized on those

---

[50] From 1929 to 1934, Chinese exports were cut almost in half. Bergère, "Chinese Bourgeoisie," 77.

[51] Sheehan, *Trust in Troubled Times*, 163.

[52] Hershatter, *Workers of Tianjin*, 35–36.

[53] Hershatter, *Workers of Tianjin*, 36.

[54] Rana Mitter, *A Bitter Revolution: China's Struggle with the Modern World* (New York: Oxford University Press, 2004), 90.

[55] Bergère, "Chinese Bourgeoisie," 100.

[56] Hershatter, *Workers of Tianjin*, 45.

living links in his sermons by calling up glorified images of their former lives, albeit in an indirect and sanitized form.

In Song's sermons the countryside became the place of righteousness. In the story of Abram and Lot, Abram had the better portion (Gen 13:10-18). On the surface, of course, Lot appeared to enjoy the better life. After immigrating to the city of Sodom, he "made his pile [of money] . . . by opening many business houses—Lot Trading Co., Lot Groceries, Lot Travel Service, Lot Banking Corporation." His daughters were "society birds," and everything seemed to fall his way.[57] Even when he faced unpleasantness, like when he was captured by marauding kings and dragged away from the city, Lot remained unshaken in his confidence in urban living, for when Abram rescued him, he quickly scampered back to the city. As it turned out, Lot was like a dog returning to its vomit.[58] For, Song reminded his listeners, Sodom was ultimately destroyed by the wrath of God. Abram, on the other hand, always "remained in the village, away from the world." He kept his distance from urban contamination because it was only when he was in rural areas that "[h]e praised God all day."[59] This symbolic sanctification of the countryside surfaced over and over again in Song's services. He depicted Nicodemus, for example, as the urbanite who looked down on Jesus, the bumpkin from the hinterlands. Or in another sermon, he paused to point out that Jesus healed a blind man only after leading him outside the city (Mark 8:22-26). "From this we can see that flourishing cities will impede people on the road of salvation. Today, we also need to leave the cities and go to the villages. Only then will we see the Lord's glory."[60]

Whereas the village became a primary symbol of purity for Song, the city was the womb of wickedness. Nothing good could come from it. Even infants "immediately perceive that it is bitter, and so open their

---

[57] Song, *Forty John Sung Revival Sermons*, 1:81.

[58] Song Shangjie, *Fenxingji* [*Revival Messages*], 6th ed. (1935; repr., Hong Kong: Bellman House, 1989), 168.

[59] Song, *Forty John Sung Revival Sermons*, 1:81. Song was not the only person exploiting the differences between the city and the countryside. Chinese novels and cinema, likewise, depicted the city as foul and corrupt, whereas the countryside was pure and uncontaminated. See Madeleine Yue Dong and Joshua L. Goldstein, eds., *Everyday Modernity in China* (Seattle: University of Washington Press, 2006); Link, *Mandarin Ducks and Butterflies*.

[60] Song Shangjie, *Peilingji* [*Devotional Messages*] (1935; repr., Hong Kong: Bellman House, n.d.), 4.

mouths and cry."[61] Just as Jericho was a prosperous but adulterous city, so also was Tianjin. "Jericho is a type of the world to be destroyed. This glittering [city] will be destroyed one day."[62] When worked into a lather, Song might even shout out that the whole world would melt by fire just like Sodom and Gomorrah.[63]

Or would it? Literalism certainly prompted Song to affirm the fiery end of the whole world with 2 Peter 3:10-12. However, his symbolic representations of the city and countryside complicated matters. Ultimately, he sided with the words of Jesus. On the Day of Judgment, believers should flee from China's cities and hide in the mountains or in the wilderness (Matt 24:16).[64] Urban areas were evil, and they would be ruined. The nation's interior, on the other hand, was a sanctuary from the corruptions of the modern world. Song spoke of a safe place to China's petty urbanites, who faced real insecurity.

Audiences lapped up Song's dichotomous and fictionalized depiction of urban and rural China. It did at least three things. For one it provided them comfort. It was a reminder that rural China was still there. "It existed before the modern city did, and still in a sense lay beneath it—almost ontologically prior," Perry Link explains. "A person could rise and fall and be hurtled about in the city, and the city itself might entirely collapse, but the countryside would always be there. One could count on it."[65] That did not mean Song's converts abandoned the city and moved back to their birthplaces in droves. They didn't. They all knew that Song's idyllic picture of the places from which they had just come was illusory. To leave the city would be an extraordinary loss. Even Song knew it. When he was not excoriating China's cities, he could admit and be humbled by the sacrifice of the handful of people he knew who actually left them in order to preach in China's interior.[66] No one really planned to depart the city. Song's elevation of village life

[61] Song Shangjie, *Moshide jidutu dang zhuyide er da wenti* [*Two Important Issues End-Time Christians Should Be Aware of*] (1936; repr., Beijing: Endiantang, 1963), 49.

[62] Song Shangjie, *Forty John Sung Revival Sermons*, vol. 2, trans. Timothy Tow (Singapore: Alice Doo, 1983), 33.

[63] Song, *Moshide jidutu dang zhuyide er da wenti* [*Two Important Issues End-Time Christians Should Be Aware of*], 18.

[64] Song Shangjie, "Yesu zailai [Jesus' Return]," as recorded by Lü Daguang, Moore Memorial Church, 1936, *Lingsheng* 2, no. 5 (May 1936): 20.

[65] Link, *Mandarin Ducks and Butterflies*, 202.

[66] Song, *Forty John Sung Revival Sermons*, 2:37.

was more like "'sweet grapes' . . . the romanticizing of an alternative one knew was secure."[67] Unsettled circumstances in urban China could not deny petty urbanites the comfort of a backup plan. Poverty, illness, violence, and boredom did not have to have the last word. If life in the city truly fell apart, then at least people could make a trip back to a rural place that Song colluded in pretending with his audience was not so bad after all.

Second, Song's sermons provided a satisfying resolution to the petty urbanites' conundrum. None of them wanted to return to their rural lives, but almost all of them were disappointed with the urban reality. Where were they to go? Time after time Song would end his services by inviting people to *"huijia ba!* [Return home!]."[68] It was not a suggestion for someone to return to her physical birthplace, but an opportunity to repent of one's sins, turn to God, and find her way to a new heavenly home—a home very much like the one Song had been romanticizing. Occasionally he might describe it as a place of wealth, health, or abundance. Far more often, though, the new home was simply a stable place where a person could truly belong. If his immigrant listeners would join "the Father's hometown," then they would be God's sons and daughters now.[69] "No one will be separated by the surnames Wang, Chen, or Huang. We will all be one family, living together and never, ever leaving one another."[70] All partings, those risky departures from home in search of a better life, could cease. God the Father was the stolid patriarch who held the new family together, whereas Jesus fulfilled the role of the mother. It fell to God the Son to weep over sinners, cuddle the brokenhearted, and coo with delight over his *baobei* [precious darlings].[71] Together the Father and the Son offered an idealized picture of the family, "a beautiful heavenly home," right here and now in the city to all who believed. Many in Song's audiences found it difficult to resist, therefore, when he asked them, "Do you want to go home? Raise your hands if you want [to]! I'm the first!"[72]

---

[67] Link, *Mandarin Ducks and Butterflies*, 229.

[68] Song, *Fenxingji [Revival Messages]*, 3.

[69] Song, *Fenxingji [Revival Messages]*, 187.

[70] Song, *Moshide jidutu dang zhuyide er da wenti [Two Important Issues End-Time Christians Should Be Aware of]*, 47.

[71] Song, *Fenxingji [Revival Messages]*, 3–4.

[72] Song, *Forty John Sung Revival Sermons*, 1:140.

Finally, Song's contrast between the city and the countryside gave petty urbanites an honorable way to maintain their rural values. Perry Link has argued that petty urbanites, more than any other group, felt pressured to act modern. Caught between the media-driven urban ideal and the reluctance to abandon rural norms, many *xiaoshimin* adopted "stylishness."[73] Chinese stylishness—the learning of a few foreign words, the purchase of a fountain pen, the watching of a movie about new-style dating, or even experimenting with such romantic attachments—allowed petty urbanites to appear modern, befitting their new life in the city.[74] Yet for all the attention such behavior received by the media, petty urbanite stylishness remained superficial. "At a deeper level, traditional values were still dear to their hearts."[75] In their eagerness to appear urbane, the *xiaoshimin* acted like they were something they were not. "They wear Western clothes, eat Western food, read Western books. . . . Whatever it is," Song pointed out, "it is all Western."[76] He, therefore, invited his audience to tear down the façade. At the end of each service, he gave listeners the opportunity to confess and repent of their artificial lives. For people to stand at the front of the meeting hall and announce that they rejected stylish facets of modern city life was to settle the unresolved dual identity that divided their souls. Tears were as much a sign of relief as they were of grief, for as penitents embraced Song's message about the idealized countryside, they were reclaiming what appeared to be the familiar rural standards of conduct on how to live.[77]

[73] Link, *Mandarin Ducks and Butterflies*, 203.

[74] Link, *Mandarin Ducks and Butterflies*, 20.

[75] Link, *Mandarin Ducks and Butterflies*, 20.

[76] Song Shangjie, "Zhude enai [The Lord's Grace and Love]," as recorded by Zhao Aiguang, *Budao zazhi* [*Evangelism*] 7, no. 4 (July–August 1934): 10.

[77] In the accounts of Song's revivals, one cannot help but notice the ever-present references to weeping and tears. Missionaries in particular drew special attention to the maudlin displays, explaining, "[This] cannot be done according to Oriental habits and opinions." (See Hendrik Kraemer, *Van Godsdiensten en Menschen* [*About Religions and People*] [Nijkerk, Netherlands: G. F. Callenbach, 1940], 179.) Nonetheless, these emotional outbursts were a regular feature in Song's services. He would note approvingly, "When I was speaking I was shedding tears. All were shedding tears and raising hands to believe in Jesus." (See Song Shangjie, March 6, 1931, SSD, TTC.) The emotional release that epitomized Song's revivals was not without a secular parallel. Song noted that popular Mandarin Duck and Butterfly fiction, which also sentimentalized the countryside, did the same thing. The difference, in his opinion, was that after crying at the end of a novel, "[T]he feeling is good, but it was only temporary; it was not more than an impulse.

A Reconstituted Morality

Moral decay was an axiomatic assumption for Song, many of his listeners, and revivalism generally.[78] Before people were ensnared by the griefs and sins of this world, something better had existed. Maybe it was back in some pristine historical era or in an Edenic paradise, but everyone presumed that a better life had existed in the past and that such a good life was possible again. Since cities became the locus and, in some ways, the source of the slide into modern debauchery, it should come as no surprise that Song felt he needed to import virtues from the countryside that predated it.[79] When juxtaposed to life in the village, the urban degradation was obvious:

> Men have become women, and women have become men; today [people] preach cohabitation, tomorrow it will be divorce; every kind of bizarre phenomena are with us. Before, there were no cigarettes, but now cities are filled with them; before sons and daughters were filial and obedient to their mother and father, now they attack them, and oppose ethical education. Before students respected their teachers, but now they attack them. Before a few famous people had syphilis, but now 606, 914, and venereal disease doctors have become ubiquitous in cities. Everything has changed. Contemporary society is messed up, and the church is even more of a wreck. Just look at one place: Shanghai. The city has tens of thousands of prostitutes. The people of today only think about attaining high positions and great wealth.[80]

Absolutely nothing of a loving heart remains." See Song, *Fenxingji* [*Revival Messages*], 8. Revivals, therefore, were the only place for petty urbanites to resolve the deep-seated anxiety that plagued their lives.

[78] Richard M. Riss, *A Survey of 20th Century Revival Movements in North America* (Peabody, Mass.: Hendrickson, 1988), 4.

[79] Rural values and urban revivalism have frequently gone hand in hand. See, for example, the studies of Lyle W. Dorsett, *Billy Sunday and the Redemption of Urban America* (Grand Rapids: Eerdmans, 1991); Thekla Ellen Joiner, *Sin in the City: Chicago and Revivalism, 1880–1920* (Columbia: University of Missouri Press, 2007); Marion L. Bell, *Crusade in the City: Revivalism in Nineteenth-Century Philadelphia* (Lewisburg, Pa.: Bucknell University Press, 1977).

[80] Song, *Peilingji* [*Devotional Messages*], 42. The mention of 606 and 914 are references to the two primary medications used to combat syphilis at the time. The numbers refer to the number of experiments carried out by the doctor who invented them, one Doctor Ehrlich of Frankfurt, Germany. The medicines, interestingly enough, cost seven yuan in 1928. They were not too expensive, but still out of reach for the lower class. This may be one more confirmation of the social status of Song's audience. It might also, though, be a popular cultural reference. The drugs were ubiquitous in Chinese advertising. Christian Henriot, *Prostitution and*

All the values Song upheld, such as honesty, respect for elders, simplicity, and obedience, were from the perspective of the city primarily "'countryside' values."[81] Thus Song's impassioned calls to repent—to turn around—were cast as appeals to return to a former way of life. People were to reject the individualistic impulses cultivated by modern consumerism and recover the communal values of the village. On the surface at least Song proclaimed a conservative and appealing moral message to those uncomfortable with their stylish lives.[82]

Even as Song extolled traditional values, he reworked them for his urban context. This was, after all, the birth of a New Man, not the resuscitation of the Old. Neither he nor his audience really expected to move back to their hometowns. His conservative moral directives, therefore, had to be reset for the city. For example, his call for obedience, the positive command he laid down more than any other except for prayer, was explained not in terms of obedience to elders, but in the context of choices people had to make in the city: people were to keep their contracts and to follow government orders to avoid demonstrations. His vice list had a similarly urban feel. To tell someone not to watch movies, go to dances, or become a lover of fashion would make no sense in the countryside. Song's morality, the ethical vision he presented as traditional and rural, was, in fact, new—freshly translated for the urban environment.

Translation, therefore, meant adaptation. The supreme virtue of filial piety, for instance, needed to be reworked in the city. Listeners no longer needed to live with their parents to show filial piety; Song conceded that. However, distance did not excuse anyone from showing his

---

Sexuality in Shanghai: A Social History, 1849–1949, trans. Noël Castelino (Cambridge: Cambridge University Press, 2001), 146–47, examined Shanghai newspapers in 1930 to see how many advertisements appeared for venereal diseases. In *Shishi xinwen*, seven advertisements were crammed into the pages; *Shenbao* had sixteen; *Xinwenbao* was virtually a catalogue for venereal disease treatments rather than an account of the daily news. It held forty-six advertisements for ways to combat the dreaded—but all too common—illnesses.

[81] Link, *Mandarin Ducks and Butterflies*, 202.

[82] Michael J. McClymond, ed., *Embodying the Spirit: New Perspectives on North American Revivalism* (Baltimore: John Hopkins University Press, 2004), 31; William G. McLoughlin, *Modern Revivalism: Charles Grandison Finney to Billy Graham* (New York: Ronald Press, 1959). Both McClymond and McLoughlin note that revivalism can be radical, but more often than not it has proven to be conservative—especially when it is tied to premillennialism.

or her parents proper respect. Song's own testimony became an example of how to uphold traditional values in a new era. He shared how he honored his parents. It did not mean living with them as Chinese tradition would have it. That was not only impractical, since he was traveling on the road most of the time, but it was also against the biblical instruction for a man to leave his father and his mother and cleave to his wife (Gen 2:24). What he could do, though, was to speak highly of them, especially his father, and he did so often. This tactic allowed Song to continue to pay lip service to the nonnegotiable virtue of Chinese society even as he vacated it of any specific behavior. In the city Song assuaged troubled consciences: filial piety was an attitude rather than an act. In so saying, Song changed a historic norm to fit with urban realities.

Song also needed to find ways of expressing traditional norms for sexual propriety with urban equivalents. In some cases he relied on a straightforward invocation of the past. Whereas some urban Chinese Christians promoted the idea that young people should be able to choose their own mates in marriage, Song rejected the idea.[83] "Are free romantic attachments love?" he queried his audience. "Free romantic attachments are sin! Look, today you have a romantic attachment, and get married, but tomorrow you are divorced."[84] In his mind urban life did not require adopting new forms of marriage. Traditional arrangements still worked just fine.[85]

At other times reworking sexual standards was more complicated. Song, for instance, condemned men for visiting urban prostitutes. That, however, was not a violation of the traditional code of conduct. Historically, Chinese society showed little "unease, embarrassment, or shame"

---

[83] On December 9, 1930, Song recorded in his diary that he heard someone speak at the East China Christian Home Forward Movement Conference about how Chinese marriages were unhappy because they were not based on the couple choosing each other. Song at the time did not report his own thoughts on the matter. While he was in the United States, he seemed disappointed that his parents were arranging his own marriage. See, for example, Tianzhen Song (Levi), ed., *The Diary of John Sung: Extracts from His Journals and Notes* (Singapore: Genesis Books, 2012), 16–17. One might expect, therefore, that Song would support people choosing their own spouses. However, once he left his rural ministry in 1931, Song's own opinion clearly solidified against free marriages.

[84] Song, *Fenxingji* [*Revival Messages*], 10. Song Shangjie, March 3, 1931, SSD, TTC.

[85] Song's own marriage was arranged while he was in the United States.

about men going to brothels.[86] Yet Song had to make the behavior sound like it deviated from custom. That was important to him. Calling people to restore an imagined past was an essential feature of his revivalism. In this case the past was relatively recent. About a generation before his revivals began, missionary preaching, the "scientific" discourse about sex, and urban realities combined to make the nuclear family the petty urbanite ideal.[87] His call to exclusive sexual relationships, therefore, did not sound innovative. It harkened back to a familiar standard, albeit a rather new one, that operated among the lower-middle class.

The sexual lives of women never came up in Song's sermons—itself perhaps a demonstration of the conservative bent in his ethic. Yet the steady drumbeat of his denunciation against such female innovations as makeup and modern haircuts, and his exaltation of sexual ideals based on the nuclear family, caused many women to make personal appointments with Song to repent of their sins. In his presence they confessed to homosexual relationships or, with surprising regularity, to "breaking the seventh commandment."[88] Renouncing such behavior was to re-enshrine rural codes of sexual conduct, even as their private and unchaperoned conversations with a man were concessions to urban ways of behavior.

This updating of rural norms for the urban environment meant Song's conservatism was never reactionary. He did not try to squeeze modern life back into an ancient garment. He tailored his conservative moral vision so that it was a fresh and creative response to the modern city. That was most powerfully demonstrated in the way Song dealt with modern forms of leisure. At first blush it appeared Song lacked vision. His pronouncements on how petty urbanites should spend their free time usually came in long lists of prohibitions: do not smoke, drink alcohol, go to movies, read novels, use opium, watch shows, attend dances, be drawn to socials, or go on picnics.[89] The lists can be read

---

[86] Henriot, *Prostitution and Sexuality in Shanghai*, 356.

[87] Yeh, *Shanghai Splendor*, 1; Peter Gue Zarrow, *China in War and Revolution, 1895–1949* (New York: Routledge, 2005), 168.

[88] See, for example, Song Shangjie, April 15, 1934, SSD, TTC.

[89] One must note that particularly around forms of leisure, Song's prohibitions lose their gender-specific nature. These sins applied to men and women alike. One thing that is worth exploring further is the relationship between these leisure activities and their spatial location in the cities. Maps of Tianjin and Shanghai, for instance, reveal how certain sections of the city were densely packed with modern entertainment options, whereas other parts had virtually none. Was Song's condemnation of the city, therefore, really an attack on certain neighborhoods?

as a dry legalism, a conservative and inflexible stance towards innovations in entertainment. For Song, however, these behaviors were not rejected because they were novel or new, but because they exacerbated the problems of the lower-middle class. Religion was not the opiate of the people. Modern leisure was what made the masses insensate.[90] How else could he explain what he saw? One man, for instance, adamantly insisted, "When I smoke I am truly happy! It is like I am in heaven!" Or Song recalled a college student falling to the ground drunk in his good clothes. "This," he asked his audience, "is happiness?" He likewise pilloried those who read novels. They become so engrossed in their books, he warned, they cannot sleep; they end up listless, suffer from headaches, and are prone to consumption.[91] Modern leisure numbs. He likened the condition of those who indulged in such things to the man possessed by a legion of demons (Mark 5:1-20):

> Evil spirits want a person to take a stone and cut himself. Does it hurt? No, it doesn't even hurt! Because he does not know pain! He still believes he is happy. Look: many people smoke, but in so doing they are just using stones to cut themselves; others read novels, but are only cutting themselves, watching movies—another way to cut themselves. . . . Does attacking oneself hurt? No! No! People still feel happy! Still feel great![92]

Contemporary hedonism, or pig-ism as Song called it, had a powerfully stultifying effect.[93] He recalled once riding to Beijing on the train. He walked the whole length, from the first-class car to the last in coach. "I saw the passengers engrossed either in smoking or reading newspapers,"

Is that one reason why the family and home—often further removed from these parts of the city—could remain sacrosanct? Further research is required, but the link between geography and sin was certainly not foreign to Song's messages (see the urban-rural divide described above). In fact, if Song's sermons were really condemning just part of the city, he was giving further justification for his listeners to stay in it—something both he and they were eager to do. See Hershatter, *Workers of Tianjin*, 182–89; Henriot, *Prostitution and Sexuality in Shanghai*, 222.

[90] Song was certainly aware of the Marxist charge against religion. In more than one sermon he denied that his revivals were opium or an anesthetic for the people. See, for example, Song, *Peilingji* [*Devotional Messages*], 79; Song Shangjie, "Xiangwo chui lingqi [May the Spirit Breathe on Me]," *Budao zazhi* [*Evangelism*] 8, no. 3 (May–June 1935): 12.

[91] Song Shangjie, "Yongyuan shifang [Eternally Set Free]," as recorded by Zhao Aiguang, *Budao zazhi* [*Evangelism*] 7, no. 3 (May–June 1934): 12.

[92] Song, "Yongyuan shifang [Eternally Set Free]," 13.

[93] Song, "Yongyuan shifang [Eternally Set Free]," 15.

Song told the audience. "Everyone looked like everyone else. I came to the end of coach. There only did I find a friend, a man seated serenely by himself. I asked him, 'Friend, are you a Christian?' He replied, 'Praise the Lord!'"[94] Only those few people who were not intoxicated by modern leisure escaped becoming insensible drones.

In opposition to modern leisure's anesthetic, Song offered a fresh, if bracing, splash of cold water. The poverty, violence, sickness, and boredom that tormented petty urbanites were not to be avoided, nor their pain deadened. Instead, Song's constituents were to endure the suffering soberly and with a clear head. In one way, Song echoed a common refrain. A leader of the May Fourth generation and the editor of the magazine *Shenghuo*, Zou Taofen, instructed petty urbanites that they must learn to *chiku*, to eat bitterness. It was the dish one had to swallow to attain success.[95] It did not go down easily, Zou admitted. He became familiar with the heartaches of China's petty urbanites as they sent him letters asking for advice. In his column he acknowledged the very real pain people experienced in the city. Women, for instance, risked their reputations simply by working alongside men in shops and business offices. Nonetheless, he encouraged young people to persevere because a brighter future was coming. But that was where Song diverged from the May Fourth era's confidence in progress. Song's premillennial eschatology held no hope for improvements in urban life. Things were not going to get better for the *xiaoshimin* or anybody else. For him suffering had a different purpose and meaning.

To eat bitterness was not a rite of passage on the way to worldly success. Suffering, Song countered, was indicative of the present crisis in history. Things were about to wrap up. Wars, rumors of wars, famines, earthquakes, and the darkening of the sun were preludes to Christ's return. For Song those promises of Jesus were even now being fulfilled.[96] Biblical predictions were materializing in detail. Not only were Jews returning to Palestine, but Song explained that the prophet Isaiah's question, "Who are these that fly like a cloud, and like doves to

---

[94] Song, *Forty John Sung Revival Sermons*, 2:33.

[95] Yeh, *Shanghai Splendor*, 105–8; Mitter, *Bitter Revolution*, 80. Song used the same vocabulary. See, for example, Song Shangjie, *Chajingji* [*Bible Study Messages*] (Hong Kong: Bellman House, 1968), 3.

[96] Song, *Peilingji* [*Devotional Messages*], 40–41.

their windows?" (Isa 60:8) referred to modern airplanes.[97] No wonder he spoke to his audience as "end-of-the-world Christians."[98] In his mind Christ would certainly return before a generation passed away.[99] In at least one case, Song was apparently even more specific: Christ would return in 1936.[100]

Song believed that when petty urbanites recognized the late hour and understood that God was employing tribulations to discover who really trusted him, they would abandon seeking temporary respite from their pain and boredom in frivolous acts of leisure. Instead, with clear eyes untainted by inebriates—whether literal or figurative—believers could look for their coming king. For those willing to accept the gospel Song proclaimed, suffering had meaning. It was the prelude to ultimate salvation. "To endure bitterness for Jesus' sake is surely the most hopeful thing one can do." He added, "In this world, endure bitterness as you are witnessing for Jesus; in the coming millennial kingdom Jesus will put a crown of wealth and honor on our heads."[101] Obviously, a heavenly crown was not the reward associated with Confucianism, the traditional moral code that Song and his audience imagined still held sway in the countryside. Song's teaching was an adaptation or translation of China's rural values into the urban idiom, and it was inflected—like all of Song's morality—by the Bible and modern circumstances. Such a message satisfied the petty urbanites' desire to stay in the city but to do so on terms that sounded familiar, safe, and—ultimately—comfortable.[102]

A Competition for Converts

Song's attempts to resolve petty urbanite anxiety about the city by inviting them to "Go home" to God's way of living (which was remarkably similar to traditional ways of life) had little impact in Tianjin, at least at

[97] Song, *Moshide jidutu dang zhuyide er da wenti* [*Two Important Issues End-Time Christians Should Be Aware of*], 9.
[98] Song, *Moshide jidutu dang zhuyide er da wenti* [*Two Important Issues End-Time Christians Should Be Aware of*], 10.
[99] Song, *Peilingji* [*Devotional Messages*], 42.
[100] F. E. Reynolds, "Dr. Song's Revival Meetings," Council for World Mission Archives, Fukien Reports, box 1-6 (H-2137), Zug. 1978, box 5, 1908–1939, no. 368, Hong Kong Baptist University, Hong Kong.
[101] Song, *Fenxingji* [*Revival Messages*], 174.
[102] Link, *Mandarin Ducks and Butterflies*, 235. In his study of literature from the time, Perry Link concluded that comfort was the chief aim of books that the *xiaoshimin* read in the 1930s.

first. Low turnouts at the Li Yuanhong Memorial Hall left Song bewailing the "lack of energy" in the meetings.[103] A week into the services, Song saw other disheartening signs. The banner which hung over the door of the Memorial Hall, announcing, "Dr. Song Great Lecture Meeting," was already taken down. That evening, after a few days of incremental increases in attendance, he saw that the petty urbanite crowd had shrunk considerably. Song left the service contemplating closing the meetings in Tianjin and moving on to Beijing. His hostess, however, Mrs. Guan, confronted him: "Ever since you arrived in Tianjin you thought first about going to Beijing, and only then asked God about it." She continued, "This decision to go to Beijing is rather your own decision. You're discouraged because the number of the people. You hold yourself up too high."[104] Her rebuke cut Song to the quick.

He repented in prayer and felt that a "heavy burden had been rolled away."[105] Reprising the role of John the Baptist, he became less so that Jesus might become more. Song embraced the disappearance of his name from the public banner. He even commissioned new flyers to be printed and handed out. Whereas before his name was emblazoned on the advertisement, now it simply announced an "Evangelistic Meeting."[106] He recorded in his journal that for the first time in almost a week he had no desire to go to Beijing.[107] The instant change in Song's attitude could be mirrored in the revival services themselves. His revivalism had that kind of flexibility.

The speed at which his revivals changed can best be appreciated when juxtaposed to another attempt at Christian renewal from the same time. The National Christian Council (NCC) of China launched the Five Year Forward Movement in 1929. The motto was, "Revive thy church, O Lord, beginning with me." Its aim was to grow and renew the church—goals similar to Song's own. In organization and operation, however, the institutional attempt at revival was totally different. It relied heavily on foreign money. Close to 75 percent of the administrative costs were borne by donations from foreign missionaries and

---

[103] Song Shangjie, April 17, 1934, SSD, TTC.

[104] Song Shangjie, April 17, 1934, SSD, TTC. Using the name of Beijing at the time, Song and Mrs. Guan referred to it as Beiping. However, I have used the ancient and contemporary name of the city so readers can recognize the location.

[105] Song Shangjie, April 17, 1934, SSD, TTC.

[106] Song Shangjie, April 18, 1934, SSD, TTC.

[107] Song Shangjie, April 17, 1934, SSD, TTC.

contributions from foreign mission boards.[108] Financial security allowed Cheng Jingyi [C. Y. Cheng], the general secretary of the NCC, to work out the movement's initiatives according to what he thought Chinese Christians needed, not necessarily what they wanted. His decision to promote evangelism, religious education, literacy, Christianizing the home, stewardship, and youth in the church reflected the priorities of the church's elites.[109] In execution the Five Year Forward Movement advanced at a ponderous pace. The NCC spent considerable time and energy producing and distributing resources that could complement its six-pronged advance.[110] It then had to rely on Christian churches and organizations, which were all rather loosely affiliated with the NCC, actually to implement the curriculum. Not surprisingly, the movement's penetration among Chinese Christians was uneven and the results disappointing.[111]

Song, by contrast, demonstrated extraordinary agility, as he could (and did) change his services literally overnight. His style of revivalism allowed instant feedback. He could see and hear when a message struck a chord; he knew, beyond a shadow of a doubt, if he had "moved" his audience.[112] If people came forward to repent of their sins and believe in Christ for salvation, he could be confident that he was addressing real needs. If the crowd was apathetic he might blame their spiritual lassitude, but he could also adjust his message. In Tianjin, Song had written down the eighteen topics he wanted to cover while he was in the city.[113] His failure to draw full houses caused him to abandon that plan, and he improvised the rest of the way. He was free to move with the Spirit and the spirit of his audience.

Song's nimble operation gave him a competitive advantage in Tianjin's religious marketplace. He could immediately tailor his revival services to supply the spiritual demands of whomever sat before him. It was a disruptive innovation. For years Christian organizations like the

---

[108] Wallace C. Merwin, *Adventure in Unity: The Church of Christ in China* (Grand Rapids: Eerdmans, 1974), 100.

[109] Merwin, *Adventure in Unity*, 98.

[110] James C. Thomson, *While China Faced West: American Reformers in Nationalist China, 1928–1937* (Cambridge, Mass.: Harvard University Press, 1969), 55.

[111] Merwin, *Adventure in Unity*, 98.

[112] Song Shangjie, "Matai fuyin di liu zhang [Matthew Chapter Six]," as recorded by Chen Zhenfan, March 31, 1931, *Shengjie zhinan yuekan* [*Guide to Holiness*] 3, no. 6 (June 1931): 10–11.

[113] Song Shangjie, April 11, 1934ff., SSD, TTC.

Tianjin Union of Churches had worked to prevent religious consumerism by spearheading a unity movement. Song's willingness to cater to the tastes of the petty urbanites shattered that convention and left the church leadership sputtering, warning their members to stay away from Song's novelties. "His extremely emotional appeal [places] an emphasis upon some divisive elements in Christian thought," the leadership cautioned the city's Christians.[114] Yet the plea to ignore Song largely fell on deaf ears. For petty urbanites who were far more integrated into the new consumer economy than the working or underclass, it must have been exhilarating to have a religious choice that fulfilled their desires. Missionaries and pastors watched helplessly as one admitted, "There is something lacking in the Gong Li Hui [ABCFM] and its leadership when a man like Dr. Song so obviously does minister to the spiritual needs of a mentionable fraction of our church membership." He concluded, "I wish we were more fervent in spirit."[115] Song had something that no one else was offering.

The leadership of the Wesley Church, which had withdrawn its offer of letting Song hold his revival on their premises, reacted to the surge in Song's popularity by promoting a hastily organized "New Birth Movement."[116] Flyers were quickly handed out around Tianjin inviting people to come to Wesley's alternative services, which were to be held at 3:00 p.m. and 7:00 p.m.—the exact times when Song led his meetings in the Li Yuanghong Memorial Hall. However, Wesley did not fare well in direct competition with Song. No one did.

In many of the cities he visited, Song's services united and invigorated existing congregations.[117] In Tianjin, however, the attempt to compete directly with him split churches. When congregational leaders forced people to make a choice either between their churches and Song's services, the frustrated revivalist instructed his audience "to leave the

---

[114] North China Conference, *Official Journal of the Forty-Second Session of the North China Annual Conference of the Methodist Episcopal Church Held at the South Gate Methodist Episcopal Church, Tientsin, Hopei, China, August 22–26, 1934* (Beijing: 1934), 333.

[115] Earle H. Ballou to Friends, June 20, 1934, ABCFM North China, 1930–1939, Letters (16.3.12 v. 51), American Board of Commissioners for Foreign Mission Archives, 1810–1961 (ABC 1–91), Houghton Library, Harvard University, Cambridge, Mass.

[116] Song Shangjie, April 28, 1934, SSD, TTC.

[117] Wenona Jett to Friends, February 1, 1936, China Records Project Miscellaneous Personal Papers Collection, record group 8, box 104, folder 6, Special Collections, Yale Divinity School Library, New Haven, Conn.

devil's church."[118] Zhang Zhouxin, one of his bourgeois backers, immediately organized the *Shenghuisuo* [the Holy Assembly Center] and welcomed all the defectors.

Churches across Tianjin witnessed a drain on their church rolls. In 1933, before Song's revival campaign, Wesley had 646 members and, on average, 550 people in worship. The following year, things were strikingly different. The annual report tried to paper over the wound. "Last year Wesley Church suffered because of a division among some of the church members. We are grateful to God that Wesley has survived this division."[119] A turn to the statistical table, though, revealed how seriously the church hemorrhaged. Membership plummeted all the way down to 285, and worship attendance sank to 121.[120] Other denominations did not fare much better. W. F. Dawson, a missionary with the London Missionary Society (LMS), lamented that baptisms had dried up. A number of people whom the mission had prepared for the rite of initiation decided to be washed clean in the newly organized church instead.[121] A "few hundred" people were gone from their old churches, he concluded, because they wanted to hear "the Gospel in the way that appeals to them."[122]

Song's revivalism replicated the dynamics of China's new consumer economy. Not only did he make salvation a choice, but he also made the gospel itself something like a product. He tailored the good news to speak to the anxieties and needs of those before him, which, in his case, was a niche market of petty urbanites. His listeners were eager to claim the moniker of New Men and New Women and wanted to do so without departing too far from tradition. Song made all that possible, using his revivals to pave a way for China's aspiring lower-middle class to enter and feel at home in the city.

[118] Song Shangjie, April 27, 1934, SSD, TTC.

[119] North China Conference, *The Official Journal of the Forty-Third Session of the North China Annual Conference of the Methodist Episcopal Church, August 21–26, 1935* (Beijing: 1935), 458.

[120] *Official Minutes of the Forty-Third Session*, 458.

[121] W. F. Dawson, LMS Annual Report, 1938, Council for World Mission Archives, North China Reports, 1926–1939, box 1-12 (H-2139), Zug. 1978, box 11-1935, no. 800, Hong Kong Baptist University, Hong Kong.

[122] W. F. Dawson, LMS Annual Report, 1935, Council for World Mission Archives, North China Reports, 1926–1939, box 1-12 (H-2139), Zug. 1978, box 11-1931, no. 798, Hong Kong Baptist University, Hong Kong.

6

A New Woman

The extraordinary success that Song had among petty urbanites created a continuous flow of invitations for him to speak elsewhere. News of his services in the cities of Xiamen [Amoy] and Guangzhou [Canton] in particular vibrated across an entire web of connections that tied Southeast Asia together. For years immigrants from Fujian and Guangdong passed through those ports on their way to and from jobs, adventures, and families in places like Taiwan, the Philippines, the Malay Straits, and the Dutch East Indies. Soon, Song was being asked to go there and recreate for overseas Chinese communities what they heard he was doing on the mainland. In May of 1935, Song made his first evangelistic tour outside of China; he spoke in Manila. In late August he set out for a more ambitious campaign. Over six weeks Song spoke in the Malay Straits, the Dutch East Indies, and Singapore before returning home.[1]

When he left Singapore in October 1935, seven hundred people dressed in white squeezed together on the quay to say goodbye. In an unusual display of emotion, some in the crowd cried, while others called out well-wishes for his journey.[2] The moment, caught by a photographer, has been an iconic image in the legacy of Song Shangjie. It stands as

---

[1] The trip's conclusion was not the end of Song's travels overseas. Over the next two years, he followed immigration and trade routes to the Chinese communities in the Straits Settlements, the Dutch East Indies, Taiwan, and Burma. These trips were relatively short, however, because Song continued to focus his ministry on mainland China until the Japanese invasion of China in 1937.

[2] *Sin Chew Jit Poh* [星州日報], October 27, 1935; *Nanyang Siang Pau* [南洋商報], October 27, 1935; *Malaysia Message*, November 1935, 14. These periodicals are all held at the National Library, Singapore.

a testimony to his mass appeal.[3] Upon closer inspection the photograph also reveals another story. Most of those lining the wharf that morning were women, many of whom clasped white flags with red crosses—the emblems of their newly formed evangelistic teams. Chinese women swelled the ranks of the newly formed Singapore Christian Evangelistic League (SCEL), creating a revivalistic movement that acted as a vehicle for ferrying them into the modern world of the Straits Settlements.

Revivalism and modernity went hand in hand in Singapore. Each one created the environment for the other to flourish. Modernizing pressures from immigration, state regulation, nuclear family formation, and contested gender expectations prompted many urban women to embrace Song's revivalism.[4] Revivalism's emphasis on evangelism, meanwhile, not only encouraged voluntary activism, but also called forth new kinds of organizational structures to spread the gospel—both factors in forging modern identities. Fueling one another, revivalism and modernity ignited a movement that women used in Singapore and in the other cities Song visited to cast new places for themselves in society.

FROM A MINORITY TO A MAJORITY

When the men of the Singapore Christian Union invited Song Shangjie to expand his ministry outside of China and come to their city in 1935, they could not have anticipated the way women would capitalize on

---

[3] The photo may be seen in Song Tianzhen, ed., *Shi'er fude de riji* [*The Journal Once Lost*] (Kowloon, Hong Kong: China Alliance Press, 2006), 253.

[4] This chapter specifically provides a description of what happened in Singapore, but all the evidence suggests what transpired there was not unique. Wherever Song went he drew a disproportionate number of female followers, and his evangelistic teams were repeatedly filled with large numbers of women. This was remarkable in a country where men outnumbered women in church membership. Kenneth Scott Latourette, *A History of the Expansion of Christianity*, vol. 7, *Advance through Storm* (Grand Rapids: Zondervan, 1970), 347. For details of the high proportion of women, one can consult Song's own diaries. Women far outnumbered men in their response to his calls for conversion. Also, see the heavy representation of women in his evangelistic bands in other parts of China: Song Shangjie, ed., *Quanguo jidutu budaotuan tuankan* [*National Christian Evangelistic League Publication*] (March 1936). Further evidence of the high visibility of women in Song's services can be glimpsed in L. G. Phillips, LMS Annual Report, 1935, Council for World Mission Archives, Fukien Reports, box 1-6 (H-2137), Zug. 1978, box 5, 1908–1939, no. 370, Hong Kong Baptist University, Hong Kong; Howard Cliff and Mary Cliff, "Dear Friends," *Bible for China* 63 (May 1933): 40.

the event by using it to help answer the "woman question."[5] The meetings suggested nothing political. They never veered into May Fourth pontifications about the need to liberate women by dismantling China's disabling hierarchy, nor did they offer a diagnosis of women's backwardness as the root of the nation's ills.[6] On the surface there was nothing radical about them.

The local newspaper only remarked on the revival's extraordinary popularity. Song's services were "hot and noisy," the ideal characteristics of any Chinese religious gathering, so observers noted how his meetings gained momentum.[7] Over fourteen days crowds grew from 600 people to over 2,000. Approximately 1,300 eager listeners were squished together inside the sanctuary while an additional 700 disappointed latecomers settled for listening to Song's voice crackle over loudspeakers placed in windowsills. Students unwilling to forego their seats camped at the church, leaving some local schools half empty for the duration of the campaign.[8] Song preached forty messages and concluded with a final healing service. The religious fervor he injected into Singapore sparked a run on Bibles and Song's revival chorus books, forcing distributors in Kuala Lumpur to rush deliveries to Singapore in order to cover the deficit.[9] Yet for all the eye-popping and attention-grabbing headlines of

---

[5] Xiaofei Kang, "Women and the Religious Question in Modern China," in *Modern Chinese Religion II: 1850–2015*, vol. 1, ed. Vincent Goossaert, Jan Kiely, and John Lagerwey (Leiden: Brill, 2015), 492–93.

[6] Gail Hershatter, *Women in China's Long Twentieth Century* (Berkeley: University of California Press, 2007), 79–80.

[7] *Sin Chew Jit Poh*, October 27, 1935; David K. Jordan, *Gods, Ghosts, and Ancestors* (Berkeley: University of California Press, 1972), 126, provides a brief and helpful introduction to the importance of *renao* ["hot and noisy"] in Chinese traditional religion.

[8] "Personals," *Malaysia Message* (August 1935): 2; Paul M. Means, "From the Editor's Desk," *Malaysia Message* (September 1935): 6; "Summary of Results of Revival Meetings Held by Dr. John Sung in Singapore in September," *Malaysia Message* (November 1935): 14; A. S. Moore Anderson, "Wake Up Malaya!" *St. Andrew's Outlook* 82 (September 1935): 41; Bobby E. K. Sng, *In His Good Time: The Story of the Church in Singapore, 1819–1978* (Singapore: Graduates' Christian Fellowship, 1980), 176–82; *Sin Chew Jit Poh*, October 27, 1935; Timothy Tow, *John Sung My Teacher* (Singapore: Christian Life Publishers, 1985), 19–40.

[9] E. Tipson, preface to *My Testimony*, by Song Siong Chiat [John Sung], trans. E. Tipson (Kuala Lumpur: Caxton Press, 1936), i.

Song's revival, "the outstanding creation of his ministry" was the establishment of evangelistic teams, as one participant later noted.[10]

As his two weeks in Singapore drew to a close, Song weighed his
enthusiastic audience from behind the pulpit of the Telok Ayer Methodist
Church. He decided to challenge his listeners to test their commitment to
Jesus: step forward, he invited them, and join an evangelistic band. Dare
to tell others what God has done for you. He proceeded to give simple
instructions. At least two people were needed to form a group. They
were to meet once a week to tell others about Jesus, whether speaking to
them on the streets, in homes, or in prisons. Unlike pastors and missionaries who were paid to preach, Song insisted band members would pay
for the privilege to preach. Thus, weekly collections were to be taken
to purchase tracts or underwrite travel expenses. Participation would
be costly, he warned, but it promised to make those who signed on
truly New.[11] When he finished speaking, the response was overwhelming. Hundreds of people pushed their way to the platform or stood at
the front of the sanctuary until approximately 10 percent of Singapore's
Chinese Protestants were crammed together, enlisting to preach the gospel.[12] Men, women, and children all solemnly pledged to evangelize the

[10] Sng, *In His Good Time*, 182.

[11] *Xingzhou jidujiao budaotuan tuankan, 1935–1936* [*Singapore Christian
Evangelistic League, 1935–1936*] (1936; repr., Singapore: 2000), 78–80, hereafter
referred to as *SCEL, 1935–1936*. What exists from Singapore was written five
months after the revival and displays more codification than Song usually supplied.
Therefore, I have only repeated his more general instructions that were consistent
with other contemporary accounts of how he organized teams. See, for example,
H. A. Wiese, "China Crusaders," *The Other Sheep* (August 1935): 12. Notice how
the attention Song gave to organization is similar to the early Chinese Communist Peng Pai, who took time to explain to rural women what it meant to *zhuzhi*,
to organize. See Christina K. Gilmartin, "Gender, Political Culture, and Women's
Mobilization," in *Engendering China: Women, Culture, and the State*, ed. Christina K. Gilmartin et al. (Cambridge, Mass.: Harvard University Press, 1994), 218.

[12] Numbers from Song's initial call are not recorded. When he held a training
a month later, 732 people attended. See *Nanyang huaqiao jidujiao peiling dahui*,
photograph, 1935, Chin Lien Seminary, Singapore. At the beginning of 1936, the
SCEL counted 600 people who signed up to be volunteer evangelists through the
teams. Both numbers are impressive. Determining the exact proportion of Chinese
Protestants in Singapore who joined a team is elusive. Since most church records
in 1935 did not differentiate Chinese from other ethnicities nor count Singapore
separately from the rest of the Straits Settlements, it is impossible to know exactly
how many Chinese Protestants were on the island. Borrowing, however, from government data that claimed that 2.7 percent of all Chinese in the Straits Settlements

island. Clergy and laity both joined. People from Guangdong and Fujian, the two Chinese provinces with the most immigrants in Singapore, were evenly represented. Several who came from other places in China signed up as well. Everyone was included, but that did not mean everyone was equally represented. Women were clearly in the majority. In the photo that captured the first enthusiastic volunteers, 54 percent were female. Seemingly a small—even negligible—edge, until one remembers that in 1935 women and girls comprised but a third of the Chinese population on the island.[13] Women dominated the evangelistic teams.

Why did they join in such disproportionally high numbers? What were women doing by aligning themselves with an evangelistic band? In 1935 a complex array of forces was threatening Chinese women's identity in Singapore. Song's evangelistic teams provided a way for women to transform those potentially destructive realities into the makings of China's New Woman.

FROM MODERN GIRL TO NEW WOMAN

To be modern, China needed a new type of woman. Intellectuals and reformers all agreed on that. However, it also filled them with enormous anxiety. Their fears were played out in short stories and novels. Time and again authors presented the modern woman as smart, aggressive,

---

were Christians, I can estimate that approximately 11,500 Chinese Christians were in Singapore. Insofar as roughly half of the Christians were Roman Catholic, there were about 5,750 Chinese Protestants on the island. If that number is fairly accurate, more than 10 percent of all Protestant Christians in Singapore were on an evangelistic team. See *Annual Report of the Straits Settlements, 1935* (Singapore: 1935), 7; Tong Chee Kiong, "Religion," in *The Making of Singapore Sociology: Society and State*, ed. Tong Chee Kiong and Lian Kwen Fee (Leiden: Brill and Times Academic Press, 2002), 370–71; Alan J. A. Elliott, *Chinese Spirit-Medium Cults in Singapore*, London School of Economics Monographs on Social Anthropology, no. 14 (London: Athlone Press, 1955), 29; and Robert Hunt, Lee Kam Hing, and John Roxborogh, eds., *Christianity in Malaysia: A Denominational History* (Petaling Jaya, Selangor Darul Ehsan, Malaysia: Pelanduk Publications, 1992).

[13] *Annual Departmental Reports, Straits Settlements* and *Straits Gazette* in Maurice Freedman, *Chinese Family and Marriage in Singapore* (1957; repr., New York: Johnson Reprint, 1970), 23–25; Aline K. Wong, *Women in Modern Singapore* (Singapore: University Education Press, 1975), 16–17. For additional information about the bands and the high visibility of women, see Joshua Dao We Sim, "Chinese Evangelistic Bands in Nanyang: Leona Wu and the Implementation of the John Sung-Inspired Evangelistic Band Model in Pre-War Singapore," *Fides et Historia* 50, no. 2 (2018): 38–65.

and attractive. She wore stylish Western clothes and makeup; her hair was cut short and permed. Readers found her fascinating, but always learned that she was ultimately destructive. In a review of May Fourth literature, Sarah Stevens concluded that the Modern Girl represented the shadow side of China's modernization: she was dangerous, alienated, and conveyed cultural loss.[14]

Song agreed. He spoke, for example, of a teacher "who told students to be honest, to believe in Jesus, to follow his example. But she herself? She had a perm, studied how to dance, and spoke about romantic love. Agh!"[15] It was impossible for Song to imagine that the teacher could choose to be both a Modern Girl and a disciple of Jesus. For him, rather, it was the young lady who repented of "her days immersed in cosmetics" who could be trusted. "She changed to all simplicity," Song crowed, "a total transformation."[16]

It might sound as if Song wanted to push women back into the home to be dutiful daughters, chaste wives, and good mothers. However, that would ignore the third option he embraced. Along with Ding Ling, the leading female author of the May Fourth era, Song imagined that the dangerous Modern Girl could turn into a productive Modern Woman.[17] In 1927 Ding Ling had written "Miss Sophie's Diary," a tale of a Modern Girl who is enamored with her own inward gaze and her ability to torture psychologically the men closest to her.[18] The book was

[14] Sarah Stevens, "Figuring Modernity: The New Woman and the Modern Girl," *NWSA Journal* 15, no. 3 (2003): 83; E. Perry Link Jr., *Mandarin Ducks and Butterflies: Popular Fiction in Early Twentieth-Century Chinese Cities* (Berkeley: University of California Press, 1981); Wolfram Eberhard, *Guilt and Sin in Traditional China* (Berkeley: University of California Press, 1967), 38. Eberhard demonstrates that the idea circulated in more than popular fiction. Morality books, circulated in temples or by religious devotees in the 1930s, described the specific hell that awaited women who wore foreign clothes and cut their hair short.

[15] Song Shangjie, *Fenxingji* [*Revival Messages*], 6th ed. (1935; repr., Hong Kong: Bellman House, 1989), 42.

[16] Song Shangjie, *Forty John Sung Revival Sermons*, vol. 2, trans. Timothy Tow (Singapore: Alice Doo, 1983), 30.

[17] In chapter 4, I noted how closely Song's messages aligned with the government's New Life Movement (NLM). However, when it came to the matter of women, Song and his revivals diverged from the state's propaganda that tried to curtail the public roles of women. See Peter Gue Zarrow, *China in War and Revolution, 1895–1949* (New York: Routledge, 2005), 261.

[18] Ding Ling, "Miss Sophia's Diary," in *I Myself Am a Woman: Selected Writings of Ding Ling*, ed. Tani E. Barlow and Gary J. Bjorge (Boston: Beacon Press, 1989).

heralded as a landmark of May Fourth fiction. However, in 1930 Ding Ling replaced the melancholy Modern Girl with a depiction of China's civic-minded New Woman. Reflecting Ding Ling's own move toward the Communist Party, Meilin, the heroine of "Shanghai, Spring 1930," discovered that her pampered, carefree, delicate, and childlike existence failed to satisfy.[19] "Action had become an instinctual need."[20] Meilin finally found purpose for her life by directing her energy into a May Day protest on the street.[21] In the closing scene, her self-absorbed and domineering paramour mused, "Oh, such a woman, so gentle and soft. Now she too had abandoned him to follow the masses."[22] Such were the sacrifices of China's New Woman. She chose public service to others over private service to any one man.

Song said it very differently, but he preached Ding Ling's same revolutionary message three times every day: "The Lord saves men, and also saves women. This is true gender equality."[23] His peculiar order of salvation, which reached its climax in converts needing to go out and evangelize, meant that women had to go into the world to save others. Song was insistent upon it.

Entering public space to help others was the preeminent virtue of the New Woman.[24] Song had witnessed such service in his own life. He commonly testified that it was a female evangelist in New York, Uldine Utley, who triggered his own spiritual transformation.[25] Closer to home,

[19] Ling, "Miss Sophia's Diary," 114, 118, 124, 132.

[20] Ling, "Miss Sophia's Diary," 133.

[21] Ling, "Miss Sophia's Diary," 133.

[22] Ling, "Miss Sophia's Diary," 138.

[23] Song Shangjie, "Shenglingde xi [Baptism of the Holy Spirit]," as recorded by Zhao Aiguang, Budao zazhi [Evangelism] 7, no. 6 (November–December 1934): 8. From the May Fourth Movement onward, the issue of women became a fixture in iconoclastic rhetoric, and gender equality became a plank in the platform of all revolutionary parties and in the ideas of most intellectuals. See Hershatter, Women in China's Long Twentieth Century, 80.

[24] Stevens, "Figuring Modernity," 83.

[25] The question of Uldine Utley's role in Song's transformation is complicated. In recounting his conversion in My Testimony, he said a girl was the catalyst. It was her preaching that he believed precipitated his conversion on February 10, 1927. Later, he explained that girl was Uldine Utley. Exactly what role her preaching played in Song's hospitalization and later reconfiguration is difficult to discern. Nonetheless, Uldine Utley has been a prominent figure in Song's biographies. Often she has been used to demonstrated Song's lineage in the Fundamentalist movement. Song, it has been said, heard her preach at Calvary Baptist Church in the pulpit

Song remembered his sister preaching on the streets to men during a revival in 1909, changing their lives.[26] During his first years as an evangelist for the Xinghua [Hinghwa] Methodist Church, he watched Elizabeth Brewster preach powerfully, calling men and women to repentance. Then Shi Meiyu [Mary Stone], the co-founder of the Bethel Mission, organized the Bethel Worldwide Evangelistic Band (BWEB) after her duties at the hospital precluded her from responding to all the invitations she received to preach.[27] Song's own ministry owed its existence to the pioneering presence of women in public spaces.

Perhaps the role of women in his own life made him sensitive to their presence in the Bible. Song preached numerous sermons that focused on the faith of female biblical characters.[28] For him they were the premier models of Christian faith. The woman at the well, for instance, was the first person to ever preach about Jesus.[29] The lady who poured out her alabaster jar on the Lord's feet would be remembered eternally:

---

of John Roach Straton, the so-called "Pope of Fundamentalism." However, that cannot be substantiated. It is true that Utley preached at Calvary Baptist while Song was at Union Theological Seminary, and he potentially heard her speak there. However, according to Song's own timeline (if it can be trusted), it is more likely that Song heard Utley preach in December at the Greene Avenue Baptist Church in Brooklyn. See "35 Are Pledged by Uldine Utley," *New York Times*, December 20, 1926; Chen Renbing, "Shisui zhengshi kaishi chuangdaode meiguo Wu Delei [American Uldine Utley Really Began Preaching at Ten Years Old]," *Budao zazhi* [*Evangelism*] 7, no. 1 (January–February 1934): 35.

[26] Song Shangjie, "Song Shangjie boshi geren jianzheng [The Testimony of Dr. Song Shangjie]," as recorded by Liao Guotian, afternoon, April 2, 1931, *Shengjie zhinan yuekan* [*Guide to Holiness*] 3, no. 6 (June 1931): 27; Song, *Fenxingji* [Revival Messages], 110; William Nesbitt Brewster, *A Modern Pentecost in South China* (Shanghai: Methodist Publishing House, 1909); William Nesbitt Brewster, *Straws from the Hinghwa Harvest* (Hinghwa, China: Hinghwa Missionary Press, 1910).

[27] Andrew Gih, *Launch Out into the Deep! Tales of Revival through China's Famous Bethel Evangelistic Bands and Further Messages* (London: Marshall, Morgan & Scott, 1938), 14–15.

[28] Kwok Pui-lan, "Chinese Women and Protestant Christianity at the Turn of the Twentieth Century," in *Christianity in China: From the Eighteenth Century to the Present*, ed. Daniel H. Bays (Stanford: Stanford University Press, 1996), 200, noted that by the end of the nineteenth century Protestant Christians in China had come to focus their messages on the Gospels. For those who had ears to hear, that meant stories of women became more prominent. The Gospels, compared to the rest of the canon, place particular emphasis on women. Song certainly preached regularly from the Gospels, but he also uncovered—even seemed to seek out—more obscure stories of biblical women.

[29] Cornelie Baarbé, *Dr. Sung, een Reveil op Java: Over de Evangelist Dr. Sung en zijn preken* (Den Haag, Netherlands: Voorhoeve, 1960), 33–35.

"[N]ot some great man, but a girl," Song reminded everyone.[30] In the end women even surpassed Jesus' twelve male disciples because they followed him all the way to the cross.[31] "Women especially have faith," Song concluded. "Their faith is greater than men's."[32]

Women so dominated Song's depiction of what service to others looked like that he made shocking statements. In one sermon about the Israelite slave girl who spoke about God to her Syrian master, Song unabashedly identified himself with the young woman. "Now I am this little slave girl tonight to tell you about the Savior."[33] Often Song presented his audiences a feminized Jesus. For instance, Song both stunned and soothed an anxious audience with the promise that "Jesus talks to sinners in a sweet voice, like a mother calling."[34] Indeed, Jesus often sounded like a coddling mother in Song's sermons. Song regularly put pet names or house names on Jesus' lips. Each person in the audience was Jesus' *baobei* [precious darling] or "little child."[35] In a particularly dramatic example of feminization, Song vividly described Jesus as a second Mary, the woman who poured her perfume on the Lord (John 12:1-8). Mary sacrificed; she loved; she faced opposition; and she laid down her body. Song reminded everyone Jesus would eventually do the same. No one could misunderstand the direction that the analogy ran. Song put it this way: "[Jesus] broke His alabaster box from which flowed that ointment of love, salvation, even His precious blood."[36] Christ followed Mary's example, not the other way around. The sermon circulated in Singapore, but when it was published in China some parts of that provocative message did not survive. Jesus no longer cried as Mary cried, and the assertion that "when our Lord was on earth, the majority of those who loved him were women" was deleted.[37] Editors tried to correct Song in order to align his outlook with their own.

[30] Song Shangjie, *Forty John Sung Revival Sermons*, vol. 1, trans. Timothy Tow (Singapore: Alice Doo, 1978), 115.

[31] Song, *Forty John Sung Revival Sermons*, 2:18.

[32] Song, *Fenxingji* [*Revival Messages*], 126.

[33] Song, *Forty John Sung Revival Sermons*, 2:13.

[34] Song Shangjie, "Saoluode meng'en [Saul Receives Grace]," as recorded by Jia Zi'an, evening of April 9, 1935, in Ertiao Presbyterian Church, Beijing, *Light in Darkness* 7, no. 11 (November 1936): 24.

[35] Song, *Fenxingji* [*Revival Messages*], 48.

[36] Song, *Forty John Sung Revival Sermons*, 2:95.

[37] Song, *Forty John Sung Revival Sermons*, 2:94, 92. It is impossible at this point to determine for sure whether the message in *Forty John Sung Revival Sermons*, 2:92–96 added the lines that glorified women and feminized Jesus or if the message

Song's affirmations of women in public ministry, however, were not so easily disguised. They proceeded automatically from three sources: his peculiar *ordo salutis*, which required evangelism; his personal experience with women who preached; and his immersion in biblical narratives. He was unfazed by the criticism he received from Ni Tuosheng [Watchman Nee] and his Little Flock for allowing women to preach.[38] He knew that Ni's indigenous Christian movement cited Paul's injunction for a woman to remain silent, but he dismissed the argument.[39] Something greater than Paul's command was at work here. The experience of full

---

in Song Shangjie, *Peilingji* [*Devotional Messages*] (1935; repr., Hong Kong: Bellman House, n.d.), 97–102 edited those lines out. Presumably both sermons were reprinted from an original text—probably a sermon that first appeared in a Christian magazine. However, I have not been able to locate that original publication. Timothy Tow, the compiler of *Forty John Sung Revival Sermons*, said the sermon he translated came from another Chinese collection that his aunt, Miss Alice Doo, had published in Singapore. I have also not been able to secure that Chinese collection, so that it has even been impossible for me to compare the message in *Forty John Sung Revival Sermons* and the sermon in *Peilingji* in the same language. Nonetheless, I am confident that the sermon Tow translated into English is based on the same text that appeared in *Peilingji*. That may not be as self-evident as it first appears. Song preached the same sermons multiple times in various places. Therefore, one sometimes runs across a sermon that sounds almost identical to another, but careful scrutiny reveals real differences—especially in the choice of sermon illustrations. No such divergences exist in the English and Chinese copies. Thus, I believe they were both reprinting the identical sermon. The differences between the two, therefore, are the comments about Jesus and women mentioned above. Did Tow add the sentences in English, or did the editor of *Peilingji* delete them in Chinese? It makes the most sense that the Chinese editor deleted them. In the forty sermons that Tow translated, I uncovered several cases where he cut out lines from Song's sermons, but found no evidence that he ever added any. It would be odd, in this one case, for him to add something that could be controversial. It makes more sense that Tow included Song's words, even though he might have disagreed with them. He warned his readers that he harbored some objections to what he translated: "Nor are some of the things [Song preached] without reproach, for after all, he was but an earthen vessel." (Timothy Tow, "Translator's Preface," in *Forty John Sung Revival Sermons*, 1:17). I suspect the editor of *Peilingji* had less tolerance for Song's countercultural notions. Unlike Alice Doo, who published the sermon in Singapore, the editor of *Peilingji* apparently felt it necessary to tone down Song's feminization of Christ and his exaltation of women.

[38] Song Shangjie, April 29, 1933, Song Shangjie Diaries, Trinity Theological College, Singapore. Henceforth this location will be referred to as SSD, TTC. Song, *Forty John Sung Revival Sermons*, 1:48, 133; Song, *Forty John Sung Revival Sermons*, 2:85; Song, *Peilingji* [*Devotional Messages*], 78.

[39] Song, *Forty John Sung Revival Sermons*, 1:133.

salvation dictated women do otherwise. To hear God's message but not proclaim it to others would be like eating without working. It "results in dropsy."[40] "Do you like to be dumb?" Song specifically asked all the women in a service. "It is agonizing not to be able to express oneself well. How much more to remain dumb. Whoever does not witness is dumb. . . . Jesus tells the dumb to speak."[41] Women, Song explained, were commanded by their Lord to preach.

Thus, he sent them out to serve China as New Women. In some ways, perhaps, Song's modernizing charge only commuted women's sentence as second-class citizens. Throughout the twentieth century, China's New Woman discovered that she was still expected to sacrifice herself, only now it was to save the nation rather than her family.[42] Even so, Song's mandate was as clear as it was modern: women were to go public and share the good news with anyone who would listen.

IMMIGRATION AND SALVATION

In 1935 many of the Chinese women who heard Song's directive to preach the gospel were new in Singapore, having only arrived after the passing of the Alien's Ordinance Act three years prior. Before that time Singapore was almost exclusively a destination for temporary male workers. Women were rare in such a fluid environment. In 1884, for instance, women comprised just 10 percent of the population.[43] The new law tried to stabilize Singapore's lopsided gender ratio by restricting Chinese male immigrants but welcoming women. In the short span between the enactment of the new government policy and Song's arrival, more than 75,000 women (not counting girls) entered the Straits Settlements colony. Their arrival en masse was not enough to bring gender parity, but it was a significant enough spike to mean that roughly one in three women in Singapore were new arrivals.[44]

Newly arrived, however, did not translate into newly home. Quite the opposite; in fact, Chinese women frequently complained that they did not

---

[40] Song, *Forty John Sung Revival Sermons*, 2:85.

[41] Song, *Forty John Sung Revival Sermons*, 2:88.

[42] Kang, "Women and the Religious Question in Modern China," 509.

[43] Sumiko Kazeno, *The Role of Women in Singapore: Collaboration and Conflict between Capitalism and Asian Values* (Midoriku, Japan: Kazeno Shoboh, 2004), 23.

[44] *Annual Report of the Straits Settlements, 1936* (Singapore: 1936), 10, 103; Wong, *Women in Modern Singapore*, 16–17.

feel settled in Singapore. While earlier male immigrants had created fictive kin structures based on common surnames or shared dialects to orient their new lives, women were largely excluded from such organizations. In one neighborhood, for example, few women belonged to any association, and of those that did, 97 percent never attended a meeting. Without traditional family structures, women remained almost entirely isolated.[45]

They were caught in the middle of the immigrant narrative that, when stripped down to its essentials, may be described as home—not home—home again. Singapore was distinctly "not home." Newly arrived Chung Lai Cheng, for instance, complained that she did "not understand where some of these Singapore customs come from."[46] Another woman noted that the behavior of people in Singapore was so different than in China, it "made her feel embarrassed."[47] However, more than culture shock was at work. For many women their experiences in Singapore undermined the possibility of ever arriving home, of completing the immigrant narrative arc. The story of Mrs. Wong is illustrative. She immigrated to Singapore to earn money to support eight siblings in China. However, after she married a gambler on the island, things fell apart. She became alienated from her home in China when she could no longer send money to her family despite their angry threats, and her hope of creating a new home in Singapore was likewise undermined when she had to sell her own children to cover her husband's debts.[48] For many women in Singapore, their lives were characterized by a seemingly irresolvable state of displacement.

The revival narrative that entered Singapore with Song Shangjie, therefore, had particular appeal. His message spoke to an aching desire: the lost could be found. Listeners could easily merge the immigrant and revival narratives, just as Song did so powerfully when he preached the archetypical sermon of the revival, the parable of the Prodigal Son (Luke 15:11-32). The biblical story of the young man going away to

---

[45] Freedman, *Chinese Family and Marriage in Singapore*, 38; John Clammer, *Singapore: Ideology, Society, Culture* (Singapore: Chopmen Publishers, 1985), 13; Barrington Kaye, *Upper Nankin Street Singapore: A Sociological Study of Chinese Households Living in a Densely Populated Area* (Singapore: University of Malaya Press, 1960), 66.

[46] Kaye, *Upper Nankin Street Singapore*, 237.

[47] Kaye, *Upper Nankin Street Singapore*, 239.

[48] Hing Ai Yun, "Resistance Narratives from Mothers of Married Daughters in Singapore," in *Motherhood: Power and Oppression*, ed. Andrea O'Reilly, Marie Porter, and Patricia Short (Toronto: Women's Press, 2005), 159.

the far country was simultaneously the immigrant narrative (home—not home—home again) and the classic revivalist narrative (lost—found). The message had overwhelming appeal. When Song preached that sermon, people were seized by conviction and shaken with sobs. The story needed no explanation in Singapore. It was the immigrant's story; it was the sinner's story; it was these women's story.[49]

Home became the central metaphor for Song's female converts. Borrowing from his revival chorus book, they repeatedly sang, "Return home! Return home! Nevermore to roam! Open your arms Heavenly Father, I am coming home!"[50] In fact, Song's songs were filled with imagery of home, and women eagerly mined them for comfort and to spread the gospel.[51] Women discovered that the revival narrative offered a powerful resolution to their spiritual and physical displacement. It gave them the vocabulary to claim, "Heaven is My Home."[52]

The heavenly home they referred to may have had an otherworldly dimension, but the evangelistic message was not "going home" deferred. The teams set about creating a new home on earth.[53] Those born again, as the language itself suggested, entered a new family. Team members called one another "brother" and "sister," or in the case of the teams' leader, [Leona] Wu Jingling, "mother."[54]

[49] Sng, *In His Good Time*, 180.

[50] *Fenxing Duangeji* [*Revival Choruses*], in *Xingzhou jidujiao budaotuan tuankan, 1946* [*Singapore Christian Evangelistic League, 1946*] (Singapore: 1946), song number 62, 183ff. Hereafter this publication will be referred to as *SCEL, 1946*.

[51] Dickson D. Bruce, *And They All Sang Hallelujah: Plain-Folk Camp-Meeting Religion, 1800–1845* (Knoxville: University of Tennessee Press, 1974), 102. In his study of American revival choruses, Bruce determined that people sang of "'home' more than anything else." The choruses were used both for comfort in the midst of a world that was perceived as being filled with trials and as a tool to encourage other people to convert and make their home in heaven. Some examples of how "home" appeared in Song's chorus book can be found in *SCEL, 1946*, 183ff., song numbers 4, 12, 62, 110, 141.

[52] *Fenxing Duangeji* [*Revival Choruses*], in *SCEL, 1946*, song number 141, 183ff.

[53] Bruce, *And They All Sang Hallelujah*, 102–6. The move of Chinese women in Singapore to make a new home on earth stood in stark contrast to the Southern plain-folk of the United States. Dickson noted that in American camp meetings, revival converts understood their heavenly home to mean a total rejection of life in the world. Chinese women in Singapore, however, understood their new heavenly home to entail the creation of a new family here and now.

[54] *Xinjiapo jidutu budaotuan jinxi jiniankan* [*Singapore Christian Evangelistic League Golden Jubilee Souvenir Magazine*] (Singapore: 1985), 10. The language

As had happened at Ginling College, Wu's alma mater, the familial discourse had a powerful socializing effect.[55] Members of the evangelistic teams imagined themselves bound together in ways that superseded other commitments and imagined communities.[56] This was visually displayed through the identical white uniforms and pins women wore when they evangelized. The outfits proclaimed each woman's identity: she was washed clean and sanctified by the blood of the Lamb.[57] Other social markers, like a woman's marital status, were subordinated in the group. What mattered was that the women were redeemed.[58] By wearing the same clothes when working collaboratively to win the lost, women intensified their united sense of "us" (the converted) against "them" (the unconverted).[59] A new family identity was forming. The frequency

of "brother" and "sister" had clear biblical precedents. The introduction of the term "mother" for Wu Jingling, however, may be an indication that the Singapore teams were drawing on the language of other social movements led by women. The Woman's Christian Temperance Union (WCTU), for instance, relied heavily on maternal language. Not only were many of its leaders called "mothers," but the women of the WCTU justified their actions in the public sphere by casting their roles as "social housekeepers." See Ian Tyrell, *Woman's World, Woman's Empire: The Woman's Christian Temperance Union in International Perspective, 1880–1930* (Chapel Hill: University of North Carolina Press, 1991), 125–27; Mary P. Ryan, *Womanhood in America: From Colonial Times to the Present*, 3rd ed. (New York: F. Watts, 1983), 142–47; 226–35.

[55] Jin Feng, *Making of a Family Saga: Ginling College* (Albany: State University of New York Press, 2009), has argued that the constantly reiterated notion of the "Ginling family" was what bound the school together despite external pressures and internal fissures. In an all-women's college, it was also the mediating idea that allowed students to imagine themselves as upholding the domestic ideal even as they expressed it as moving into the public sphere to mother the nation.

[56] Melissa Wei-Tsing Inouye, *China and the True Jesus: Charisma and Organization in a Chinese Christian Church* (New York: Oxford University Press, 2019), 121.

[57] Alvyn Austin, *China's Millions: The China Inland Mission and Late Qing Society, 1832–1905* (Grand Rapids: Eerdmans, 2007), describes the power of the color system missionaries introduced to China through the Wordless Book. Although white had other connotations in China, it also became associated with holiness through Christianity.

[58] White uniforms have frequently acted as signs of purity for women whose situation was ambiguous. See, for example, Cheryl Townsend Gilkes, "'Together and in the Harness': Women's Traditions in the Sanctified Church," *Signs* 10, no. 4 (1985): 685. Isabel Mukonyora, *Wandering: A Gendered Wilderness* (Berne, Switzerland: Peter Lang, 2007), 92, also notes the power of white uniforms to undermine authoritarian power structures imposed on women and minorities.

[59] *SCEL, 1935–1936*, 103.

of meetings each week spurred on close identification with other team members, and the introduction of snacks and tea before they set out to evangelize replicated the gathering of a family around a meal. An alternative home was created that had remarkable appeal.

Women discovered a new sort of family not only within their evangelistic team, but across teams as well. Despite linguistic differences, all the evangelistic bands began to use the same translation of the Bible—the one Song used and sold. Furthermore, the revival chorus book that he introduced had a significant unifying effect. A woman who had attended Song's revival as a girl remembered, "He was able to lead people in singing, even though they didn't know the song. . . . The song would be translated into Hokkien, and then people would sing simultaneously in both Mandarin and Hokkien."[60] To join an evangelistic team was to share in a common Christian identity, not simply a regional or linguistic one. Through their teams, women expanded the space wherein they found a place to belong.

A Modernizing Religion

The need for a place to belong was augmented by women's search for a spiritual refuge. The Smashing Superstition Movement in China, whence many women recently came, intensified the pressure for women to change, to modernize. Beginning in 1928 the Nationalist government set out to eradicate all religious practices that appeared nonscientific, or more specifically, those aspects of Chinese life that appeared as roadblocks to modernity. Political progressives and intellectual elites dispatched forces to destroy temples and suppress "superstitious" behavior. Since the anti-superstition campaigns were primarily directed against traditional religion, which was popularly considered "women's business," women were particularly vulnerable to attack and easily painted as hampering the Nationalist aims for a modern Chinese society.[61] Politically, therefore, women found it advantageous to

[60] Tay Poh Luan (Mrs.), interview, February 27, 2000, access number 002239, reel 4, National Archives of Singapore.

[61] Freedman, *Chinese Family and Marriage in Singapore*, 45. In her detailed study of the Smashing Superstition campaign, Nedostup noted how the state demonized practitioners of popular religion and through its propaganda highlighted the negative role of women. One poster, for instance, was a drawing of an outrageously opulent Chinese temple filled exclusively with female devotees. The poster urged people to not waste their money at temples, but give their resources to "build the nation instead." Women were presented as especially susceptible to superstition and heterodoxy. Rebecca Nedostup, *Superstitious Regimes: Religion*

distance themselves from the stigma of traditional religion. Yet most were uncertain how to modernize spiritually.[62]

Many women finally found a desirable religious option in the Singapore revival of 1935. Since Song's evangelistic identity had been formed during the Smashing Superstition Movement in China, he had learned to capitalize on his Ph.D. in chemistry from a Western university, and he promoted his capacity to distinguish scientific truth from superstition. Song used his extremely rare scientific credentials as a way to argue that even his spiritual teachings were modern. Despite the fact that the state wanted to marginalize healings, otherworldly visions, and supernatural forces that could reveal the future, Song extolled them all. His degree made him untouchable, so he could pull much of popular Chinese spirituality into the Christian church. Women who joined his evangelistic teams, therefore, did not have to abandon all their traditional, so-called "superstitious" beliefs. They saw in Song's Christianity a way to incorporate familiar practices into a new, "modern" religion.

The inclusion of traditional religious elements in Song's style of Christianity allowed female converts to express their religious concerns in the same gendered categories as before. Whereas men struggled to transfer their concerns about "bad luck" in business or gambling to the God of Jesus Christ, women seamlessly moved their requests about unfaithful husbands, wayward children, and physical illnesses to their new Lord.[63] Women found it natural to ask for God's intervention in healing the sick and restoring family harmony.[64] They also rejoiced that the Christian God communicated in familiar ways through dreams and visions. The women spoke easily about Jesus or an angel delivering messages to them and to those they evangelized. Their awareness of supernatural forces frequently appeared in team reports. One team of women, for instance, having shared the gospel with a family who did not immediately accept the good news, reveled in the fact that

> three days later, in the middle of the night a dark shadow suddenly pulled a woman from her bed, knocking her out as she fell to the floor. Meanwhile, her daughter-in-law continued to sleep. Unexpectedly, [the

---

and the Politics of Chinese Modernity (Cambridge, Mass.: Harvard University Press, 2009), 199–200, 222.

[62] Yoshiko Ashiwa, "Positioning Religion in Modernity," in *Making Religion, Making the State*, ed. Yoshiko Ashiwa and David L. Wank (Stanford: Stanford University Press, 2009).

[63] Elliott, *Chinese Spirit-Medium Cults in Singapore*, 90.

[64] For illuminating examples, see *SCEL, 1946*, 45, 49–50, 62–63, 69–71, 76–78.

daughter-in-law] felt someone clothed in white hit her on the head, waking her up. She arose, and saw her mother-in-law lying on the floor. She got her up and prayed for her. They received the Lord's grace, and the woman was completely healed. The whole family accepted the Lord.[65]

The account was certainly about extraordinary events, but the description of demonic forces, angelic beings, and physical healing was not unusual. They had precedent in traditional Chinese religion. Women recognized that for themselves, at least, conversion to Christianity was a transfer of allegiance, not the abandonment of popular feminine spirituality.

THE DOUBLE BIND OF GENDER EXPECTATIONS

Women faced conflicting pressures as the nuclear family system evolved in Singapore. When the multigenerational-family ideal failed to take shape on the island, women were bombarded with messages and images produced by reforming elites: seize this opportunity and break with custom to become a New Woman.[66] An essay published during the time of Song's evangelistic campaign demanded that "Women arise!" and throw off traditional conceptions of domesticity.[67] Advertisements in the newspaper dangled modern portraits before Singaporean women as they depicted Chinese ladies outside mixing with men, or—if inside—creating lavish, Western-style homes for their nuclear families.[68]

However, conflicting messages were just beneath the surface. An essay calling for women's liberation would be placed next to an advertisement for a resort that promised the availability of women who would cater to a male customer's every desire. Newspaper articles with titles such as, "Women Should Work!" were complemented in subsequent issues with, "The Modern Chinese Girl: A Model Wife and Perfect Mother."[69]

[65] *SCEL, 1935–1936*, 27.

[66] May Fourth radicals wanted women to break away from family control, escape from their inner chambers, and reject arranged marriages. Janet Ng, *The Experience of Modernity: Chinese Autobiography of the Early Twentieth Century* (Ann Arbor: University of Michigan Press, 2003), 54.

[67] "Nürenmen, qilai!" *Sin Chew Jit Poh*, October 5, 1935. This periodical is held at the National Library, Singapore.

[68] "Doan's Backache," *Sin Chew Jit Poh*, October 30, 1935; "Ovaltine," *Sin Chew Jit Poh*, September 9, 1935. This periodical is held at the National Library, Singapore.

[69] P. S. Choo, "Women Should Work!" *Malay Tribune*, February 7, 1931; Miss Julian, "The Modern Chinese Girl: A Model Wife and Perfect Mother," *Malay Tribune*, May 9, 1931. This periodical is held at the National Library, Singapore.

Advertisements were frequently ambiguous. In one popular promotion, for example, a woman was clad in a bathing suit and standing on a horse. At one level the image could be interpreted as a bold visual representation of a modern woman. On another level, however, the woman simply appeared like a circus performer.[70] Not long before the advertisement appeared, May Wong, an American-born Chinese woman, had visited Singapore. She noted that no women were on the streets or even in the markets. When she entered a restaurant by herself, she received curious stares until she overheard someone remind everyone else, "The circus is in town."[71] Her presence, like the advertisement, was socially acceptable only insofar as it could be relegated to a fringe character.

In whatever format it was delivered, the implicit message communicated to Chinese women was as clear as it was impossible to adopt in practice: women in Singapore were to become modern without disrupting tradition.

Women freed themselves from that double bind, however, by joining an evangelistic team. *God* commanded them to move outside of domestic places and into public spaces. The words of Mark 16:15 were more than an adornment on the cover of the first publication produced by the teams; they were a divine permission slip for women to create new modern identities.[72] God ordered them to "[g]o into all the world and preach the good news to all peoples."

SAVED TO SERVE

As women joined evangelistic teams, they were not only neutralizing various pressures, but were actively constructing and embodying a new, modern way of life. By organizing evangelistic teams, women who had for centuries been identified almost exclusively as daughter, wife, or mother were now also recognized for their elected functions: team leader, secretary, and treasurer.[73] Likewise, women's creative efforts to meet their own

---

[70] *Sin Chew Jit Poh*, October 19, 1935.

[71] May Wong, interview, access number 000093, reel 8, National Archives of Singapore.

[72] *SCEL, 1935–1936.*

[73] Kwok Pui-lan, "Claiming Our Heritage: Chinese Women and Christianity," *International Bulletin of Missionary Research* 16, no. 4 (October 1992): 151. The pattern was not without precedent among women connected with revivalism. A similar extension of women's roles had happened in the United States as women, inspired by Holiness revivalism, began practicing "tactics of recruitment,

financial costs for evangelism allowed many team members to attain powers previously unknown.[74] Having disposable money meant that numerous women entered the public sphere of economic exchange for the first time—even if in a limited fashion.[75] Teams also forced women to assume new public positions. They were all now evangelists, whether they called people to faith through preaching, teaching, singing, or prayer. Being part of a team also meant internalizing and spreading a modern form of individualistic piety. These new positions, piety, and public presence through preaching and evangelism were all but first signs that Christian women were becoming New Women in Singapore.[76]

PIETY

Revival choruses indelibly marked the language, and therefore the piety, of female evangelistic teams. Words and phrases from Song's chorus book that were used by all the teams seeped into reports and were borrowed to express spiritual longings. Women sang choruses before going out to evangelize; they sang them to attract curious crowds. Women introduced choruses before and even during their preaching in order to capture the essence of their message. They also used them to welcome a new convert, comfort themselves in the face of rejection, or express jubilation. Song's chorus book saturated evangelistic bands and played a formative role in shaping women's piety and their new self-understanding.

The choruses were filled with intensely personal expressions of devotion. The songs led women to cry out, "For me! For me! Christ died

---

organization, fund raising, propagandizing, and petitioning." See Nancy F. Cott, *The Bonds of Womanhood: "Woman's Sphere" in New England, 1780–1835* (New Haven: Yale University Press, 1977), 7–8; Dana L. Robert, *American Women in Mission: A Social History of Their Thought and Practice* (Macon, Ga.: Mercer University Press, 1997), 144–48.

[74] Women in Chinese society seldom had direct access to financial resources. According to May Wong, the American born Chinese lady who visited Singapore in the early 1930s, men even did the shopping for fruits and vegetables because they controlled all the money (May Wong, interview, access number 000093, reel 8, National Archives of Singapore). That context inspired the Chinese Communists' first piece of legislation passed on May 1, 1950: "Both husband and wife shall have equal rights in the possession and management of family property." See Judith Thornberry, "Women in China," *Church and Society* 65, no. 3 (January–February 1975): 42.

[75] *SCEL, 1935–1936,* 77.

[76] *SCEL, 1935–1936,* 77.

upon the cross. He suffered, bled and died alone, His suff'rings were for me, for me, for me."[77] Other songs instilled confidence in one's personal capacity: "I can, I will, I do believe."[78] This modern form of individualistic piety was in some measure offset by the fact that women sang the songs not only alone, but also together as a group. Nonetheless, revivalism's assumptions about individualism and voluntarism were repeatedly presented as the norm.[79]

The emphasis the songs placed on home also empowered the women to extend the domestic sphere into the world. Song's converts sang with assurance that heaven was now their home.[80] As they did so, they relativized their earthly homes. Women were no longer *neiren*, literally "inside people," bound by definition to their houses. Instead, revived women were inside-Christ people. They could venture into parks and markets or stand on the streets. According to revivalistic piety, such places were as much home as a woman's house, because if she was already spiritually home in Jesus Christ then physical spaces no longer needed to bind her. If anything, she needed to help the lost find their way to the heavenly home she had recently come to occupy. The move was a deft extension of home, the domestic sphere, to include the broader Singaporean society.[81]

[77] *Fenxing Duangeji* [*Revival Choruses*], in *SCEL, 1946*, song number 118, 183ff.

[78] *Fenxing Duangeji* [*Revival Choruses*], in *SCEL, 1946*, song number 42, 183ff.

[79] Bruce, *And They All Sang Hallelujah*, 95. Camp-meeting revival choruses were "highly redundant and quite brief." Their structure and brevity meant that camp-meeting songs could convey only a small amount of information. What they taught, therefore, were only "those matters about which the community was in substantial agreement." Redundancy and brevity were hallmarks of Song's choruses as well, and the cumulative message was that each individual could and should choose for salvation.

[80] Bruce, *And They All Sang Hallelujah*, 96, has argued that "all [revival choruses] were expressions of the assurance of salvation felt by the singers."

[81] Extensive literature exists on this phenomenon. Chinese Redemptive Societies gave women ways to expand ideas about "home" into "society." Likewise, women in Europe and the United States found ways to extend the domestic sphere. The reasons given were different than those created in Singapore, but the result was very much the same. See, for example, Prasenjit Duara, "Of Authenticity and Woman: Personal Narratives of Middle-Class Women in Modern China," in *Becoming Chinese: Passages to Modernity and Beyond*, ed. Wen-hsin Yeh (Berkeley: University of California Press, 2000), 354–56; Cott, *Bonds of Womanhood*; Mary P. Ryan, *Cradle of the Middle Class: The Family in Oneida County, New York, 1790–1865* (Cambridge: Cambridge University Press, 1981); Jane Hunter, *The Gospel of Gentility: American Women Missionaries in Turn-of-the-Century China* (New Haven:

The chorus book was the crucial medium for passing on a new spiritual vocabulary to women. It played a decisive role in creating their revivalistic and socially active piety. Thus, an evangelistic team of women rejoiced when during one of their campaigns "forty Bibles were sold, and three hundred hymnals."[82] They were undisturbed by the obvious disproportion, for the chorus books were not only less expensive, but as the unique possession of Song's evangelistic teams, they were the central device for instilling his revivalistic and modern form of spirituality.[83] When one woman converted through the ministry of an evangelistic band, her transformation was condensed into saying she "prayed and studied the songs."[84] The chorus book, even more than the Bible, was the formative document of the movement. Women were able to extract from it the language necessary to describe the momentous shifts transpiring in their personal lives.

PUBLIC APPEARANCES

While women who joined evangelistic teams embraced a new piety, the real novelty of their Christian identity was in their conspicuous spread across Singapore. Almost every team was based in the urban core with members living somewhere close to the busy harbor, but groups were never confined there.[85] As female teams moved out, some shared the gospel publicly.[86] They confronted people at temples or in parks; they preached in the

---

Yale University Press, 1984); Tyrell, *Woman's World, Woman's Empire*; Megan Smitley, *The Feminine Public Sphere: Middle Class Women in Civic Life in Scotland, c. 1870–1914* (Manchester: Manchester University Press, 2009).

[82] *SCEL, 1935–1936*, 10.

[83] Russell E. Richey, "Revivalism: In Search of a Definition," *Wesleyan Theological Journal* 28, nos. 1–2 (1993): 165–75. Richey has convincingly argued that revivalism is a modern phenomenon. Unlike revivals or revitalization, which have a longer history, revivalism is a particular form of religious activity that is built on movements and assumptions that are associated with the modern world. Pietism and voluntarism would be two primary examples of revivalism's connection to modernity.

[84] Richey, "Revivalism," 36.

[85] The SCEL gathered copious information about its teams, including addresses.

[86] It must be noted that teams were not necessarily gender exclusive. Some women were part of male-led teams, and several males—most likely boys who were children of female team members—traveled with predominantly women's teams. Nevertheless, most teams led by women had female membership. See Tay Poh Luan (Mrs.), interview, February 27, 2000, access number 002239, reel 3, National Archives of Singapore.

streets.[87] One team operated by designating a different member each week to select any destination she wished. The team would then send out one or two members to explore the place and make contact with people in the area in order to prepare the neighborhood for the full team's arrival a day or two later.[88] The plan was well suited for spreading into unfamiliar territory, something many women did often. Some teams reported traveling to rural areas and outlying islands. In their reports on such trips, women described these peripheral zones as especially superstitious and beholden to written charms or idols, suggesting that for Singaporean women their urban/modern identity was intertwined with their Christian identity.[89] They believed it was incumbent upon them, therefore, to take the gospel from the modern city to the hinterlands of the earth.

Despite the highly visible evangelistic efforts of such groups, other female teams were more reluctant to enter open spaces. They preferred to evangelize inside homes, hospitals, antidrug associations, or shops, accommodating cultural expectations that proper women should be inside.[90] Nonetheless, their piety, preaching, and evangelism continued to instill a new identity. Revivalistic evangelicalism and modernity were merging together.

Preaching and Teaching

Whether in recognizably public or private spaces, women were proclaiming the gospel. They frequently reported it as "lecturing," though sometimes the word "preaching" slipped into their vocabulary.[91] They were announcing the good news. They normally began with the story of the Prodigal Son. In part women used the story to address undesirable behaviors in men.[92] Gambling, in which more than 200,000 yuan could

[87] SCEL, 1935–1936, 45.

[88] SCEL, 1935–1936, 32.

[89] See for example, SCEL, 1935–1936, 32, 39, 43–44, and 47.

[90] For a variety of examples of how and where women evangelized inside, See SCEL, 1935–1936, 17; 24–25; 46–47.

[91] Compare, for example, the report of team 3, a men's team, with similar female accounts from teams 20 and 29. See SCEL, 1935–1936, 14, 17, 25–26.

[92] It is worth noting that revivalism and social reform have an intertwined history, and women have frequently stood at the intersection. Reforming male society became the task and burden for a number of women inspired by nineteenth-century Holiness revivalism in the United States. One suspects that something similar was happening in Singapore in the wake of Song's revivals, especially as both tended to focus on male vices that disrupted the home and threatened social cohesion. Women in both revivals felt it incumbent to create a

pass through hands each day, almost entirely in small sums, was an acute family issue, as was prostitution and opium addiction.[93] Women could easily link the actions of many men in Singapore with the reprobate choices of the Prodigal Son.[94] However, the story appealed to women as well as it described how the immigrant/sinner could finally return home. The gospel they preached was not only a rebuke to destructive behavior, but also an invitation to be saved and a chance to go home.[95]

In their sermons or lectures, women often ventured further. Their messages had particular nuances that distinguished them from male sermons. For instance, team 9, composed of men, stated,

> We often preached the following themes: (A) God is the creator of the universe; (B) Humanity has sinned, but God sent his only Son to pay the price for humanity's sin; and (C) Preached that only by believing in Jesus Christ will people be able to give up wickedness and return to righteousness.[96]

On the same page, a team of women reported their messages very differently. They did not attempt to recreate the narrative of creation, fall, and redemption through a series of sermons. They contentedly reported that

---

new community. See Timothy L. Smith, *Revivalism and Social Reform in Mid-Nineteenth Century America* (New York: Abingdon Press, 1957); Bruce, *And They All Sang Hallelujah*, 47; Ryan, *Cradle of the Middle Class*; Nancy A. Hardesty, "Minister as Prophet? Or as Mother? Two Nineteenth Century Models," in *Women in New Worlds*, vol. 1, ed. Hilah F. Thomas and Rosemary Skinner Keller (Nashville: Abingdon Press, 1981), 97.

[93] Elliott, *Chinese Spirit-Medium Cults in Singapore*, 21. It is interesting to note that some female teams worked with antidrug associations. Churches in Singapore avoided collaborating with Chinese organizations that battled opium in part because the nationalistic language of the anti-opium associations made Western missions uncomfortable, and possibly in part because the denominations were dependent on the tax revenue generated by the sale of the drug for the support of their Christian schools. Since the Evangelistic League was neither affiliated with Western denominations nor had ambitions for starting a school, teams may have been free to forge new bonds against the sale and use of opium among Chinese immigrants. See also Robert Hunt, "The Churches and Social Problems," in *Christianity in Malaysia: A Denominational History*, ed. Robert Hunt, Lee Kam Hing, and John Roxborogh (Petaling Jaya, Selangor Darul Ehsan, Malaysia: Pelanduk Publications, 1992).

[94] Mary P. Ryan, "A Women's Awakening: Evangelical Religion and the Families of Utica, New York, 1800–1840," in *Religion and American Culture*, ed. David G. Hackett (New York: Routledge, 1995), 147–66, captures the familiar pattern of women using revivals to control the behavior of men.

[95] See for illustrative examples, *SCEL, 1935–1936*, 25, 28, 43, 55, 58.

[96] *SCEL, 1935–1936*, 17.

"[o]ur message was the loving and gracious God," a theme they believed could "illumine the hearts of the listeners and cause them to trust, believe and be saved."[97] Female teams also went beyond the stock evangelistic message of sin and redemption, and they included sermons on topics like Ruth's love for her mother-in-law, Naomi. On one hand the content of such a message affirmed traditional Chinese domestic values with its emphasis on the daughter-in-law submitting to her mother-in-law. On the other hand, the act of a woman preaching any sermon undermined all domestic values as women went outside their homes to spread the gospel. Venturing into preaching/lecturing held contradictions for women even as it solidified their new identities.

EVANGELISM

The stated goal of all this preaching was to make converts. The number of people reached by all the evangelistic teams during their first six months is impossible to determine. Based solely on the hard numbers supplied, the SCEL held 780 services in and around Singapore with 40,429 people listening.[98] Since many reports were incomplete, a better estimate would probably double both figures. Teams impressively canvassed the island's 450,000 Chinese immigrants, declaring to all who would listen that Jesus saves.

The women met mixed reactions. Curious if somewhat mocking observers gathered easily enough to watch the spectacle of women in uniforms marching through streets, waving flags, and singing songs. However, an audience's attention was difficult to maintain. People could easily wander off halfway through a sermon. Stiffer opposition was not uncommon: sermons were derailed by listeners who argued with the message or by whispers that Jiang Jieshi [Chiang Kai-shek] forbade people to follow Christ.[99] On an outlying island, inhabitants refused to allow women who came without a male chaperone to disembark from their boat.[100] Children were more receptive, but female evangelists still

---

[97] *SCEL, 1935–1936,* 17.

[98] *SCEL, 1935–1936.*

[99] *SCEL, 1935–1936,* 47. This charge was particularly interesting because Z. T. Kuang of the Southern Methodist Church had baptized Chiang Kai-shek in 1930. The event, however, was not publicized in China as the newspapers were under strict military censorship. See "Chiang Kai Shek: Why He Became a Christian," *Sydney Morning Herald,* January 10, 1931, 7.

[100] *SCEL, 1935–1936.*

reported being cautious: "We also sometimes taught little kids to sing hymns but only after we watched for the right time, and then made a move."[101] Teams tried to remain optimistic, but disappointment surfaced as women recognized that "evangelizing and planting seeds is hard."[102]

Nevertheless, after just six months, 961 people, or 2.5 percent of those who heard teams speak, responded in some positive way to the evangelistic message. Among those who expressed interest in the gospel, evangelistic teams discovered they had almost always followed some prior inroad to the listener's heart. Teams learned, for example, that if a person had been exposed to the Christian message beforehand she was far more likely to show interest in the gospel. Converts, therefore, were disproportionately represented by people who had gone to Christian schools in China, those who had grown up Roman Catholic, or persons who had formerly attended church.[103] Female evangelists also generated converts through family connections—when they existed in Singapore.[104] Lin Youcai, for example, convinced her mother-in-law Xu Yanniang to cast out her idols, and likewise converted her father-in-law shortly thereafter. Another member in the same team convinced her younger sister to abandon witchcraft and follow Jesus.[105] However, since most people in Singapore did not have ready access to their extended families, they maximized other social relations. When a team traveled to the village of Wanli on a distant island, for instance, they stayed with acquaintances and relied on them as translators in order to testify to the good news. By operating through preexisting relationships, the team saw remarkable results. Sixty-six people were converted, approximately 10 percent of all the Chinese in that community.[106] The pattern was clear: female teams utilized networks already present to share the gospel. Cold calls and street preaching, which men tended to do, never produced as many new Christians as did spreading the gospel through personal relationships and across social networks.[107] Since women generally preferred

---

[101] SCEL, 1935–1936, 50.
[102] SCEL, 1935–1936, 44.
[103] SCEL, 1935–1936, 10, 27, 33, 38, 45.
[104] SCEL, 1935–1936, 33–34.
[105] SCEL, 1935–1936, 33–34.
[106] SCEL, 1935–1936, 10.
[107] Ryan, Cradle of the Middle Class, described something similar in the United States. Women were very effective in using "maternal evangelism" to lead family and friends to a conversion.

more intimate settings with family and friends, they witnessed twice as many conversions as their male counterparts. Energized by the steadily rising tide of converts, (Leona) Wu Jingling created a mathematical formula proving that if teams and their converts continued to make new converts, then the entire world would be converted to Christ in twenty-five years.[108] For a while, at least, Song's evangelistic teams in Singapore appeared to be a popular spiritual movement that was transforming the world.

Legacy

Optimism about the movement's future, however, was premature. The SCEL soon lost momentum. Several forces contributed to its decline. First, the sharp rise in women's voluntary religious commitment and their assumption of modern gender roles became normalized. By requiring all team members to participate in specific evangelistic practices, the thrill and anxiety surrounding cultural transgression gradually diminished. It became routine. Conceivably, teams could have renewed that initial excitement by incorporating new converts or starting new teams—vicariously enjoying newcomers' enthusiasm. However, because of a lengthy and complicated order of salvation, those who did respond to the gospel were generally excluded from joining an evangelistic band. For instance, despite the fact that one woman had "ceased to worship idols, and now prays every day . . . [and] has led other people to hear the message," the team that evangelized her still prayed that the "Holy Spirit [would] open the eyes of her heart, so that soon she will turn to the Lord and become a citizen of heaven." To them she did not appear converted, even though they said, "She enjoys progressing in the way of the Lord."[109] More and more teams faded away as the months passed, with few replacements able to join the diminished ranks. At its apex, 111 teams simultaneously marched out of the Telok Ayer Methodist Church at the end of one of Song Shangjie's services and filled Singapore with testimonies to Jesus Christ. Three months later, the number of operating teams was closer to 50. By the time the Japanese invaded the island on February 15, 1942, the emaciated organization "imperceptibly and quietly came to a standstill."[110]

---

[108] *Xinjiapo jidutu budaotuan yingxi jiniankan* [*Singapore Christian Evangelistic League, Silver Anniversary, 1960*] (Singapore: n.p., 1960), 1.

[109] *SCEL, 1935–1936*, 51.

[110] *SCEL, 1946*, 83.

Second, although the League reconvened after the war, it was never again a truly popular movement. Numbers remained down, and the tone of members' testimonies understandably shifted from highly wound evangelistic zeal to exhausted sighs of relief that the occupation was over.[111] Furthermore, Singapore had changed in the decade since evangelistic teams first canvassed the island. Women could now find alternative ways to settle into a modern society. The demands of postwar reconstruction, for example, helped women solidify their acceptance as part of the modern workforce. Evangelistic teams were no longer necessary social innovators.

Third, when the American fundamentalist Carl McIntire visited Singapore a few years after the war, he invited the Evangelistic League to join his International Council of Christian Churches (ICCC). Although not a church itself, the League was nonetheless drawn by McIntire's vehement denunciation of the liberalism in the World Council of Churches (WCC), a theological poison of which Song had warned his converts.[112] Shortly thereafter, on March 18, 1950, the SCEL voted to affiliate with the ICCC.[113] When the majority of churches in Singapore rejected similar invitations and chose to cooperate with the WCC instead, the Evangelistic League was almost entirely isolated. Its strict policy of separation from WCC affiliates meant that the Evangelistic League, which had originally leavened many Protestant denominations, withdrew into a small enclave and only forged a direct relationship with the Singapore Bible Presbyterian Church. In their seclusion the surviving evangelistic teams became marginal to Singaporean Protestant Christianity.

CONCLUSION

For a brief time, women made Song Shangjie's evangelistic teams a modernizing spiritual movement. In the face of forces that put them in seemingly impossible positions, female converts used the band's structure and mandate to mold themselves into New Women. Teams transformed women's identities as they integrated immigrants into a new family, giving them an alternative home. They provided spiritual refuge as women

---

[111] *SCEL, 1946*, 83.

[112] *SCEL, 1946*, i.

[113] Wilbur Morse Jr., "East Asia Crippled by Communism Rev. McIntire Says," *Christian Beacon* 15, no. 1 (February 16, 1950): 5; Quek Kiok Chiang to McIntire, T. T. Shields and Arie Kok, March 20, 1950, MacIntire Papers, box 383, folder 9, Princeton Theological Seminary Archives, Princeton, New Jersey.

escaped the charge of being "superstitious" by becoming Christians. They also helped women resolve anxieties about their gender roles by giving them divine sanction to assume modern female identities. In addition, Song's revival equipped women to extend the concept of home and service into the public sphere, which thereby released them to move around Singapore proclaiming the gospel and spreading revival across preexisting networks.

Although Singapore's history influenced the particular trajectory of the evangelistic teams on the island, the transformative power of female preaching bands was not altogether different in other places Song visited. The extant materials are less complete than in Singapore, but in one place after another, records bubble with wonder over the prominent role women played during and after his meetings. Wherever he went, Song joined other May Fourth radicals and reformers in promoting new places for women in Chinese society. In some ways he was suspicious of the modernizing militants celebrated by the likes of Ding Ling, but in the end he advocated that women in his meetings should become a kind of soldier too—a soldier of the cross. Both types of women broke with custom. That is what made them New. In Song's mind, though, female evangelists put their bodies in public not to make them seen, but to use them as pointers to the transformative power of Jesus Christ.

7

A New Body

After Song Shangjie left Singapore on October 16, 1935, he returned to mainland China. The ship ride home was a rare break in his otherwise punishing schedule. By the time Chen Rongzhan heard him speak just seven months later, Song had led another four hundred or so revival services in twenty-two different locales. Chen caught up with the indefatigable revivalist in Taishan, Guangdong. It was a perfect opportunity for the curious spectator to record part of what happened during a single day in China for an upcoming publication, and almost a sure way to guarantee that the essay he submitted would be published alongside 468 others, which cumulatively tried to document the scope of what happened on May 21, 1936. In his report Chen likened Dr. Song Shangjie to a "traveling medicine peddler."[1] Trying to make sense of what he saw for a general audience, Chen said virtually nothing about Song's sermon, but twice in his brief essay he drew comparisons between Song and the itinerant medicine sellers who were active in China's cities.[2] One can easily detect the condescension in his description. Chen submitted his essay to be published as a depiction of China's superstition, but what is not so easily dismissed is his decision to cast Song as a type of medical practitioner. The fast-talking revivalist did not awaken in him associations with

---

[1] Chen Rongzhan, "Notes on Dr. Song's Preaching," in *One Day in China, May 21, 1936*, ed. Sherman Cochran, Andrew C. K. Hsieh, and Janis Cochran (New Haven: Yale University Press, 1983), xiii, 186–88.

[2] Sherman Cochran, *Chinese Medicine Men: Consumer Culture in China and Southeast Asia* (Cambridge, Mass.: Harvard University Press, 2005), 39; T. J. Hinrichs and Linda L. Barnes, eds., *Chinese Medicine and Healing: An Illustrated History* (Cambridge, Mass.: Belknap Press of Harvard University Press, 2013), 153.

other preachers or even teachers of the dharma. Chen may have doubted the efficacy of what Song and other medical hucksters had to offer, but he understood Song to be first and foremost a kind of healer.

Chen was not alone. Song's reputation for healing was a core component of his popularity. Press reports highlighted his sensational and miraculous cures. Christian magazines carried personal testimonies that vouched for the efficacy of his services. All the attention lavished on Song's ministry of healing made several of his friends and later biographers uncomfortable. They were afraid people were fixating on the physical transformations that happened through his work and thereby missing the spiritual significance of his ministry.[3] For Song, the two were never so neatly separated. Like others in his country who were trying to make all things new, Song understood that a New Man or a New Woman must also have a New Body.

The idea was almost axiomatic in China. Men had cut off their long queues in defiance of the Qing dynasty. A modern woman bobbed her hair and put on makeup and a *qipao*.[4] Changing the body had become a critical way to signify that a person "was an active participant in the grand effort to construct a new order."[5] Physical alterations mattered in China. They were the visible expression of a person's new identity.

It turned out they were also only skin-deep. By the 1930s modern hairstyles, clothes, and cosmetics were so common in China's cities that questions arose as to why people were changing their appearance. Was

[3]   See William E. Schubert, China Records Project Miscellaneous Personal Papers Collection, record group 8, box 185a, tape 6.1, Special Collections, Yale Divinity School Library, New Haven, Conn (hereafter referred to as YDSL); Leslie T. Lyall, *A Biography of John Sung* (Singapore: Genesis Books, 2004); Cornelie Baarbé, *Dr Sung, een Reveil op Java: Over de Evangelist Dr. Sung en zijn preken* (Den Haag, Netherlands: Voorhoeve, 1960). All three biographers went to great lengths to minimize the prominence of Song's healing ministry, explaining to readers how seldom he practiced it. Although he seldom dedicated a service strictly to healing, he always offered a divine touch to whoever asked for it.

[4]   Louise Edwards, "Policing the Modern Woman in Republican China," *Modern China* 26, no. 2 (April 2000): 131. A *qipao* was a dress that invoked equality with men as it mimicked the *changpao* of the men's wardrobe. This gender parity was part of what made a Woman New [*xin nüxing*] or Modern [*xiandai funü*] (the terms were interchangeable).

[5]   Christina K. Gilmartin, "Gender, Political Culture, and Women's Mobilization," in *Engendering China: Women, Culture and the State*, ed. Christina K. Gilmartin et al. (Cambridge, Mass.: Harvard University Press, 1994), 201; Edwards, "Policing the Modern Woman in Republican China," 131.

it because they wanted to be radical, or was it because they wanted to be beautiful? Retailers had managed to make the modern look fashionable, so petty urbanites regularly appeared in the new style. However, when Japan encroached on the nation's territory, economy, and political institutions in the early 1930s, those clad in the new look offered little resistance. Reformers complained that people had refashioned their bodies, but beneath the linen and the lipstick they were no different. Real change, they began to emphasize, would not just redecorate the body, but transform it. In order to survive, China did not need fashionable bodies; it needed stronger and healthier ones.

Song agreed. Anyone can dress up the body. He dismissed Western clothes and cosmetics as hypocrisy: cheap ways to masquerade as a New Man or New Woman.[6] Real change had to go deeper. But what would it look like? How would an inner transformation visibly manifest if not by the cut of a man's clothes or the arrangement of a woman's hair? Song's services pointed to health and healing. China's New Man and New Woman would have a strong and healthy body, and faith in Jesus Christ would make it so. It was a provocative claim that challenged the powers in China which claimed that they alone had the legitimate means to "strengthen the race and to strengthen the nation."[7] Song insisted he had something better. New Bodies for a New China would not come through Western medicine, Chinese medicine, or any other medical option, but it would come through the healing power of Jesus Christ.

RECONFIGURING THE MEDICAL LANDSCAPE

WESTERN BIOMEDICINE

After the May Fourth Movement, there was a general consensus among Marxist radicals, pro-Western liberals, and conservative nationalists that "'science' had to play a leading role in twentieth-century China, if

---

[6] Song Shangjie, *Forty John Sung Revival Sermons*, vol. 1, trans. Timothy Tow (Singapore: Alice Doo, 1978), 50; Song Shangjie, *Forty John Sung Revival Sermons*, vol. 2, trans. Timothy Tow (Singapore: Alice Doo, 1983), 12; Song Shangjie, "Saoluode meng'en [Saul Receives Grace]," as recorded by Jia Zi'an, evening of April 9, 1935, in Ertiao Presbyterian Church, Beijing, *Light in Darkness* 7, no. 11 (November 1936): 23.

[7] Andrew D. Morris, "'The Me in the Mirror': A Narrative of Voyeurism and Discipline in Chinese Women's Physical Culture, 1921–1937," in *Visualizing Modern China*, ed. James A. Cook et al. (Lanham, Md.: Lexington Books, 2014), 108.

there was to be a China in the twentieth century."[8] Zealots of science especially promoted Western biomedicine as the way to improve bodies and thereby strengthen the nation. "Every body knows that modern China needs science," opined a university student: "Modern medicine is a branch of science, whereas 'old style' medicine is but a fool's philosophy."[9]

Such a statement would have been inconceivable fifty years prior. Medical missionaries who first introduced Western biomedicine to China initially met resistance. Their techniques were inexplicable, and their surgeries obscene. The idea of cutting the human body, a gift from one's parents, contravened filial piety. Because Chinese doctors were loath to perform operations, Western doctors found a niche treating problems like cataracts with simple surgeries. Their successes quickly led to an increased demand for their services.[10]

Doctors trained in biomedicine multiplied in the late nineteenth and early twentieth centuries. The presence of medical missionaries in China grew from 19 in 1881 to 462 by 1920. The number of Chinese doctors trained in biomedicine also ballooned. In 1909, the country had only 400 students learning Western medicine, almost all of whom studied abroad. Two decades later thousands had supplemented the ranks of those early graduates. In 1927 China had 3,000 doctors trained in Western medicine. In 1937 the number reached 9,000. The rise of Western medicine was meteoric.[11]

Even so, the increasing number of doctors paled in comparison with China's enormous population. In the 1930s England's ratio of doctors using biomedicine to the general population was 1 in 1500, and in the United States it was 1 in 800. China, on the other hand, had only one

[8] Ralph C. Crozier, *Traditional Medicine in Modern China: Science, Nationalism, and the Tensions of Cultural Change* (Cambridge, Mass: Harvard University Press, 1968), 1.

[9] Chang Tsung-Liang, essay in *Yi yao zhi ye zheng wen ji. Di san jie* [*"Old Style" versus "Modern" Medicine in China: Which Can Do More for the Health and Progress of the Country, and Why?*] (Shanghai: Wei sheng jiao yu hui, 1926), 7.

[10] Michelle Renshaw, *Accommodating the Chinese: The American Hospital in China, 1880–1920* (New York: Routledge, 2005), 196; Croizier, *Traditional Medicine in Modern China*, 26–27.

[11] John Stewart Barwick, "The Protestant Quest for Modernity in Republican China" (Ph.D. diss., University of Alberta, 2011), 113; Crozier, *Traditional Medicine in Modern China*, 48.

doctor trained in Western medicine for every 80,000 people in the country.[12] The disproportion was even further imbalanced by the fact that almost all doctors trained in Western medicine settled in China's relatively few urban centers. Shanghai alone accounted for almost a quarter of all biomedical doctors in the nation.[13] Thus, the impact of Western medicine on the general population was uneven. It was in the cities—where the density of biomedical experts was highest and Western medicine was visible—that biomedical ideas about diagnosing and treating illnesses found powerful cultural allies.

May Fourth intellectuals championed Western medicine and savaged traditional medicine before the public. In articles and speeches, reformers ridiculed Chinese medicine for its unfounded premises and diagnoses, which were little more than guesswork. Chen Duxiu, the editor of *New Youth* and eventual co-founder of the Communist Party in China, complained that Chinese medicine did nothing more than "confuse the world and delude the people."[14] A professor of psychiatry at the Peking Union Medical College, the leading biomedical facility in Asia, went further. He suggested that the persistent belief in the unscientific methods of Chinese medicine was potentially a sign of psychological illness.[15] Lu Xun, one of China's most celebrated authors, portrayed China's historic healing arts darker still. In his short story "Medicine," parents of a young man acquire at considerable cost a special Chinese medicine: a bun dipped in human blood. The ill boy ate the sure cure, but died. With little subtlety the story not only attacked the ineffectiveness of Chinese medicine, but also linked it to cannibalism. Choosing to use Chinese medicine instead of Western biomedicine was akin to drinking the lifeblood out of the nation.[16]

[12] J. A. Jewell, "The Development of Chinese Health Care, 1911–1949," in *Health Care and Traditional Medicine in China, 1800–1982*, ed. S. M. Hillier and J. A. Jewell (Boston: Routledge, 1983), 48.

[13] C. C. Chen, *Medicine in Rural China: A Personal Account* (Berkeley: University of California Press, 1989), 27, 61; Jewell, "Development of Chinese Health Care," 49.

[14] Chen Duxiu, "My Solemn Plea to the Youth," quoted in Crozier, *Traditional Medicine in Modern China*, 71.

[15] John Z. Bowers, *Western Medicine in a Chinese Palace: Peking Union Medical College, 1917–1951* (Philadelphia: Josiah Macy Jr. Foundation, 1972), 196.

[16] Lu Xun, "Yao [Medicine]," in *Lu Xun quan ji* (Beijing: Ren min wen xue chu ban she, 1981), 440–49.

Indeed, the life of the nation was precisely what was at stake. Articles and advertisements flooded the masses with a simple message: China had to produce New Bodies, better bodies, if it were to compete with stronger nations. Essays argued that focusing on education and industry was doomed to fail for "only the development of the physical health of the individual will raise [a person] to a standard high enough to save China."[17] But which kind of medicine could most help the country, as the Shanghai Association for Hygiene Education asked in their pamphlet *"Old Style" versus "Modern" Medicine in China: Which Can Do More For the Health and Progress of the Country, and Why?* Was China's hope in "old style" or "modern" medicine?[18] Framed that way, the pretense of intellectual debate became obvious. The association, like other urban reform movements, had already decided that "[f]or the benefit of the individual, of society, and of China, 'modern' medicine should be adopted without hesitation."[19] It was necessary to turn to something different, because "The hollow-breasted and humpbacked, the pale-faced and slender-limbed . . . the award of the very title of 'The Far Eastern Sick Person' [are] . . . direct gifts of the old-style medicine to China."[20] Social Darwinism required China to change medical systems or else the country would never survive. Only biomedicine could save the nation.

Corporations marketed the same idea. Kiazin, for example, was a Western-style medicine sold to treat the symptoms of tuberculosis and other ailments. Advertisements for the drug depicted a Chinese man bound and gagged; he was a prisoner. Who imprisoned him was intentionally vague, but the product's byline promised that Kiazin could return vigor to the patient and to the nation as a whole.[21]

---

[17] Chow Teh Lin, essay in *Yi yao zhi ye zheng wen ji. Di san jie* [*"Old Style" versus "Modern" Medicine in China: Which Can Do More for the Health and Progress of the Country, and Why?*] (Shanghai: Wei sheng jiao yu hui, 1926), 27.

[18] Chow, essay in *Yi yao zhi ye zheng wen ji . . .* [*"Old Style" versus "Modern" Medicine in China . . .*].

[19] Chow, essay in *Yi yao zhi ye zheng wen ji . . .* [*"Old Style" versus "Modern" Medicine in China . . .*], 27.

[20] Chang, essay in *Yi yao zhi ye zheng wen ji . . .* [*"Old Style" versus "Modern" Medicine in China . . .*], 9. The English wording clarified the association's bias. "Old Style" was their English translation of *zhongyi*, literally "Chinese medicine."

[21] Bridie J. Andrews, "Tuberculosis and the Assimilation of Germ Theory in China, 1895–1937," *Journal of the History of Medicine* 52 (January 1997): 144.

The merger of biomedicine and Chinese nationalism attracted a potent political ally. The Nationalist government saw Western medicine as a means to create a stronger and healthier citizenry. Better bodies—like those produced through the biomedical measures used in Japan, Europe, and the United States—might give China a fighting chance against imperialist incursions. Thus, the government turned to Western-trained doctors for guidance when it set up the first Ministry of Health in China's history. At the National Health Conference held in 1929, the prominence of Western biomedicine within the Nationalist government became exceedingly clear. The delegate Yu Yunxiu motioned "to abolish the old style practice in order to remove the obstacles to medicine and public health."[22] The proposal, which was unanimously approved, went on to outline how traditional medical associations would be outlawed and newspapers and magazines would be prohibited from publishing "reactionary views" or "unscientific propaganda" (i.e., advertisements for traditional medicine). The document also suggested that those who currently practiced medicine in China would need to study Western medicine and complete that course of study within three years in order to get a medical license. All who failed to comply would be banned from plying their trade. In other words, the Ministry of Health—stacked with people trained in Western medicine—voted to eliminate its medical competition. Biomedicine, they agreed, was the only way to give Chinese people a New Body.[23]

CHINESE MEDICINE

Medical practitioners not trained in Western medicine were easy targets for modernizing nationalists. Their status in society was tenuous. For centuries physicians had appeared in Chinese theatre in the role of *chou*, clown-like characters who provided comic relief. "The sarcasm was aimed at the low level of their medical skills and even lower level of their medical ethics."[24] Since licensing was a foreign concept, anyone

[22] Ye Xiaoqing, "Regulating the Medical Profession in China: Health Policies of the Nationalist Government," in *Historical Perspectives on East Asian Science, Technology and Medicine*, ed. Alan K. L. Chan, Gregory K. Clancy, and Hui-chieh Loy (Singapore: Singapore University Press, 1999), 200.

[23] Ye, "Regulating the Medical Profession in China," 199–200; Crozier, *Traditional Medicine in Modern China*; Bridie J. Andrews, "The Republic of China," in Hinrichs and Barnes, *Chinese Medicine and Healing*.

[24] Ye, "Regulating the Medical Profession in China," 199.

could claim to be trained in Chinese healing arts. That made Chinese doctors appear as greedy opportunists, preying on the ill, known to kill more than to cure.[25]

The proposal "Abolishing Old-Style Medicine in Order to Clear Away the Obstacles to Medicine and Public Health," however, galvanized the diffuse Chinese medical community. In fact, the government's plan to eliminate Chinese medicine had the opposite effect. It created *guoyi*, or National medicine—what we recognize as Chinese medicine today. In response to the not-too-subtle declaration of war on indigenous medicine, Chinese medical practitioners mobilized opposition. A month after the Ministry of Health unanimously passed a resolution to phase out medical alternatives, the alternatives appeared in Shanghai with force. Representatives from over one hundred medical associations across China descended on Shanghai. Two thousand Chinese-style pharmacies went on strike for half of the day to show their support for the nation's traditional doctors. The protesting medical community grabbed hold of the influential rhetoric of nationalism, which the Ministry of Health used to justify its sponsorship of biomedicine, and turned it against the government office. Western medicine was not the savior of the country, but its enemy. Biomedicine was part of the imperialist invasion, traditional doctors warned. The government proposal to forbid Chinese medicine was a capitulation to the desires of foreign powers to sell more of their own drugs in China's vast market. National strength was not found in ideas or healing practices that originated outside the country; it would come by capitalizing on the country's own medical resources. Real patriotism meant embracing indigenous medicine. It alone was untainted by foreign interests, so only it could build the kind of bodies that would be free of imperial exploitation.[26]

Those who gathered in Shanghai founded a nationwide organization of Chinese medical doctors. The name they took for themselves was significant: Institute of National Medicine (INM). Henceforth, they were not going to be associated with "old-style" medicine (the English

[25] Manfred Porkert, "The Intellectual and Social Impulses behind the Evolution of Traditional Chinese Medicine," in *Asian Medical Systems: A Comparative Study*, ed. Charles Leslie (Berkeley: University of California Press, 1976), 70; Crozier, *Traditional Medicine in Modern China*, 32–33.

[26] Sean Hsiang-lin Lei, "When Chinese Medicine Encountered the State, 1910–1949" (Ph.D. diss., University of Chicago, 1999); Andrews, "Republic of China," 225–26.

translation of the word *zhongyi*, which is literally "Chinese medicine"). Instead, they would be the country's National medicine, *guoyi*. With the language of nationalism in their arsenal, the INM battled the Ministry of Health to a standstill. It won over enough politicians to ensure that the proposal to abolish Chinese medicine never became law.

In order to achieve a stalemate, however, the INM did have to concede to other demands. It became necessary for Chinese doctors to gain credibility for their craft by making it scientific. This was more difficult than early enthusiasts anticipated since science was understood to be secular. How could a doctor of National medicine prove his practice was not tainted by religion when his very precepts were rooted in Chinese religiosity? If the human body was a microcosm of the cosmos, animated by the same psychophysical stuff called *qi*, and a participant in the sacred network that tied Heaven, Earth, and Human Beings together in a dynamic relationship of co-creation, how was that going to be expressed in materialist terms?[27] The need to speak in naturalistic language was not going to be easy.

Chinese doctors tried several things as they worked to modernize their image. Some claimed science helped them shed the superstitious accretions that had made Chinese medicine the unstable alloy people despised. This allowed doctors to pick and choose ideas from ancient medical texts. Others tried to reinterpret their medical work in modern language. *Yin* and *yang*, one doctor suggested, referred to positive and negative electrical charges.[28] He argued that Chinese medicine was already scientific—one just needed to see the modern ideas beneath those allegorized in the historic medical textbooks. Others conceded that Chinese medicine was not scientific, but Chinese drugs were.[29] Soon, however, that argument, too, ran into difficulties as "[m]agic and ritual play[ed] too large a role in drug formulas to ignore."[30]

In the end, regardless of the method by which Chinese doctors tried to align their practices with science, all of them worked together

[27] Linda L. Barnes, *Needles, Herbs, Gods and Ghosts: China, Healing, and the West to 1848* (Cambridge, Mass.: Harvard University Press, 2005), 4.

[28] Crozier, *Traditional Medicine in Modern China*, 97.

[29] Crozier, *Traditional Medicine in Modern China*, 84–86, 125.

[30] William C. Cooper and Nathan Sivin, "Man as Medicine: Pharmacological and Ritual Aspects of Traditional Therapy Using Drugs Derived from the Human Body," in *Chinese Science: Explorations of an Ancient Tradition*, ed. Shigeru Nakayama and Nathan Sivin (Cambridge, Mass.: MIT Press, 1973), 206.

to standardize, unify, and secularize their field. Before the twentieth century, multiple healing traditions could have been described as Chinese medicine. The INM, however, symbolized the push to limit Chinese medical pluralism. Traditional medical textbooks were edited to suppress contradictions that led to divergent practices.[31] More importantly, they also removed the multiple and lengthy passages concerned with "external" imbalances: sicknesses caused by spirits, fate, or other supernatural powers. Instead, textbooks concerned themselves with how to redress the "internal" imbalances which surfaced as seasons changed, people aged, food intake varied, and the like. The important thing in terms of gaining their own political allies was that National medicine excluded ideas that might sound religious or, worse, superstitious.

By creating the illusion of a Chinese medicine that had a well-defined and secular theory of health that was easily put into practice, National medicine appeared modern. Its proponents could now argue that it, rather than biomedicine, had the unique capacity to produce the New Body that the government pursued so obsessively. The state, caught between convincing advocates from both sides, finally acquiesced to having two very different medical systems operate in China.

MEDICAL ALTERNATIVES

Although both Western medicine and the freshly secularized National medicine emerged as winners in the contest to make China's New Body, that did not mean there were no losers. The state had little tolerance for health practices that reached beyond a strict materialism. It opposed systems that accounted for "external" imbalances or supernatural forces. It had to; it was a matter of state security. The continuation of old practices would only produce the same old bodies that had left China weak in the first place. Officials argued that the nation needed something new and better than religious healing, which had been the most dominant medical system in China for millennia.[32] It was time to rethink Daoist priests, who were described as "physicians and dispensers of medicines."[33] It

[31] Andrews, "Republic of China," 222.

[32] Paul U. Unschuld, *Medicine in China: A History of Ideas* (Berkeley: University of California Press, 1985), 216.

[33] J. J. M. de Groot, *The Religious System of China: Its Ancient Forms, Evolution, History and Present Aspect, Manners, Custom and Social Institutions Connected Therewith* (1892–1897; repr., Taipei: Ch'eng Wen, 1969), 1165.

was important to sever the link that drew doctors and pharmacies to temple sites.[34] Worshippers, of whom 95 percent prayed for the healing of a disease, needed to be turned from the temple to the hospital.[35] The state wanted citizens to make new and modern medical choices.

That became especially urgent after Japan muscled past Chinese troops and seized control of all Manchuria in 1931–1932. China was weak. The state produced songs and printed propaganda that blamed geomancers, fortune-tellers, and healing-ritual specialists. They were responsible for China's miserable bodies. What began as criticism later turned to suppression. The state's ambitious Hygiene Movement targeted religious professionals who performed healing services and dispensed supernatural medicines. They were labeled as peddlers of superstition and, therefore, enemies of the state. The Guomindang also passed laws against "divination, geomancy, mediumistic ritual, folk healing, and even the use of spirit money and firecrackers."[36] It became illegal to improve the body through supernatural channels.

Yet for all the money and effort put into propaganda, the weak state's declaration of war against religious healing was a statement of intent rather than fact. It had little power to counter the multiple healing options that thrived in what became a gray market of healing.[37] Bone-setter shops persisted; family potions and other do-it-yourself techniques remained popular. Acupuncture flourished after adopting Western anatomy in the 1930s. Quackery proliferated, and shamans continued to draw crowds. In cities where the state operated medical facilities open to the public, officials groused, "[W]hen people are sick or have some matter they cannot figure out, they go to diviners or those who understand the spirits, and make their decisions through prayer, consulting

---

[34] John Shyrock, *The Temples of Anking and Their Cults: A Study of Chinese Religion* (Paris: Librairie Orientaliste Paul Geuthner, 1931), 127.

[35] C. K. Yang, *Religion in Chinese Society: A Study of Contemporary Social Functions of Religion and Some of Their Historical Factors* (Berkeley: University of California Press, 1961), 15.

[36] Rebecca Nedostup, *Superstitious Regimes: Religion and the Politics of Chinese Modernity* (Cambridge, Mass.: Harvard University Press, 2009), 194.

[37] For example, virtually no religious healer was arrested during the state's campaigns to eliminate religious healing, save a handful of charismatic figures who had become fabulously rich through their services. Nedostup, *Superstitious Regimes*, 218.

divination sticks, fortune reading, or diagramming characters."[38] Despite the state's efforts to neutralize religious healing, all kinds of illicit techniques persisted. Presumably, patients wanted something secularized medicine could never offer: a divine cure.

DIVINE HEALING

Song Shangjie's healing ministry emerged in and capitalized on the medical matrix of the 1930s. His work was something of a hybrid. On the one hand, it looked like a medical alternative: a religious practice that filled the void that was created when the state decided only to sanction medical systems that were avowedly secular. In particular his services converged with those of serious gray-market players, temple shamans. Shamans were ritual specialists who channeled deities while in a trance. They claimed that they were not the ones at work in healing encounters; the gods borrowed them. When a heavenly spirit would take control of their bodies, shamans would breathe heavily and jump around rhythmically.[39] Song did the same. In fact, when asked why he jumped around during his revival meetings, Song explained, "When I preach it is not really I who preach, but God's Spirit who manifests himself through my body."[40] In the same way, when he laid his hands on people, he believed he was not to be the agent of healing. "I am nothing more than a piece of wood," Song wrote in his journal. "God's power borrows me to make itself manifest."[41]

Like shamans, Song also relied on talismans. In the temple setting, a charm was an edict written down by the possessed shaman that commanded the afflicting spirit to leave the sick person alone. It was the command of a greater god over a lesser.[42] Song used the Bible in similar ways. He would recite Scripture because the word of God had authority

---

[38] Nedostup, *Superstitious Regimes*, 219, quoting from "*Haimen fengsu diaocha* [*Haimen County Customs Survey*]," 1935, Second Historical Archive 12(6): 18261.

[39] Emily M. Ahern, *Chinese Ritual and Politics* (Cambridge: Cambridge University Press, 1981), 49.

[40] Song Shangjie, *Peilingji* [*Devotional Messages*] (1935; repr., Hong Kong: Bellman House, n.d.), 31.

[41] Song Shangjie, December 10, 1931, Song Shangjie Diaries, Trinity Theological College, Singapore. Henceforth this location will be referred to as SSD, TTC.

[42] Ahern, *Chinese Ritual and Politics*, 24; Emily M. Ahern, "Sacred and Secular Medicine in a Taiwan Village: A Study of Cosmological Disorders," in *Culture and Healing in Asian Societies: Anthropological, Psychiatric and Public Health Studies*, ed. Arther Kleinman et al. (Cambridge, Mass.: Schenkman Publishing, 1978), 33.

over sin, sickness, and evil spirits. He also promoted the Bible as a sacred book imbued with special power. Traditionally, Daoist and Buddhist texts were used in homes to ward off evil, but the Bible could do even more.[43] In a sermon on the woman who was healed after bleeding for twelve years, Song explained to those assembled, "If you want your issue of blood to be healed you must touch Jesus' garment every day. . . . Jesus' garment is the Bible. Just as power went out of Jesus when the woman touched him, so if we read the Bible every day, Jesus' power is able to flow into our bodies."[44] Song promoted Scripture as religiously potent and bodily efficacious.

In addition, Song's healing ministry was a public event. He worked before an audience just as shamans operated before family, friends, and curious onlookers.[45] Even when people sought Song's help before or after a service, he usually had seekers cluster together in groups. Divine healing was not hidden in private examination rooms, but was a social event that welcomed spectators. In key ways Song behaved like a traditional religious healer.

He often thought like one too. Crowds were welcome at a healing ceremony because Song treated illness primarily as a social rather than a biological reality. Family conflicts, financial difficulties, personal loss, and the like were at the root of disease. It was paramount, therefore, to treat the person rather than the pathogen.[46] This outlook meant Song and shamans took sin seriously. The presence of sickness was indicative of some moral failing. Modern biomedicine criticized such an idea for creating a "blame culture of illness."[47] Many people in China, however, found the idea that sin caused sickness preferable to Western medicine's externalization of the cause.[48] To think that illness struck because of the inhalation of germs or bacteria reduced sickness to chance. It deprived patients of the opportunity to find a reason for and a meaning in their

[43] Michel Stickmann, *Chinese Magical Medicine*, ed. Barnard Faure (Stanford: Stanford University Press, 2002), 187, 96.

[44] Song Shangjie, "Zhiyao yangwang yesu [Just Look to Jesus]," as recorded by Xiao Liangtong, November 8, 1933, in Changsha, *Budao zazhi* [*Evangelism*] 7, no. 1 (January–February 1934): 9.

[45] Arthur Kleinman, *Patients and Healers in the Context of Culture: An Exploration of the Borderland between Anthropology, Medicine, and Psychiatry* (Berkeley: University of California Press, 1980), 220.

[46] Kleinman, *Patients and Healers in the Context of Culture*, 240.

[47] Stickmann, *Chinese Magical Medicine*, 2.

[48] Stickmann, *Chinese Magical Medicine*, 2.

suffering. Thus, most Chinese people continued to hold to traditional messages captured in *shanshu*, ubiquitous books on moral improvement that were passed out for free by those wanting to acquire merit. "Misfortune or good luck have no need for doors—man himself calls them in. The rewards for good and bad are like the shadow which follows the object."[49] The belief in the causal connection between sin and sickness rarely created such thorough consistency as to send those with common temporary ailments on a quest to purify their souls. It did mean, however, that when a particularly painful or intractable illness brought a person low, he or she could explain it and pursue a religious solution—just as gray-market actors like Song and shamans said.

It takes little imagination to see how Song looked and sounded like other religious healers in China in the 1930s. His performance was like a shaman's.[50] On the other hand, his purpose was more like the state's. Song did not set out to restore a sick body to the way it was, but to transform it. He wanted more than to make someone better; he wanted to make a person New. It is no coincidence that Song's healing ministry began while he was in Manchuria during the Japanese invasion of 1931, the precise moment when government officials threw up their collective hands in exasperation and desperation.[51] Chinese bodies had to be remade. More of the same would never do. Song understood that, and he challenged audiences to pursue a complete reconstitution. It was ridiculous to settle for a return to normal. Later he likened such an act to the folly of a woman who hoped Song would ease her suffering. Song delivered her from her affliction; however, because the lady did not change her entire life, her poor condition not only returned but

---

[49] Wolfram Eberhard, *Guilt and Sin in Traditional China* (Berkeley: University of California Press, 1967), 14.

[50] For more on this, see Lian Xi, *Redeemed by Fire: The Rise of Popular Christianity in Modern China* (New Haven: Yale University Press, 2010).

[51] Like with so much, the beginning of Song's healing ministry has been obscured by his own self-promotion. He dated the beginning of his healing services to December 10, 1931, some weeks after he left Manchuria. It was a convenient date, as on that evening Song performed one of his most dramatic and well-documented healings of a crippled woman. However, closer inspection of his diaries reveals that he was seeking the gift of healing in April 1931 and then began praying for people to experience divine healing on his tour through Manchuria in September 1931. See Daryl R. Ireland, "John Sung: Christian Revitalization in China and Southeast Asia" (Ph.D. diss., Boston University, 2015), 297–300.

worsened.[52] Divine healing would never settle for restoring the status quo, Song explained. Its purpose was to produce new creations. The government imagined these new people as stronger than their political or military opponents. Song pictured them as witnesses. Their new bodies testified to what he preached: God delivers a person wholly.

THE PROMISE OF A NEW BODY

Cultural, political, and commercial forces converged in the 1930s to put extraordinary emphasis on the human body in China's cities. Whether one used athletic programs, hypodermic needles, or applied creams, lotions, and toothpastes, the message was clear: the human body could and should be improved. Health and beauty were available if one used the right technique.

Certain Christian ideas compounded the pressure and promise that China's millions have a New Body. Chinese Protestants generally accepted the veracity of miraculous cures in the Bible and presumed God could do the same for them.[53] But the Bethel Mission, with whom Song was associated when his healing ministry began, went further. The people of Bethel were not content with the possibility that someone could be healed; they promoted everyone should be healed. Jennie Hughes, the co-founder of Bethel, was deeply embedded in the American Holiness movement, where her father, George Hughes, was the editor of the popular Holiness periodical *Guide to Holiness*.[54] The magazine was one of the foremost organs for working out a theology of divine healing in the early twentieth century and for publicizing accounts of miraculous cures. The concept occupied a significant amount of space in the periodical, appearing in essays on the subject and even more commonly as personal testimonies.[55] Before leaving for China, Jennie Hughes had worked for the *Guide to Holiness*, and when she opened the Bethel Mission she started her own version, *Shengjie zhinan* [*Guide to Holiness*]. Her popular magazine was no less committed to insisting on the importance of

[52] See, for example, Song, *Forty John Sung Revival Sermons*, 2:78.

[53] Melissa Wei-Tsing Inouye, "Miraculous Mundane: The True Jesus Church and Chinese Christianity in the Twentieth Century" (Ph.D. diss., Harvard University, 2011).

[54] "Personals," *Christian Advocate* 84, no. 37 (September 16, 1909): 1478.

[55] Harold Y. Vanderpool, "The Wesleyan-Methodist Tradition," in *Caring and Curing: Health and Medicine in the Western Religious Traditions*, ed. Ronald L. Numbers and Darrel W. Amundsen (New York: Macmillan, 1986), 318.

divine healing for China. For whenever Bethel spoke, whether through its magazine or the Bethel Worldwide Evangelistic Band (BWEB), it would always deliver the whole gospel: the good news that Christ's atonement dealt definitively with sin and also with sickness.[56]

That did not mean medicine had no place in the Christian life. After all, Hughes' closest friend and co-founder of Bethel was Shi Meiyu [Mary Stone], a medical doctor. Hughes took pride in Bethel's hospital and nursing school. Nonetheless, she also fully believed in divine healing. Reformation arguments that miracles had ceased after the apostolic era held no interest for her or other Holiness people. To them the Spirit who inaugurated the apostolic era was the selfsame Spirit who now animated their hearts. What amazing things God did in the past, God was still doing now.

Pentecostals temporarily led Song to associate God's transformative presence with speaking in tongues. The Bethel Mission, however, caused him to conclude that the foremost demonstration of God's stupendous power was not babbling and infantile sounds but the miracle of entire sanctification.[57] The Pilgrim Holiness Church, whose general superintendent ordained Jennie Hughes and Shi Meiyu [Mary Stone] in Shanghai in 1926, defined entire sanctification as a second work of divine grace that was instantaneous, and it was God's way of "cleansing the heart of the recipient from all sin, setting him apart and enduing him with power for the successful accomplishment of all to which he is called."[58] Such a

---

[56] "Bentuan xuanyan," *Shengjie zhinan yuekan* [*Guide to Holiness*] 3, no. 4 (April 1931): 9.

[57] Song had at least three experiences that he described as losing control of his lips and speaking in another language. However, when asked about speaking in tongues, he took a traditional Holiness position: the fruit of the Spirit is more important than the gift of the Spirit. Love is primary; speaking in tongues is secondary and, therefore, unnecessary. See Song Tianzhen (Levi), ed., *Shi'er fude de riji* [*The Journal Once Lost*] (Kowloon, Hong Kong: China Alliance Press, 2006), 209.

[58] *Manual of the Pilgrim Holiness Church* (Easton, Md.: Easton Publishing, 1926), 15. The *Bethel Newsletter*, 1951, Biographical Files, "Jennie Hughes," General Commission on Archives and History, United Methodist Church, Madison, N. J. (hereafter referred to as UMC), reported that Jennie Hughes and Mary Stone were ordained by Seth Rees in Shanghai in 1926. Rees was a newly elected general superintendent of the Pilgrim Holiness Church. Rees had extensive connections to the Holiness movement and was something of a representative of its multiple forms. He became popular at Holiness camp meetings as a Quaker revivalist. Later, Rees promoted the more radical Holiness message of his friend and colleague Martin Wells Knapp as they cofounded the International Holiness Union

description of inward purity and power inevitably caused people to seek external signs of the sanctifying grace. What would Christian perfection look like in the world? "Stringent behavioral norms," Jonathan Baer concluded, "provided the main way for the holy to enact and guard their purity."[59] Modest and simple clothes, strict observance of the Lord's Day, avoidance of card playing, and complete abstinence from polluting substances like alcohol and tobacco headed the list. An additional sign of total inward healing from sin was evinced in a healthy body.[60] A pure heart and a pure body went together.[61] That was where Hughes' openness both to human agency and divine healing came together. One Holiness leader of the time expressed it thus: "God made no distinction between healing with or without means."[62] It did not matter how it happened, whether it came through a doctor or a prayer. What was critical was that God wanted a holy person well. That message stamped Song's ministry with a distinctive imprint. Holy people were to be healthy people, and he was the agent through which God would produce both.

Some people recognized this as a departure from Song's earliest years of ministry. The London Missionary Society (LMS) missionary F. E. Reynolds, who heard Song preach in 1929, for example, lamented that when he heard him again in 1935, physical healing now competed with the spoken word.[63] Song, however, saw healing as the logical extension of his

---

and Prayer League. After he departed from Cincinnati where he worked with Knapp, Rees joined the Church of the Nazarene. Not long thereafter, though, the fledgling denomination expelled him. Rees started his own Pilgrim Temple, which he eventually led into the International Holiness Church (the child of his earlier work with Knapp). In the merger, the new denomination took the Pilgrim Holiness Church as its moniker.

[59] Jonathan R. Baer, "Perfectly Empowered Bodies: Divine Healing in Modernizing America" (Ph.D. diss., Yale University, 2002), 175.

[60] Baer, "Perfectly Empowered Bodies," 185.

[61] See, for example, Jennie Hughes, ed., *Bethel Heart Throbs of Revival* (Shanghai: Bethel Mission, 1931), 72; Andrew Gih, *Launch Out into the Deep! Tales of Revival through China's Famous Bethel Evangelistic Bands and Further Messages* (London: Marshall, Morgan & Scott, 1938), 36, 42.

[62] J. B. Chapman, *With Chapman at Camp Meeting: Sermons Preached by J. B. Chapman at Camp Meeting* (Kansas City, Mo.: Beacon Hill Press, 1961), 19.

[63] Reynolds was not the only one to object to the introduction of healing. Stanley Carson, a Methodist missionary in Xinghua [Hinghwa], lamented that when Song returned home after traveling around China and Southeast Asia for seven years, it was obvious that his healing ministry had come to overshadow more "spiritual matters." Jeanette Veldman, a missionary in Xiamen, Fujian, regretted the damage Song's healing services did to those who were not cured. She recalled the pain of a mother who left his

work. The Lord "called me to preach, heal, and drive out spirits every-where," he told his audiences.[64] They were all of one cloth. Song never approached healing or praying for the possessed as if they were add-ons to his preaching ministry. "If what you preach is true," he explained, "it will be evidenced with miracles."[65] Divine healings were not a distraction from or a corruption of his preaching ministry; they were its confirmation—the fulfillment of God's promise to make all things New.

A THEOLOGY OF HEALING

A New Body did not come without a price. It could only happen if a person "has faith and is willing to confess his sins, to ask for forgive-ness, then that person's sickness will be made better."[66] There was no reversing the order. In other parts of the world, and even in China, many people used healing as a way to prompt a conversion.[67] For them heal-ing was evangelistic. After someone was healed, he or she was likely to convert to Christianity. Song rejected that idea. Health sprang out of holiness, not the other way around.

---

healing service crying. Her baby was not made well, and she could do nothing more than lash herself with the question, "Am I lacking faith?" Elizabeth Brewster, the mis-sionary who had responsibility for Song and his evangelistic work in Xinghua when he first returned from the United States, criticized Song for that very reason. "Some have lost their faith in their disappointment," she grieved. "I wish he had not added healing to his wonderful preaching ministry." In her mind, it was not an essential component of his call to preach the gospel, but an undesirable and harmful "tangent." See F. E. Reynolds, LMS Annual Report, 1935, Council for World Mission Archives, Fukien Reports, box 1-6 (H-2137), Zug. 1978, box 5, 1908–1939, no. 362, Hong Kong Baptist University, Hong Kong; Stanley Carson to Frank Cartwright, Octo-ber 28, 1937, United Methodist Church (U.S.), *Missionary File: Methodist Church, 1912–1949*, Hinghwa, Carson, F. S. (continued) to Cole, W. B. (Wilmington, Del.: Scholarly Resources, 1999), roll 74; Jeannette Veldman, "To God Be the Glory," Western Theological Seminary, W89–102, Veldman, Jeannette (1901–1994), Papers, 1912–1989, Joint Archives of Holland, Holland, Mich.; Eva M. Brewster, *Her Name Was Elizabeth*, unpublished manuscript, China Records Project Miscellaneous Per-sonal Papers Collection, record group 8, box 28, file 13, YDSL.

[64] Song Shangjie, *Fenxingji [Revival Messages]*, 6th ed. (1935; repr., Hong Kong: Bellman House, 1989), 8.

[65] Song, *Forty John Sung Revival Sermons*, 1:124.

[66] Song, *Fenxingji [Revival Messages]*, 72.

[67] Gotthard Oblau, "Divine Healing and the Growth of Practical Christianity in China," in *Global Pentecostal and Charismatic Healing*, ed. Candy Gunther Brown (Oxford: Oxford University Press, 2011).

To say otherwise was to peddle a "heal-the-outside" gospel. "The modern, so-called famous leaders of the church," Song bitterly observed, "were consumed with building hospitals, education programs, and negotiating church unions."[68] Such programs were doomed to failure, for they tried to work from the outside in. Song insisted that "healing the outside is not as important as healing the inside."[69] Freeing a body from sickness was temporary and superficial if it did not come as the result of a freed soul.

He tried to illustrate the point. One time he was confused and then dismayed by the answer a young woman gave to the most important question she would ever be asked in her life: Have you been born again? She replied, "I had a stomach ache once. I prayed and got well again."[70] A ludicrous response, he told people. The girl had been tricked into thinking that a mended body meant she had a mended soul, that a nice outside meant everything was well inside.

Song protested vehemently, probably because the girl's logic was a distorted version of his own. Whereas she imagined that a healthy body was a sign of a healthy spirit, Song taught that it was a sick body that was the sign of a sick spirit. Health, by itself, had no clear meaning. Sickness, on the other hand, was always symptomatic of something sinister. He said it bluntly: "You should know, no matter what kind of sickness you have, it comes from sin! If you have sin, you have sickness. No sin, no sickness!"[71] In all of history, Song only knew of two people who were exceptions to that rule: Job and the man who was born blind in order to show forth God's glory when Jesus healed him (John 9). In all other cases, sickness was the result of unresolved sin.[72] It became his primary objective, therefore, to help people deal decisively with the sin in their inner lives, having them expunge it through confession at one of his regular revival services, in personal interviews, or during a special

[68] Song Shangjie, "Make di'erzhang [Mark Chapter Two]," as recorded by Chen Zhenfan, *Shengjie zhinan yuekan* [*Guide to Holiness*] 3, no. 9 (September 1931): 19.

[69] Shangjie, "Make di'erzhang [Mark Chapter Two]," 19.

[70] Song, *Forty John Sung Revival Sermons*, 1:52.

[71] Song Shangjie, "Xiangwo chuilingqi [May the Spirit Breathe on Me]," as recorded by Zhao Aiguang, *Budao zazhi* [*Evangelism*] 8, no. 3 (May–June 1935): 1; Song, *Fenxingji* [*Revival Messages*], 72.

[72] See, for example, Song, Shangjie, April 14, 1934, SSD, TTC; Song, *Forty John Sung Revival Sermons*, 1:89, 129; Song, *Forty John Sung Revival Sermons*, 2:7–8; Song Shangjie, *Wode jianzheng* [*My Testimony*] (1933; repr., Hong Kong: Bellman House, 1991), 108–9.

healing service. Anything less, any attempt to relieve a person's external pain while not eliminating the source, would be an empty gesture.

The good news that Song held out was that God promised so much more than temporary physical relief. The death and resurrection of Jesus was the double cure for the soul and the body. "Jesus does not only conquer when sin has made our *spirit* ill," Song rejoiced with his audience: "[h]e also conquered over the weakness and misery of the *body*."[73] Christ's death dealt with sin—the root of the problem—and therefore with sickness. Christ's atonement secured salvation and health, but the New Body always came in that order.

THE PRACTICE OF HEALING

Everything hung on confession. In the penultimate or last service in a city, Song would usually preach on sin and sickness and then explain Mark 16:17-18 and James 5:14-15. The verses from Mark reminded the audience that God promised to heal the sick as a sign to those who believed the gospel. The passage from James outlined the biblical conditions for healing: the presence of the elders of the church (which Song identified as himself), prayer, anointing the sick person with oil, and confession.[74] Prayers for healing would come to nothing, Song emphasized, if people did not first name their errant behaviors so that Jesus could remove the sins that were obstructing God's healing power.

Before he would pray for anyone, Song slowed the service down. An appropriate chorus, such as "*shizijia, shizijia* ["The Cross, the Cross"]," would be sung collectively—sometimes for thirty minutes.[75] By repeating the song's simple message about how a person could be completely cleansed from sin, the mind of the audience became fixed on the awful medium by which God defeated the power of sin and sickness.[76] Then, at the climax of the service, those assembled were told to pray simultaneously, fervently and out loud, verbalizing their sins.[77] The eradication of sin had to precede the eradication of sickness. In the minutes that followed, a rumble of voices would fill the sanctuary, as supplicants pled, cried, and sometimes shouted for mercy. The vehemence of the prayers

---

[73] Baarbé, *Dr Sung, een Reveil op Java*, 37 (italics original).
[74] Baarbé, *Dr Sung, een Reveil op Java*, 36.
[75] F. E. Reynolds, LMS Annual Report, 1935.
[76] F. E. Reynolds, LMS Annual Report, 1935.
[77] Song, *Forty John Sung Revival Sermons*, 2:48.

could be unsettling, but as the roar of confession descended from its crescendo, a deep stillness settled on the assembly.[78]

In the quietness, Song would kneel on the platform facing the audience. He required those who wanted to come for healing to write down their name, address, and particular affliction. An assistant would read out the name of a sick person from the stack of cards collected. When a person's name was called, he or she would go—or be carried—up to the platform and kneel before Song. He would then pour oil into his hand and usually rub it over the sick person's forehead, though some observers noted he occasionally smacked the side of the person's head with his oiled palm. Song then prayed, frequently quoting a verse from the Bible, and commanded the illness to leave "In Jesus' name!" When he finished, the person before him moved off the platform, and the next name was announced.[79]

These services took hours, as three to four hundred people commonly waited for God to renew their health and strength. Those hundreds of people, though, represented but a portion of seekers who visited Song for healing. Many, perhaps even the majority, sought God's miraculous intervention during personal interviews with the evangelist. Although it was extraordinarily taxing to lead a service for two hours in the morning, speak personally with scores of people, and then repeat the process again in the afternoon and evening, Song encouraged it. Whenever he concluded a revival service, he dismissed the people with the rather curt announcement: "The meeting is over." He added, though, "Those who are troubled in heart stay and I will pray for [you]."[80]

The people who lingered behind for personal interviews usually sought healing. Song placed just as much emphasis on confession in those conversations as he had in the public assembly. In Beijing, for instance, Song led those who wanted an audience with him to the

---

[78] F. E. Reynolds, LMS Annual Report, 1935. Reynolds found the individual prayers uttered collectively to be extremely unnerving. He felt "the practice of all kneeling at the same time and praying loudly in their own words in a frenzied manner [was] calculated to completely unbalance the mentally weak."

[79] S. A. van Hoogstraten, "Dr John Sung in Soerabaia," De Opwekker 84, no. 10 (October 1939): 548.

[80] Lily N. Duryee, "Dr. Sung's Revival Meetings in Amoy Feb-March 1935," Western Theological Seminary, W88–0315, China Mission, Papers, 1888–1979, Joint Archives of Holland, Holland, Mich.

neighboring home of James Leynse, a Presbyterian missionary. In a letter to his friends, Leynse described what ensued:

> Between meetings our living room, dining room, hall, study—even upstairs bedrooms were converted into sanctuaries where burdened souls knelt to find salvation. Humphrey and Wally, back from the school, wandered sometimes in awe among those who wept and pled while waiting for a personal interview.[81]

When the wait was over and a person was called to speak to Song for about fifteen minutes, Song always ensured that he helped his visitor "thoroughly repent."[82] For men these confessions were usually a catalogue of vices. Li Qisheng, for instance, told Song that he smoked, gambled, went to shows, and visited prostitutes. Once he had named all his misdeeds, Song prayed for his physical healing.[83] Most women took a broader approach. They not only confessed their sins to Song, but situated them amidst the struggles of their lives. Wang Wangming, for example, told Song that she had stolen, but also how she had borrowed money, and that her husband was dead. Song dealt with her bad foot the same as he did all the others: he laid his hands on her and prayed.[84]

The way Song let his patients name their problems—whether in the assembly hall or in a personal interview—inverted the common medical encounter. Doctors of National medicine were supposed to be able to tell a patient what was wrong by taking his or her pulse and maybe looking at the tongue.[85] Physicians trained in biomedicine were to be the experts on disease. They might ask a few questions to understand the symptoms, but they determined what was wrong.[86] Divine diagnoses from shamans were little different, for who on earth can challenge insights revealed from heaven? Medical encounters in China ensured that someone other

---

[81] James P. Leynse to Friends, Christmas 1932, China Records, record group 8, box 115, folder 6, YDSL.

[82] Donald MacInnis, "Will Schubert," Donald MacInnis Papers, record group 204, box 8, folder 89, YDSL; Song's journal entries frequently used the language that he helped people "thoroughly repent." While he was in Tianjin, for instance, it was a common refrain virtually every day. Song Shangjie, SSD, TTC, April 11–27, 1934.

[83] Song Shangjie, April 27, 1934, SSD, TTC.

[84] Song Shangjie, April 17, 1934, SSD, TTC.

[85] Kleinman, *Patients and Healers in the Context of Culture*, 279.

[86] Andrew Cunningham and Bridie Andrews, eds., *Western Medicine as Contested Knowledge* (Manchester: Manchester University Press, 1997), 6.

than the patient always defined the illness. Song, by contrast, allowed each person to name his or her own affliction. Whether writing the name of their sickness on a card, or sharing the general struggles of their lives in an interview with Song, his patients determined what they suffered from. He gave them power in the healing process and granted them freedom to conceive of their sickness however they pleased.

The multiple cases of tuberculosis that Song faced are instructive on this point. Tuberculosis was a slippery concept in Chinese. The first Western doctor to translate biomedical ideas into Chinese worked before the bacteria that caused tuberculosis were identified. When he translated "consumption," he selected the word *lao* from the Chinese medical vocabulary, because the symptoms—coughs, shortness of breath, phlegm, fever, vomiting of blood, etc.—were similar to the indicators used to diagnose consumption. In Chinese medicine, however, *lao* was caused by malevolent spirits that fed on a person's heart and lungs. Japanese doctors, who were trained in Western biomedicine but who used Chinese characters, decided that the ideas associated with *lao* perpetuated superstition. After the discovery of the bacteria that caused tuberculosis, they coined a neologism, *feijiehe* [lung tubercule]. It was a sterile term, bereft of any ideas about evil spirits. It was also incomprehensible to patients. The upshot was that tuberculosis was problematic. If a doctor diagnosed the disease using the Japanese terminology, it was strictly scientific, but the words made no sense to Chinese patients. Alternatively, to use the ancient Chinese term could introduce unwanted associations with spirits or outdated ideas about consumption.[87]

Medical doctors may have struggled with this linguistic conundrum, but Song's approach completely sidestepped it. He allowed those who came to him to tell him what they had, and his journals show that they spoke of their lung diseases in a whole variety of terms. In one afternoon those who came for healing told Song they had *feibing* [lung sickness], *laobing* [wasting sickness], *laozheng* [consumption], *lao* [exhaustion], and *tuxie* [spitting blood].[88] All probably referred to tuberculosis, but Song recorded their self-diagnoses precisely as given to him. He did not try to convince them that, in fact, they suffered from *feijiehe*. He simply jotted down their own terms for their own illnesses. Whether his

[87] Andrews, "Tuberculosis and the Assimilation of Germ Theory in China," 114–57.

[88] Song Shangjie, April 28, 1934, SSD, TTC.

patients were thinking of consumption, an evil spirit, or bacteria made no difference to the revivalist. God, after all, could defeat every enemy.

Song demonstrated similar latitude when he dealt with evil spirits. He spoke of them frequently and prayed for people to be delivered of them regularly, but what precisely he meant by a demon, devil, or evil spirit was ambiguous. On the one hand, he sometimes displayed a secularizing tendency on the subject. Song suggested that demon possession in the Bible might be parallel to mental illness.[89] He had a penchant for speaking of evil spirits in figurative terms. He peppered his sermons with calls for people to be delivered from "the opium devil, the gambling devil, the adultery devil, the lying devil, etc."[90] Or, he could write in his journal, "This morning I cried and confessed my sins, and in that way drove off the evil spirit [of discouragement]."[91] When Song named the spirits, he often allegorized them according to behaviors or attitudes that worked against the purposes of God. On the other hand, Song also spoke of spirits as external agents who inflicted harm on people. One boy, he remembered, ran afoul of supernatural powers when he hacked off the hand of a temple god in his modernizing zeal. The young man was, in turn, afflicted with a crippled hand.[92] Song also took seriously the work of other ritual specialists. He believed they harnessed supernatural power when they interacted with gods, spirits, and magic formulas. Their problem was that to invoke the spirits was ultimately to become the subject of them. A woman Song knew in Fujian, for instance, used to make her living casting out demons until she herself was possessed by them.[93]

Regardless of whether he or his audience thought in secular or spiritual terms about spirits, demons, and devils, Song delivered a consistent message: God's power was at work in him to cast out all evil. Deliverance from the spirit of smoking and from the spirit of a deity occurred through the same process, or ritual, and it was used in all of Song's healing encounters. At any time during his revival campaign, a person could take the initiative and come to Song for help. He would ask the person to confess her sins and name her afflictions; Song then touched the sick or possessed person and prayed. In fact, Song used the same technique in

---

[89] Song Shangjie, "Yongyuan shifang [Eternally Set Free]," as recorded by Zhao Aiguang, *Budao zazhi* [*Evangelism*] 7, no. 3 (May–June 1934): 14.

[90] Song, *Peilingji* [*Devotional Messages*], 85.

[91] Song Shangjie, April 17, 1934, SSD, TTC.

[92] Song, *Wode jianzheng*, 26–27.

[93] Song, *Forty John Sung Revival Sermons*, 2:47–48.

every circumstance, no matter if a person came to him to be saved, filled with the Holy Spirit, healed, or delivered from a demon. "The Great Physician," as Song called Jesus, made people well.[94] The type of affliction did not matter. A person could define his trouble in whatever way made sense to him. The problem could be germs, spirits, bad attitudes, immoral behaviors, or devils. Whatever it was, Song's practice of healing invited people to be made whole in spirit and thereby restored in body.

THE NATURE OF DIVINE HEALING

Healings were often dramatic. A woman who had been paralyzed for eighteen years stood up after Song prayed for her. "She arose immediately and walked from the missionary's home where the prayer took place over to the church, and has been walking ever since," assured Southern Baptist missionary Mary Crawford.[95] A photo of Mrs. Loa, standing erect and unsupported, accompanied Crawford's report—visual proof that after two years of investigation, Loa's New Body was not a hoax or a temporary phenomenon inspired by psychological suggestion. Magazines, which provided the bulk of information about Song's healings, had less time and resources to confirm every miracle. They just reported the constant thread of news that followed Song wherever he went: withered hands were restored, congenital illnesses cured, skin diseases disappeared, and mute mouths opened.[96] Divine healing could be amazing.

Yet until the transformation was described as God's work, someone could chalk it up to spontaneous remission, potent magic, the natural course of the disease, or the like. In order for a cure to be connected to divine intervention, someone had to declare that it was God who made him, her, or another well. Paradoxical as it may seem, testimonies after the fact were required to create a miraculous healing. God had to be narrated into the story of a person's physical change. Song provided those opportunities by always setting apart time in his services for people to ascend the platform and give a brief word about their spiritual and physical healing. Whoever took that opportunity implicitly agreed with Song that the change in their body was due to a divine touch. Those who

[94] Song Shangjie, ed., *Quanguo jidutu budaotuan tuankan* [*National Christian Evangelistic League Publication*] (March 1936): 7.

[95] Mary K. Crawford, *The Shantung Revival* (Shanghai: China Baptist Publication Society, 1933), 57.

[96] Song, *Quanguo jidutu budaotuan tuankan* [*National Christian Evangelistic League Publication*].

were not saved or healed would have nothing to say; they did not bother to come forward. That meant that healing testimonies were uniformly positive, though they tended to move in one of three directions.

The first narrative of divine healing was the most awesome. Song always required a person's testimony to be brief, and only a few words were necessary for this type of witness. "As [Dr. Song] put his hands on me, I saw a red light follow his hands and come down. Six years of asthma was cured all at once."[97] Others even testified without words, since in the context of a divine healing service it was unnecessary to explain that God had done the miracle. One man, for example, simply pulled off his shirt in jubilation and allowed everyone to marvel that the giant carbuncle, which had protruded out from his belly, was gone.[98] Each person joyfully expressed what God had done in brief, idiosyncratic, and highly personal ways. Enthusiasm, even elation, can be heard in their words and pictured in their faces. Sickness had taken on a new meaning. It was no longer about loss, but about gain: God had been found at the point of their weakness.

The second type of testimony witnessed to a different kind of healing. The illness was not gone, persons admitted, but their suffering was now seen in a different light. For instance, a man with bad eyes did not recover his sight, but he did rejoice in his realization that he needed only his mouth to preach the gospel.[99] A terminal patient gave thanks for her ailment, because she had been able to use all the attention that was lavished on her as she approached death to lead her entire family to faith in Jesus Christ.[100] Or, in an extreme case, Song praised God even after a young woman died, because the deceased youth had appeared to her mother and classmate on a divine errand to spread the gospel.[101] Not everyone was healed, these testimonies acknowledged, but Song's services

---

[97] Song, *Quanguo jidutu budaotuan tuankan* [*National Christian Evangelistic League Publication*], 21.

[98] "Fujian Gutian Shenggong jie Meihui tongju dahui qianren mengen [The Episcopal and Methodist Churches of Gutian, Fujian Hold a Joint Revival wherein 1,000 People Receive Grace]," *Nanchang* [*Southern Bell*] 10, no. 5 (May 1937): 21.

[99] Song, *Forty John Sung Revival Sermons*, 1:152.

[100] Song Shangjie, "Zhude enai [The Lord's Grace and Love]," as recorded by Zhao Aiguang, *Budao zazhi* [*Evangelism*] 7, no. 4 (July–August 1934): 13.

[101] Song, *Forty John Sung Revival Sermons*, 1:59–60.

still offered audience members a way to rethink their losses so that they were not meaningless but part of a cosmic vision of redemption.[102]

The third way to respond was to muddle through an inconclusive cure. Hints of the ubiquity of this third type of response surfaced in the scores of generic reports that appeared in various Christian publications. One from 1937, for instance, declared, "Mr. Song rubbed oil on and prayed for 479 sick people. We truly saw God's great glory: 200–300 people received the Lord's amazing healing."[103] Two conclusions can be drawn from such a printed statement. First, not everyone was healed. A significant gap existed between those who sought healing and those who claimed to receive it. Second, divine healing was a very imprecise term.

The specific number of "479 sick people" stood in stark contrast to the vague "200–300 people" who received healing. Why was that? Most likely because it was difficult to determine if someone was truly made well. If a person was addicted to opium, did the fact that he did not crave it the next day, the day of the testimony service, signify that he was miraculously cured? It would be difficult to say. For one or two there was little doubt of divine intervention, so they became the focus of the reports. The man with the carbuncle that disappeared, the lame woman who walked, or the person whose obviously crooked spine was straightened headlined the papers. Less often one might find a reference to someone who found meaning in his or her continued state of ill health.[104] For everyone else it became necessary either to conclude that they were not healed or to push forward in hope that their body would eventually prove to be new.

Evidence suggests that most people who experienced uncertain healings, those in the loose "200–300" category, tried to put the best face on the vagueness of their physical transformation. They made their way onto the platform to give thanks to God, but unlike those who could describe what happened using their own words, this group of people

---

[102] Amanda Porterfield, *Healing in the History of Christianity* (Oxford: Oxford University Press, 2005), 4.

[103] "Fujian Gutian Shenggong jie Meihui tongju dahui qianren mengen [The Episcopal and Methodist Churches of Gutian, Fujian Hold a Joint Revival wherein 1,000 People Receive Grace]," 21.

[104] Song, *Quanguo jidutu budaotuan tuankan* [*National Christian Evangelistic League Publication*]; M. A. Alt, "De Boodschaap van Dr. John Sung: Impressies I [The Message of Dr. John Sung: Impressions I]," *Gouden Schoven* 12, no. 20 (October 15, 1939), 4–7.

tended to borrow language from the Bible. In one case a boy clutched to Song's suggestion that for a miracle to be made manifest a person must first testify in faith to God's healing touch. "I can see!" he therefore dutifully insisted after the healing service: "I can see [John 9:25]!" Evidence to the contrary did not dampen the vehemence with which he staked his claim nor the jubilation among the crowd. When the young man failed to identify how many fingers were held before his face or what objects were in someone's hands, those closest to him dismissed it. "People said that it was not remarkable that, never having seen, he could not identify objects."[105] Only after Song had left the city did the boy finally admit that he was trying to believe himself into seeing.

In another case someone borrowed biblical words to describe what happened to others. One missionary enthusiastically wrote home about Song's services in an article called "Blind Receives Sight, the Dumb Speaks [Matt 15:31]." Two girls, he reported, proved that Jesus still healed just "the same as in the Holy Land during Bible times."[106] A more sober colleague pointed out that the blind girl "did not have the best control of her eyes" and that the dumb girl "did not have perfect control over her voice."[107] So what was one to say in such cases? Were the girls healed? It was hard to say, so most people chose to superimpose biblical language on top of the ambiguity. It was a way to trust God, and it invited those yearning for a change to live into the promise that their bodies were new.

Song himself dealt with disappointment using similar techniques. When a woman died during a service, he tried to resurrect her based somewhat loosely on biblical precedent: "In the Name of Jesus Christ, I command you to arise [Acts 3:6]!" When repeated efforts failed to re-set the situation via a biblical phrase, he switched tactics. He confessed that, like the audience, he wanted the woman to live again. Indeed, his efforts brought her to the brink of returning to life—just ask those surrounding her how warm she had become during his heated prayers—but at the last moment her resuscitation was cut short because God had better

---

[105] C. Stanley Smith, "Modern Religious Movements," in *China Christian Year Book, 1934–1935*, ed. Frank Rawlinson (Shanghai: Christian Literature Society, 1935), 107–8.

[106] Leon C. Osborn, "God's Blessings at Fan Hsien," *The Other Sheep* 23, no. 3 (September 1935): 17.

[107] H. A. Wiese, "Blind Receives Sight, Dumb Speaks," *The Other Sheep* 23, no. 11 (May 1936): 21.

plans for her in heaven.[108] For those with ears to hear, Song was making a larger point about the ambiguous nature of divine healing: God's touch achieves its purpose, though sometimes it produces unexpected results.

SICK UNTO DEATH

A significant proportion of people did not receive what they asked for at Song's healing services, but his popularity as a religious healer never waned. In fact, as his fame spread, some missionaries worried that people were starting to come to his revivals for no other reason than to be healed.[109] Song recognized the shift, too, and tried to rebuff those who came for literally carnal reasons.[110] Still, day after day he met with those broken in body and distraught in spirit, taking time to lay his hands on up to 1,710 sick people in a single day.[111]

Drawing such enormous crowds eventually became impossible in China, for in July 1937 Japanese soldiers invaded eastern China from several entry points. As they raced inward they pushed Song's services further and further west, away from the urban centers where his revivals flourished. The Methodist periodical in Southeast Asia, *Southern Bell*, reported that Song was now "working in a war zone," though in reality he carefully avoided it.[112] He skipped from place to place, staying sometimes months and other times only weeks ahead of the invading Japanese forces.

Song managed to avoid the Japanese, but even in their absence the invading army was palpably present wherever he went. "Not a bomb has been dropped amongst us. But Fear—fear of the coming invasion from the Yangtze—has had the whole countryside in a fever of anxiety," wrote missionary Robert McClandiss from Huaiyuan, Anhui Province. "The people are moving homes and families and possessions from town to country and back again. Thousands have fled from the city to

---

[108] "Cora Martinson," Midwest China Oral History and Archives Collection (St. Paul, Minn.: Archives-Gullixson Hall, 1980), 77–78.

[109] Harry P. Boot to Dr. Potter, February 18, 1935, Western Theological Seminary, W88–0012, Boot, Harry P. (1874–1961), Papers, 1900–1954, Joint Archives of Holland, Holland, Michigan.

[110] Song, *Peilingji* [*Devotional Messages*], 1.

[111] Song Shangjie, *The Journal Once Lost—Extracts from the Diary of John Sung*, trans. Thng Pheng Soon (Singapore: Genesis Books, 2008), 284.

[112] *Southern Bell* 11, no. 3 (March 1938): 16–17.

escape bombing."[113] Although McClandiss wrote his letter right after Song's services in 1937, not a word about his revival or healing ministry was mentioned. Instead, McClandiss focused on the preparations for war. "Both of our middle schools are closed, and practically all the students and some of the faculty are gone. . . . Our shell-proof—and perhaps bomb-proof—underground shelter has been completed."[114] For the moment people were more concerned about saving the body than remaking it.

Cities were hard hit by the war. The Japanese purposely sought to control urban areas, even if by the time they occupied them many were empty shells. M. H. Box from the LMS explained that in Zhangzhou, Fujian, "all families in the city who could, moved away, either to Amoy, Hongkong, the Straits, or into the villages."[115] Hence, even when Song managed to visit a city before it was captured, the dynamics were totally different. Most had turned into ghost towns months before the first shells began to fall. "The city was practically empty, shops were closed, the streets deserted and Church services held for about twenty odd people in those churches which carried on," A. E. Lindsay reported in the spring of 1938.[116] It was impossible, under those conditions, to do mass evangelism or hold large-scale healing services.

Faced with bleak conditions in eastern and central China, Song finally went to the western frontier. He held services in Yunnan Province, where the non–Han Chinese ethnic groups predominated. He organized several revivals over the summer of 1938, but found little receptiveness to his message among Tibetans or the other minority groups that populated the rural region.[117] When he returned home to the French Concession in Shanghai in the fall of 1938, an islet of freedom in the midst of the Japanese occupation, Song decided he had seen enough. He

[113] Robert McClandiss, Christmas 1937, China Records Project Miscellaneous Personal Papers Collection, record group 8, box 366, YDSL.

[114] Robert McClandiss, Christmas 1937, China Records Project Miscellaneous Personal Papers Collection, record group 8, box 366, YDSL.

[115] M. H. Box, March 1938, Council for World Mission Archives, Fukien Reports, box 1-6 (H-2137), Zug. 1978, box 5, 1908–1939, no. 370, Hong Kong Baptist University, Hong Kong.

[116] A. E. Lindsay, Council for World Mission Archives, Fukien Reports, box no. 1-6 (H-2137), Zug. 1978, box 5, 1908–1939, no. 370, Hong Kong Baptist University, Hong Kong.

[117] Lyall, *Biography of John Sung*, 211.

concluded that he had to leave the mainland. Almost all the cities of the nation were in the hands of the Japanese.[118]

Thus, for the next sixteen months he spent his time in Southeast Asia. The decision was logical. Song had made periodic visits to the region earlier in his career, and the Chinese communities in Nanyang, or the South Seas, were an extension of mainland China in many imaginations. The Republic of China maintained seats in the Legislative Yuan for residents of Nanyang. Migrant workers as well as trade kept connections very much alive between China and Southeast Asia. And churches, although geographically separated, saw themselves as part of a single work. The Methodists, for example, celebrated the first century of Chinese Methodism (1847–1947) by writing about churches in both the mainland and Nanyang.[119] Similarly, Chinese churches organized by Dutch missionaries in the East Indies voted to join the Church of Christ in China, the largest denomination in the mainland.[120]

The shared imaginative space that linked the cities of the South Seas and urban China meant Song could resume his best work. He no longer had to flounder about, trying to energize China's rural inhabitants. In Bangkok, Kuala Lumpur, and Jakarta, he could speak once again to audiences eager to become New Men and New Women. Furthermore, in the wake of Japan's successes in the mainland, Song's promise of a New Body took on new urgency. In 1938 and 1939, audiences in Singapore, the Straits Settlements, Thailand, and the Dutch East Indies were desperate for transformation. Letters from missionaries, reports from pastors, and magazines reveled again and again in Song's miraculous cures and how "Pentecostal power and Miracles are not out of date in the age of Science."[121] Collectively, they left the impression of frenzied scenes as Song contended with the demand for physical healing.

---

[118] Peter Gue Zarrow, *China in War and Revolution, 1895–1949* (New York: Routledge, 2005), 310.

[119] Editorial Committee of the Centennial Celebration, *Zhonghua jidujiao weiligonghui baizhou jiniankan, 1847–1947* [*Methodist Centennial in China, 1847–1947*] (Foochow, Fukien, China: Editorial Committee of the Centennial Celebration, 1948).

[120] A. R. Kepler to H. A. C. Hildering, September 28, 1938, file 6493, Raad voor de zending (1102-2), Het Utrechts Archief, Utrecht, Netherlands; A. C. Hildering to the National Christian Council of China, October 29, 1939, file 6493, Raad voor de zending (1102-2), Het Utrechts Archief, Utrecht, Netherlands.

[121] Kru Sook to Mr. and Mrs. Landon via Margaret C. McCord [October 1938, Phet Burl, Thailand], SC/38 box 94, folder 9, Wheaton College Special Collections, Wheaton, Ill.

Even the Dutch Reformed missionaries, who tended to understate, were shocked by what they observed. The powerful and emotional responses Song stirred among people caused the careful linguist and cautious missiologist Hendrik Kraemer to shake his head in disbelief: "[This] cannot be done according to Oriental habits and opinions."[122] Yet crowds did push forward, eager to name their sins in public and thereby secure salvation and health. In a rising crescendo, Song performed services that led to the deaf hearing, the crippled walking, the blind receiving sight, and those on their death bed rising to new life.[123]

With such demonstrative displays of divine power, other pathways to a New Body appeared expensive, painful, slow, and redundant. That did not mean that medicine was bad. At least the numerous physicians trained in National medicine and Western biomedicine, who supported Song's ministry, never understood him to say such a thing.[124] It was just that their methods of healing were superseded. In Song's mind relying on human agents for healing was superfluous at best, a sign of faithlessness at worst. In one telling example, he rebuked a man who came to be healed of his poor eyesight. Right as Song stretched out his hands to anoint the supplicant with oil, he caught a glimpse of the man's glasses in his shirt pocket. He quickly withdrew his arms and rebuked the petitioner: "You should have thrown [your glasses] away if you really believed!"[125] Human medicine, in any of its various forms, was like those glasses. A person could use it as a crutch, but why limp along when God offered a complete transformation?

Song spoke as if what was happening in Nanyang was just the beginning. Could God not do the same the world over? He told churches in Vietnam that the Holy Spirit was urging him "to go to India, Africa and elsewhere to revive the Church of Jesus Christ and prepare her for

---

[122] Hendrik Kraemer, *Van Godsdiensten en Menschen* [*About Religions and People*] (Nijkerk, Netherlands: G. F. Callenbach, 1940), 179.

[123] Kraemer, *Van Godsdiensten en Menschen* [*About Religions and People*]; Mrs. D. I. Jeffrey, "Dr. John Sung," *Alliance Weekly* 73, no. 47 (November 19, 1938): 745; Alt, "De Boodschaap van Dr. John Sung: Impressies I [The Message of Dr. John Sung: Impressions I]," 4–7; Baarbé, *Dr Sung, een Reveil op Java*, 35–38.

[124] Twelve percent of those who joined the National Evangelistic League, which sprang out of Song's revivals, worked as dentists, pharmacists, nurses, doctors trained in Western biomedicine, or doctors trained in traditional Chinese medicine. See Song, *Quanguo jidutu budaotuan tuankan* [*National Christian Evangelistic League Publication*].

[125] Lyall, *Biography of John Sung*, 171.

the soon return of her Bridegroom."[126] But in reality, his ministry was already at the end.

Since his time in the United States, Song suffered from an anal fistula. He had received operations in America to address the problem, but it never really went away. The possibility of receiving additional treatment ceased when Song started his healing ministry for the sick. To ask for human aid, he maintained, would contradict his own message of divine healing. Instead, he put his efforts into following his own prescription. He furiously raked his own heart to uncover any unconfessed sins. He pled for mercy, admitting that he threw children out of his services if they were disruptive; he exaggerated whenever he told his testimony— "hoping that people would be saved"; his devotional times had become mechanical; he stole God's glory; he looked down on others and thought too highly of himself; and the donations he collected through his evangelizing had not been given to God as holy.[127]

When such thorough confessions still brought no relief, Song turned to self-care. He used a sharp stick to puncture the abscess that would form near his anus and thereby find some relief as the pus drained. He had become the living illustration from one of his own sermons. He was the woman who had bled for twelve years. Song understood what it felt like to have vitality literally "flowing out of you."[128] No matter how many times he reached out to Jesus or touched the Bible, he was not made well. He took to washing his underwear in the privacy of his own room. He dearly wanted to hide the soggy mess he peeled off after every service. His diligence in the matter may have hidden the blood, but he could not disguise the weakness. In December 1939, Song was so weak he preached lying down on a cot.

Days later he was laid on a steamship headed back to Shanghai. Song's career was over. The fistula had grown to be the width of a human fist and had carved a tunnel into his body a foot deep. Still, Song resisted medical intervention. It took the promise of friends that God had given them special revelations that he needed a doctor for Song to concede his body not only to the Lord, but also to physicians. For the last four years of his life, he received help from Western biomedicine, National medicine, six surgeries, the passing of time, and many prayers. None of

---

[126] Jeffrey, "Dr. John Sung," 745.
[127] Song Shangjie, February 12, 1940, SSD, TTC.
[128] Song, "Zhiyao yangwang yesu [Just Look to Jesus]," 9.

it reversed the course of his condition. Song died August 18, 1944; he was forty-two years old.

What lived on, however, was the offer that Song made to more Chinese people than any other person in the first half of the twentieth century. Anyone could have a New Body through repentance and faith in Jesus Christ. In large part due to his eight years of delivering divine cures, Christian healing squeezed into the crowded medical marketplace in China. It did not sweep the alternatives away. In fact, many—like Song himself—ultimately relied on biomedicine, National medicine, *gongfu*, or other medical practices. Sometimes prayer and pills were used simultaneously, and sometimes sequentially. That did not subtract from his innovative message or method. What was important was that Song bequeathed a new way of dealing with illness to China and Chinese communities in Southeast Asia. He was not the only Christian to practice divine healing, but since he more than anyone else transcended geographical boundaries and sectarian proclivities, it was his ministry which popularized it. Song offered people a way to possess a New Body, the kind which the government, commerce, and Christ so wanted China to have.

Conclusion

Modern Chinese Christianity

The Chinese Communist government has observed that the nation has a case of "Christianity fever."[1] On any given Sunday there are now more Protestants in church in China than in all of Europe, and there is no indication that the spread of the faith is contained.[2] On the contrary, according to the most conservative estimates more than one million Chinese people convert to Christianity ever year.[3]

This seems counterintuitive, of course. Christianity in China experienced a great shock in the middle of the twentieth century. The Communist victory in 1949 inaugurated a series of devastating setbacks. By 1950 virtually every missionary was gone. In the years immediately following, roughly twenty thousand Protestant churches and chapels were forcibly united under the Three-Self Patriotic Movement (TSPM), and the state closed many congregations due to redundancy. It reasoned that since the Methodist, Baptist, Presbyterian, Lutheran, Nazarene, and Mennonite churches were now duplicates of the TSPM it made no sense to have competing facilities.[4] Then in 1958, 90 percent of the churches that had

---

[1] Alan Hunter and Kim-Kwon Chan, *Protestantism in Contemporary China* (Cambridge: Cambridge University Press, 1993), 4.

[2] Daniel H. Bays, "Chinese Protestant Christianity Today," *China Quarterly* 174 (July 2003): 488.

[3] Katrin Fiedler, "China's 'Christianity Fever' Revisited: Towards a Community-Oriented Reading of Christian Conversions in China," *Journal of Current Chinese Affairs* 39, no. 4 (2010): 72.

[4] Roman Catholics were eventually merged into an organization known as the Catholic Patriotic Association in 1957. Both the Catholic hierarchy and the

survived the initial pruning were shuttered. By then the entire population needed to focus exclusively on making the Great Leap Forward into
an industrialized economy. The Cultural Revolution finished off what
little visible presence of Christianity remained in the country. Beginning
in 1966, the People's Liberation Army and the nation's youth ran amok
for a decade as they destroyed the four olds: old ideas, old culture, old
customs, and old habits. Down came the few remaining churches, those
signs of bygone days when foreigners exploited the superstitious masses,
and out went the Christians to labor camps, public-humiliation ceremo-
nies, and struggle sessions. Jiang Qing, Mao's wife and an instigator of
the Cultural Revolution, observed the cumulative destruction and pro-
nounced religion in China dead.

It turned out to be one of the great exaggerations of history. As the
suffocating restrictions on religion were eased at the end of the 1970s, it
became clear that Christianity had not only survived, but had not even
diminished in size. And since given a little breathing space, Christianity
has grown at an astonishing rate. Protestants have mushroomed from
one million in 1979 to approximately ninety million today.[5] The surge
in conversions has revealed one of the great surprises of the twentieth
century: religion is resilient.

Efforts to explain the extraordinary growth of Chinese Christianity have led scholars to identify several features that are central to its
durability and dynamism.[6] First, they observe, contemporary Chinese

---

fact that most Catholics were in rural areas where entire villages would often be
Catholic made the years following 1949 different for Catholics than for Protestants. What both groups shared in common were widespread closures or seizures
of property, heavy regulations, and periodic persecutions. For a brief history of
the Roman Catholics in Communist China, see Daniel H. Bays, *A New History of
Christianity in China* (Malden, Mass.: Wiley-Blackwell, 2012), 169–78.

[5] Todd M. Johnson and Gina A. Zurlo, *World Christian Encyclopedia*, 3rd ed.
(Edinburgh: Edinburgh University Press, 2019), 195. Protestants numbered one
million in 1949 and just over one million in 1979.

[6] Significant literature has been produced in the last twenty years on this topic,
examining both the registered and unregistered churches in China. See, for example, Wayne TenHarmsel, *China's Registered Churches: Flourishing in a Challenging Environment* (Eugene, Ore.: Wipf and Stock, forthcoming); Fenggang Yang,
Joy K. C. Tong, and Allan H. Anderson, *Global Chinese Pentecostal and Charismatic Christianity* (Leiden: Brill, 2017); Brent Fulton, *China's Urban Christians*
(Eugene, Ore.: Pickwick Books, 2015); Bays, *New History of Christianity in
China*; Lian Xi, *Redeemed by Fire: The Rise of Popular Christianity in Modern
China* (New Haven: Yale University Press, 2010); Fiedler, "China's 'Christianity

Christianity is centered on charismatic figures, often itinerant evangelists who operate free from institutional control. The requirements are not stringent. A man, woman, or child needs no formal theological education or official licensure. The gifting is what is important. Does a person have the capacity to help someone experience God's immediate presence? Thus, the state's attempt to manage and limit ordination makes little impact on the spread of Christianity. The Chinese church is not built around its few trained leaders, but is energized by a huge host of believers who are firmly Bible-based and Christ-centered and have the capacity to allegorize Scripture so that the Word of God is always experientially close.

Second, faith healing plays an important role in Christianity's growth. Probably no other phenomenon attests to the experiential immediacy of God like divine healing. Many Chinese Christians, therefore, make it prominent in their ministries. It is evidence of the veracity of their message and a desirable medical choice for many in China who find public health provisions inaccessible or unaffordable after the market reforms of the 1980s. Many believers—in some places up to 90 percent of converts—testify to the role of a miraculous cure in their conversion.

Third, it almost goes without saying that Chinese Christianity places extraordinary emphasis on evangelism. It is not possible to grow fifty times faster than the general population without persistent and productive evangelism. Chinese women have been especially effective at evangelizing their social network, but most Christians would agree: to be a Christian is to be a witness. The two are inseparable.

Fourth, Christianity has multiplied as it has urbanized. Market liberalization under Deng Xiaoping created new economic opportunities in China's cities, and more than one hundred million people have immigrated to urban centers in hopes of a better future. The transition has been difficult for many. Competition, corruption, the collapse of traditional support systems, and the like have pushed many people to seek some kind of meaning system that can make sense of the city. Christianity has

Fever' Revisited"; Fenggang Yang, "Lost in the Market, Saved at McDonald's: Conversion to Christianity in Urban China," *Journal for the Scientific Study of Religion* 44, no. 4 (December 2005): 423–41; Ryan Dunch, "Protestant Christianity in China Today: Fragile, Fragmented, Flourishing," in *China and Christianity: Burdened Past, Hopeful Future*, ed. Wu Xiaoxin and Stephen Uhalley (Armonk, N.Y.: M. E. Sharpe, 2001); Hunter and Chan, *Protestantism in Contemporary China*.

emerged as a popular choice. In places like Shenzhen or Shanghai, which have been rapidly integrated into the global market economy, Christianity is seen as a cosmopolitan religion. It can transcend the traditional, conservative, and restrictive forces that seem to retard success in the city. Thus, among the rising middle class, Christianity is perceived as progressive, liberating, and modern. To them, Christianity has become associated with all things New.

At first, this seems like a stunning reversal. In the pell-mell rush to remake China in the wake of the May Fourth Movement of 1919, Christians were almost lost in the stampede. Their few voices were largely drowned out in the cacophonous shouts for change. Anarchists clamored alongside socialists. Champions of an avant-garde culture clashed with those who promoted cultural reforms. While some hailed science as a savior, others demanded China rise above vulgar materialism. Mainline Protestants entered the fray through the mouthpieces of Christian missions. In their periodicals and publications, they advanced a modernizing and social gospel: China could be renewed by overhauling its social, economic, and political institutions. However, like almost all the other May Fourth programs for national salvation, their vision eventually foundered. Already in 1922 it was beached as the Anti-Christian Movement ebbed liberal Protestant influence away. Detractors pointed out that plans to supplant Chinese cultural institutions with Christian institutions was really only a front for importing Western ones. Then, in 1949, the entire enterprise sank as it was smashed by the rising tide of Communism. The close association between the YMCA, mainline mission boards, and the Nationalist regime tainted Christian progressives as enemies of the people. Christianity, as the Cultural Revolution painted it, was just another old idea, old custom, old habit.

But even as the Protestant establishment broke apart, there was another Christian tradition ready to take its place. Formed in the decades following May Fourth, this type of Christianity was not primarily worked out in periodicals or reform programs, but in the furnace of revivals. Under the pounding words of itinerant evangelists like Song Shangjie, the features of modern Chinese Christianity were first hammered into place. Song made Jesus experientially close. A person need only step out in faith to become a New Man or a New Woman; the old could all be left behind. That included a sick or weakened body. In a revival, if a soul was made well then the body was too. Converts needed to share the good news of their transformation with others. Failure to do so was to slip back already into a former way of life. But China's lower-middle class did not want to go back; petty urbanites were trying to move forward. Faith in Christ, then, became a way to start something New.

Perfected in Song's revivals, those features are now the fundamental building blocks of contemporary Chinese Christianity. Of course, it is impossible to prove that Song is their only source or that he is the father of all the Christian communities that claim to be his heirs— too much of the historical record in China was disrupted or destroyed in the middle of the twentieth century to cinch that point.[7] But what is clear, with eight decades of hindsight, is that Song appears as the archetype and exemplar of what came to be the most popular Chinese expression of the Christian faith. To know the story of John Song and how he became a New Man is to understand the formation of modern Chinese Christianity.

---

[7] Yalin Xin, *Inside China's House Church Network: The Word of Life Movement and Its Renewing Dynamic* (Lexington, Ky.: Enoch Press, 2009), 26.

Bibliography

"35 Are Pledged by Uldine Utley." *New York Times*, December 20, 1926.

Abbott, Paul R. "Revival Movements." In *China Christian Year Book, 1932–1933*, edited by Frank Rawlinson, 175–92. Shanghai: Christian Literature Society, 1934.

Administrative file for Sung Siong Ceh, [aka] John Sung, UTS STM incomplete, 1926, 1926–2003, series 10A, box 4, folder 9, UTS2 Union Records, Burke Library, Union Theological Seminary, New York.

Ahern, Emily M. *Chinese Ritual and Politics*. Cambridge: Cambridge University Press, 1981.

————. "The Power and Pollution of Chinese Women." In *Women in Chinese Society*, edited by Margery Wolf and Roxane Witke, 193–214. Stanford: Stanford University Press, 1975.

————. "Sacred and Secular Medicine in a Taiwan Village: A Study of Cosmological Disorders." In *Culture and Healing in Asian Societies: Anthropological, Psychiatric and Public Health Studies*, edited by Arthur Kleinman et al., 17–39. Cambridge, Mass.: Schenkman Publishing, 1978.

A. I. D. "Wonderbaarlijke genezingen. De Chineesche Evangelist. [Miraculous Healings. The Chinese Evangelist.]" *Gouden Schoven* 12, no. 7 (April 1939): 14–15.

Alt, M. A. "De Boodschaap van Dr. John Sung: Impressies I [The Message of Dr. John Sung: Impressions I]." *Gouden Schoven* 12, no. 20 (October 15, 1939): 4–7.

————. "Dr. John Sung en zijn boodschaap: Impressies II [Dr. John Sung and His Message: Impressions II]." *Gouden Schoven* 12, no. 21 (November 1, 1939): 4–5.

————. "Dr. John Sung en zijn boodschaap: Impressies III [Dr. John Sung and His Message: Impressions III]." *Gouden Schoven* 12, no. 22 (November 15, 1939): 4–6.

————. "Dr. John Sung en zijn boodschaap: Impressies IV [Dr. John Sung and His Message: Impressions IV]." *Gouden Schoven* 12, no. 23 (December 1, 1939): 4–6.

American Board of Commissioners for Foreign Missions Archives, 1810–1961 (ABC 1–91). Houghton Library, Harvard University, Cambridge, Mass.

Anderson, A. S. Moore. "Our Chinese Church in Singapore and Jahore." *St. Andrew's Outlook* 81 (July 1935): 54.

————. "Wake Up Malaya!" *St. Andrew's Outlook* 82 (September 1935): 41.

Andrews, Bridie J. *The Making of Modern Chinese Medicine, 1850–1960.* Vancouver: UBC Press, 2014.

————. "The Republic of China." In *Chinese Medicine and Healing: An Illustrated History*, edited by T. J. Hinrichs and Linda L. Barnes, 209–19. Cambridge, Mass.: Belknap Press of Harvard University Press, 2013.

————. "Tuberculosis and the Assimilation of Germ Theory in China, 1895–1937," *Journal of the History of Medicine* 52 (January 1997): 114–57.

Annual Report of the Straits Settlements, 1935. Singapore: 1935.

Annual Report of the Straits Settlements, 1936. Singapore: 1936.

"Apartment Erected by Union Settlement." *New York Times*, October 24, 1926.

Archives of the YMCA: Student Division, RG 58, Box 79, Folder 1024, Special Collections, Yale Divinity School.

Ashiwa, Yoshiko. "Positioning Religion in Modernity." In *Making Religion, Making the State*, edited by Yoshiko Ashiwa and David L. Wank, 43–73. Stanford: Stanford University Press, 2009.

Austin, Alvyn. *China's Millions: The China Inland Mission and Late Qing Society, 1832–1905.* Grand Rapids: Eerdmans, 2007.

Baarbé, Cornelie. *Dr. Sung, een Reveil op Java: Over de Evangelist Dr. Sung en zijn preken.* Den Haag, Netherlands: Voorhoeve, 1960.

Baer, Jonathan R. "Perfectly Empowered Bodies: Divine Healing in Modernizing America." Ph.D. diss., Yale University, 2002.

Barnes, Linda L. *Needles, Herbs, Gods and Ghosts: China, Healing, and the West to 1848.* Cambridge, Mass.: Harvard University Press, 2005.

Barwick, John Stewart. "The Protestant Quest for Modernity in Republican China." Ph.D. diss., University of Alberta, 2011.

Batumalai, Sandayandy. *A Bicentenary History of the Anglican Church of the Diocese of West Malaysia (1805–2005): In the Province of South*

East Asia. Melaka, Malaysia: Syarikat Percetakan Muncul Sisterm Sdn. Bhd., 2007.

Bays, Daniel H. "Chinese Protestant Christianity Today." *China Quarterly* 174 (July 2003): 488–504.

———. "Christian Revival in China, 1900–1937." In *Modern Christian Revivals*, edited by Edith L. Blumhofer and Randall Balmer, 161–79. Urbana: Illinois University Press, 1993.

———. "The Growth of Independent Christianity in China, 1900–1937." In *Christianity in China: From the Eighteenth Century to the Present*, edited by Daniel H. Bays, 307–16. Stanford: Stanford University Press, 1996.

———. *A New History of Christianity in China*. Malden, Mass.: Wiley-Blackwell, 2012.

Bell, Marion L. *Crusade in the City: Revivalism in Nineteenth-Century Philadelphia*. Lewisburg, Pa.: Bucknell University Press, 1977.

Benson, Carlton. "The Manipulation of *Tanci* in Radio Shanghai during the 1930s." *Republican China* 20, no. 2 (1995): 117–46.

"Bentuan xuanyan." *Shengjie zhinan yuekan* [*Guide to Holiness*] 3, no. 4 (April 1931): 8–10.

Bergère, Marie-Claire. "The Chinese Bourgeoisie, 1911–1937." In *The Cambridge History of China*, vol. 12, part 1, edited by John K. Fairbank. Cambridge: Cambridge University Press, 1983.

———. *The Golden Age of the Chinese Bourgeoisie, 1911–1937*. Translated by Janet Lloyd. Cambridge: Cambridge University Press, 1989.

"The Bethel Evangelists." *Missionary Review of the World* 56, no. 3 (March 1933): 163.

Biographical Files. "Jennie Hughes." General Commission on Archives and History. United Methodist Church, Madison, N.J.

Bishop Correspondence. United Methodist Archives and History Center, Madison, N.J.

Bissonnette, W. S. "A Little Child Shall Lead Them: Child Evangelist Uldine Utley." In *The Contentious Triangle: Church, State, and University: A Festschrift in Honor of Professor George Huntston Williams*, edited by Rodney L. Petersen and Calvin A. Pater, 307–17. Kirksville, Mo.: Thomas Jefferson University Press, 1999.

———. "The Revival in the Kutien Field." *China Christian Advocate* 24, no. 12 (December 1937): 11.

Blumhofer, Edith L., and Randall Balmer, eds. *Modern Christian Revivals*. Urbana: University of Illinois Press, 1993.

Bodenhorn, Terry L. *Defining Modernity: Guomindang Rhetorics of a New China, 1920–1970*. Ann Arbor: Center for Chinese Studies, University of Michigan, 2002.

Boot, Harry P., to Dr. Potter. February 18, 1935, Western Theological Seminary, W88–0012, Boot, Harry P. (1874–1961), Papers, 1900–1954, Joint Archives of Holland, Holland, Michigan.

Børdahl, Vibeke. "Professional Storytelling in Modern China: A Case Study of the 'Yangzhou Pinghua' Tradition." *Asian Folklore Studies 56*, no. 1 (1997): 7–32.

———. "The Storyteller's Manner in Chinese Storytelling." *Asian Folklore Studies 62*, no 1 (2003): 65–112.

Borenham, F. W. "Xingyang yu yiyao [Faith Healing]." Translated by Chen Renbing. *Budao zazhi [Evangelism]* 10, no. 1 (January 1937): 22–25.

"Boteli budaotuan baogao dongbei shibian [Bethel Evangelistic Band Report on Changes in the Northeast]." *Xinghua bao* 28, no 2. (January 27, 1932): 32–33.

"Boteli huanyou budaotuanzhi [Report of the Bethel Traveling Evangelistic Band]." *Xinghua bao* 28, no. 23 (July 29, 1931): 37–38.

"Boteli huanyou budaotuan fengxian dianli dahui ji." *Shengjie zhinan yuekan [Guide to Holiness]* 3, no. 4 (April 1931): 4–40.

"Botelijiaohui xinzu huanyou budaotuan [Bethel Church Creates a New Traveling Evangelistic Band]." *Xinghua bao* 28, no. 1 (January 21, 1931): 31.

Bowers, John Z. *Western Medicine in a Chinese Palace: Peking Union Medical College, 1917–1951.* Philadelphia: Josiah Macy Jr. Foundation, 1972.

Boynton, Charles L. "Five Year Movement." In *China Christian Year Book, 1932–1933*, edited by Frank Rawlinson, 203–11. Shanghai: Christian Literature Society, 1934.

Boynton, Charles Luther, and Charles Dozier Boynton, eds. *1936 Handbook of the Christian Movement in China under Protestant Auspices.* Shanghai: Kwang Hsueh Publishing House, 1936.

Brauer, Jerald C. "Revivalism and Millenarianism in America." In *In the Great Tradition: Essays on Pluralism, Voluntarism, and Revivalism*, edited by Joseph D. Ban and Paul R. Dekar, 147–60. Valley Forge, Pa.: Judson, 1982.

Brewster, William Nesbitt. *A Modern Pentecost in South China.* Shanghai: Methodist Publishing House, 1909.

———. *Straws from the Hinghwa Harvest.* Hinghwa, China: Hinghwa Missionary Press, 1910.

Brown, William A. "The Protestant Rural Movement in China (1920–1937)." In *American Missionaries in China*, edited by Kwang-Ching Liu, 217–48. Cambridge, Mass.: Harvard University Press, 1966.

Bruce, Dickson D. *And They All Sang Hallelujah: Plain-Folk Camp-Meeting Religion, 1800–1845.* Knoxville: University of Tennessee Press, 1974.

"Buoteli jiaohui lishi [The History of the Bethel Church]." In *Jiushizhounian ganen tekan* [*90th Anniversary Thanksgiving Publication*]. Hong Kong: Bethel, 2011.

Butterfield, Fox. "A Missionary View of the Chinese Communists (1936–1939)." In *American Missionaries in China*, edited by Kwang-Ching Liu, 249–302. Cambridge, Mass.: Harvard University Press, 1966.

Cai Jianyuan, ed. *Zhonghua quanguo jidutu budaotuan huananqu chajingdahui baogoshu* [*The National Evangelistic Association Southern Division Bible Study Meeting Report*]. Fuzhou, Fujian: Shiming Shuguan, 1937.

Carlberg, Gustav. *China in Revival*. Rock Island, Ill.: Augustana Book Concern, 1936.

Carpenter, Joel A. *Revive Us Again: The Reawakening of American Fundamentalism*. New York: Oxford University Press, 1997.

Carter, Allene G., and Robert L. Allen. *Honoring Sergeant Carter: A Family's Journey to Uncover the Truth about an American Hero*. New York: Amistad, 2004.

Caschera, Martina. "Chinese Cartoon in Transition: Animal Symbolism and Allegory from the 'Modern Magazine' to the 'Online Carnival.' *Studies in Visual Arts and Communication: An International Journal* 4, no. 1 (2017): 2.

Chang Tsung-Liang. Essay in *Yi yao zhi ye zheng wen ji. Di san jie* [*"Old Style" versus "Modern" Medicine in China: Which Can Do More for the Health and Progress of the Country, and Why?*]. Shanghai: Wei sheng jiao yu hui, 1926.

Chao, Jonathan. "The Chinese Indigenous Church Movement, 1919–1927." Ph.D. diss., University of Pennsylvania, 1986.

Chapman, J. B. *With Chapman at Camp Meeting: Sermons Preached by J. B. Chapman at Camp Meeting*. Kansas City, Mo.: Beacon Hill Press, 1961.

Chen, C. C. *Medicine in Rural China: A Personal Account*. Berkeley: University of California Press, 1989.

Chen Chonggui. "Bianji zhihou [Editor's Notes]." *Budao zazhi* [*Evangelism*] 7, no. 1 (January–February 1934): 110.

———. "Bianji zhihou [Editor's Notes]." *Budao zazhi* [*Evangelism*] 7, no. 4 (July–August 1934): 110.

———. "Budao zazhi lainiande jihua [*Evangelism* Magazine's Plan for the Coming Years]." *Budao zazhi* [*Evangelism*] 4, no. 6 (November–December 1931): 1.

Chen, Janet. *Guilty of Indigence: The Urban Poor in China, 1900–1953*. Princeton, N.J.: Princeton University Press, 2012.

Ch'en, Jerome. "The Communist Movement 1927–1937." In *The Cambridge History of China*, vol. 13, edited by Denis Twitchett and John K. Fairbank, 168–229. Cambridge: Cambridge University Press, 1986.

Chen Jinghuang. "Boteli disi xialingdahuizhi shengkuang [The Highlights of Bethel's Fourth Summer Conference]." *Shengjie zhinan yuekan* [*Guide to Holiness*] 3, no. 9 (September 1931): 1–2.

Chen Pingyuan. *Touches of History: An Entry into 'May Fourth.'* Leiden: Brill, 2011.

Chen Renbing. "Shisui zhengshi kaishi chuangdaode meiguo Wu Delei [American Uldine Utley Really Began Preaching at Ten Years Old]." *Budao zazhi* [*Evangelism*] 7, no. 1 (January–February 1934): 35–42.

Chen Rongzhan. "Notes on Dr. Song's Preaching." In *One Day in China, May 21, 1936*, edited by Sherman Cochran, Andrew C. K. Hsieh, and Janis Cochran, 186–88. New Haven: Yale University Press, 1983.

Chen, Yuan-Song. *Return to the Middle Kingdom: One Family, Three Revolutionaries, and the Birth of Modern China.* New York: Union Square Press, 2008.

———. "Shall the Five Year Movement Succeed?" *Bulletin of the National Christian Council* 40 (March 23, 1932): 1–2.

Chiang Kai-Shek. "A Message to the Students of China." *China Christian Advocate* 18, no. 1 (January 1931): 3–4.

———. *Outline of the New Life Movement.* Translated by Madame Chiang Kai-Shek. Nanchang: Association for the Promotion of the New Life Movement, 1934.

"Chiang Kai Shek: Why He Became a Christian." *Sydney Morning Herald,* January 10, 1931, 7.

China and the Gospel: The Glory of Thy Kingdom. Report of the China Inland Mission. Edinburgh: R & R Clark, 1933.

China Mission. W88–0315. Papers, 1888–1979. Western Theological Seminary. Joint Archives of Holland, Holland, Mich.

China Records Project Miscellaneous Personal Papers Collection. Record group 8. Special Collections. Yale Divinity School Library, New Haven, Conn.

"A Chinese 'Billy Sunday.'" *Missionary Review of the World* 58, no. 7 (July 1935): 377.

Chinese Methodist Church, Seremeban, 106th Anniversary 1901–2007. Seremban: 2007.

Chinese Recorder 64, no. 6 (1934). [Issue on finding common ground with Communism.]

The Chinese Students' Christian Association Year Book: Commemorating the Sixteenth Anniversary of the C.S.C.A. in North America. New York: CSCA, 1925.

Choo, P. S. "Women Should Work!" *Malay Tribune,* February 7, 1931.

Chow Teh Lin. Essay in *Yi yao zhi ye zheng wen ji. Di san jie* [*"Old Style" versus "Modern" Medicine in China: Which Can Do More for the Health and Progress of the Country, and Why?*]. Shanghai: Wei sheng jiao yu hui, 1926.

Chow, Tse-Tsung. *The May Fourth Movement: Intellectual Revolution in Modern China.* Cambridge, Mass.: Harvard University Press. 1960.

Cio, L. D. "Five Year Movement." In *China Christian Year Book, 1931,* edited by Frank Rawlinson, 126–29. Shanghai: Christian Literature Society, 1931.

Claassen, Ryan L., and Benjamin Highton. "Policy Polarization among Political Elites and the Significance of Political Awareness in the Mass Public." *Political Research Quarterly* 62, no. 3 (September 2009): 538–51.

Clammer, John. *Singapore: Ideology, Society, Culture.* Singapore: Chopmen Publishers, 1985.

Cliff, Howard, and Mary Cliff. "Dear Friends." *Bible for China* 63 (May 1933): 39–40.

Cochran, Sherman. *Chinese Medicine Men: Consumer Culture in China and Southeast Asia.* Cambridge, Mass.: Harvard University Press, 2005.

———, ed. *Inventing Nanjing Road: Commercial Culture in Shanghai, 1900–1945.* Cornell East Asia Series. Ithaca, N.Y.: Cornell University, 1999.

Cole, W. B. "Sienyu Notes." *China Christian Advocate* (June 1929): 15.

Cooper, William C., and Nathan Sivin. "Man as Medicine: Pharmacological and Ritual Aspects of Traditional Therapy Using Drugs Derived from the Human Body." In *Chinese Science: Explorations of an Ancient Tradition,* edited by Shigeru Nakayama and Nathan Sivin, 203–72. Cambridge, Mass.: MIT Press, 1973.

Cott, Nancy F. *The Bonds of Womanhood: "Woman's Sphere" in New England, 1780–1835.* New Haven: Yale University Press, 1977.

Council for World Mission Archives. Fukien Correspondence Files (in/out), 1928–1939, Fukien Reports, North China Correspondence Files (in/out), 1908–1939, North China Reports, 1926–1939, South China Correspondence Files (in/out), 1928–1939. Hong Kong Baptist University, Hong Kong.

Crawford, Mary K. *The Shantung Revival.* Shanghai: China Baptist Publication Society, 1933.

Crozier, Ralph C. "The Ideology of Medical Revivalism in Modern China." In *Asian Medical Systems: A Comparative Study,* edited by Charles Leslie, 341–55. Berkeley: University of California Press, 1976.

———. *Traditional Medicine in Modern China: Science, Nationalism, and the Tensions of Cultural Change.* Cambridge, Mass.: Harvard University Press, 1968.

Culpepper, Charles L. *The Shantung Revival.* Dallas: Baptist General Convention of Texas, 1968.

Cunningham, Andrew, and Bridie Andrews, eds. *Western Medicine as Contested Knowledge*. Manchester: Manchester University Press, 1997.

Cunningham, Floyd, ed. *Our Watchword and Song: The Centennial History of the Church of the Nazarene*. Kansas City, Mo.: Beacon Hill Press, 2009.

Dean, Kenneth, and Zheng Zhenman. *Ritual Alliances of the Putian Plain*. Vol. 1, *Historical Introduction to the Return of the Gods*. Leiden: Brill, 2010.

"De Evangeliesatie-arbeid van Dr. Sung (overgenomen uit: Soerb. Handelsblad) [The Evangelistic Work of Dr. Sung (as it appeared in the Soerbaja business newspaper]." *Gouden Schoven* 12, no. 22 (November 1, 1939): 16–17.

de Jong, Christiaan G. F. *De Gereformeerde zending in Midden-Java, 1931–1975: een bronnenpublicatie*. Zoetermeer: Boekencentrum, 1997.

de Jong-Maasland, H. "Dr. John Sung de Chineesche Evangelist [Dr. John Sung the Chinese Evangelist]." *De Opwekker* 84, no. 1 (January 1939): 8–17.

Ding Ling. "Shanghai, Spring 1930" and "Miss Sophia's Diary." In *I Myself Am a Woman: Selected Writings of Ding Ling*, edited by Tani E. Barlow and Gary J. Bjorge. Boston: Beacon Press, 1989.

Dirlik, Arif. "The Ideological Foundations of the New Life Movement: A Study in Counterrevolution." *Journal of Asian Studies* 34, no. 4 (August 1975): 945–80.

Discharge Book. Vol. 2: Bloomingdale Hospital, 1921–1933. Medical Center Archives of New York-Presbyterian/Weill Cornell.

"Doan's Backache." *Sin Chew Jit Poh* [星州日報], October 30, 1935.

Dong, Madeleine Yue, and Joshua L. Goldstein, eds. *Everyday Modernity in China*. Seattle: University of Washington Press, 2006.

"Dongjiang jinxin lianhehui xiaoxi." *Zhenguang* [*True Light*] 31, no. 6 (June 1932): 87–89.

Doraisamy, Theodore R., ed. *Forever Beginning: One Hundred Years of Methodism in Singapore*. Singapore: The Methodist Church in Singapore, 1985.

Dorsett, Lyle W. *Billy Sunday and the Redemption of Urban America*. Grand Rapids: Eerdmans, 1991.

Dreyer, F. C. H. "The Revival in North China." *Moody Bible Institute Monthly* 33, no. 11 (July 1933): 496.

Du Mez, Kristin Kobes. "The Beauty of the Lilies: Femininity, Innocence, and the Sweet Gospel of Uldine Utley." *Religion and American Culture* 15, no. 2 (2005): 209–43.

Duara, Prasenjit. "Knowledge and Power in the Discourse of Modernity: The Campaigns against Popular Religion in Early Twentieth-Century China." *Journal of Asian Studies* 50, no. 1 (February 1991): 67–83.

———. "Of Authenticity and Woman: Personal Narratives of Middle-Class Women in Modern China." In *Becoming Chinese: Passages to Modernity and Beyond*, edited by Wen-hsin Yeh. Berkeley: University of California Press, 2000.

Dunch, Ryan. "Protestant Christianity in China Today: Fragile, Fragmented, Flourishing." In *China and Christianity: Burdened Past, Hopeful Future*, edited by Wu Xiaoxin and Stephen Uhalley, 195–216. Armonk, N.Y.: M. E. Sharpe, 2001.

Eberhard, Wolfram. *Guilt and Sin in Traditional China*. Berkeley: University of California Press, 1967.

Eddy, Sherwood. "Letter to John Sung." *Chinese Recorder* 66 (February 1935): 124–25.

Editorial Committee of the Centennial Celebration. *Zhonghua jidujiao weiligonghui baizhou jiniankan, 1847–1947* [*Methodist Centennial in China, 1847–1947*]. Foochow, Fukien, China: Editorial Committee of the Centennial Celebration, 1948.

"Editorial Notes." *Bible for China* 70 (July–August 1934): 1–5.

Edwards, Louise. "Policing the Modern Woman in Republican China." *Modern China* 26, no. 2 (April 2000): 115–47.

Elliott, Alan J. A. *Chinese Spirit-Medium Cults in Singapore*. London School of Economics Monographs on Social Anthroplogy, no. 14. London: Athlone Press, 1955.

Embrace the World, Redeem the Time: Centennial Celebration & 20th Mission Conference of the Chinese Methodist Church, Klang, December 10–13, 1998. N.p., 1998.

"Evangelism in Siam." *Missionary Review of the World* 62 (December 1939): 579.

F. K. "Fuxing yundongzhongde san yaodian [Three Necessary Points for a Revival Movement]." *Xinghua bao* 30, no. 50 (December 27, 1933): 5–7.

Fairbank, John K. *The Cambridge History of China*, vol. 12. Cambridge: Cambridge University Press, 1983.

Fan Mingjing. "Huangxian jiaohui kongqianzhi dafenxing [Huang County Church's Unprecedented Revival]." *Zhenguang* [*True Light*] 31, no. 2 (February 1932): 79–80.

Feng, Jin. *Making of a Family Saga: Ginling College*. Albany: State University of New York Press, 2009.

"Fenxing xiaoxi [Revival News]." *Nanzhong* [*Southern Bell*] 8, no. 5 (October 1935): 1–2.

Fewsmith, Joseph. *Party, State, and Local Elites in Republican China: Merchant Organizations and Politics in Shanghai, 1890–1930.* Honolulu: University of Hawaii, 1985.

Fiedler, Katrin. "China's 'Christianity Fever' Revisited: Towards a Community-Oriented Reading of Christian Conversions in China." *Journal of Current Chinese Affairs* 39, no. 4 (2010): 71–109.

Fitzgerald, John. *Awakening China: Politics, Culture, and Class in the Nationalist Revolution.* Stanford: Stanford University Press, 1996.

"The Five Year Movement." *Bulletin of the National Christian Council* 34 (November 1929): 7–10.

Flores, Edward Orozco, and Pierrette Hondagneu-Sotelo. "Chicano Gang Members in Recovery: The Public Talk of Negotiating Chicano Masculinities." *Social Problems* 60, no. 4 (2013): 476–90.

Freedman, Maurice. *Chinese Family and Marriage in Singapore.* 1957. Reprint, New York: Johnson Reprint, 1970.

"Fujian Gutian Shenggong jie Meihui tongju dahui qianren mengen [The Episcopal and Methodist Churches of Gutian, Fujian Hold a Joint Revival wherein 1000 People Receive Grace]." *Nanchang [Southern Bell]* 10, no. 5 (May 1937): 21.

Fulton, Brent. *China's Urban Christians.* Eugene, Ore.: Pickwick Books, 2015.

Generaal deputaatschap voor de zending. Archief van Generale Deuptaten voor de Zending onder heidennen en mohammedanen. Het Utrechts Archief, Netherlands.

Gernet, Jacques. *A History of Chinese Civilization.* Cambridge: Cambridge University Press, 1996.

Gibson, T. Campbell. "Missions and All That." *St. Andrew's Outlook* 82 (September 1935): 38–40.

Gih, Andrew. *Launch Out into the Deep! Tales of Revival through China's Famous Bethel Evangelistic Bands and Further Messages.* London: Marshall, Morgan & Scott, 1938.

Gilkes, Cheryl Townsend. "'Together and in the Harness': Women's Traditions in the Sanctified Church." *Signs* 10, no. 4 (1985): 678–99.

Gilmartin, Christina K. "Gender, Political Culture, and Women's Mobilization." In *Engendering China: Women, Culture, and the State,* edited by Christina K. Gilmartin et al. Cambridge, Mass.: Harvard University Press, 1994.

Goossaert, Vincent, and David A. Palmer. *The Religious Question in Modern China.* Chicago: University of Chicago Press, 2011.

Groot, J. J. M. de. *The Religious System of China: Its Ancient Forms, Evolution, History and Present Aspect, Manners, Custom and Social*

Institutions Connected Therewith. 1892–1897. Reprint, Taipei: Ch'eng Wen Publishing, 1969.

Habermas, Jürgen. *The Philosophical Discourse of Modernity*. Cambridge, Mass.: MIT Press, 1987.

Hall, Donald E., ed. *Muscular Christianity: Embodying the Victorian Age*. Cambridge: Cambridge University Press, 1994.

Hardesty, Nancy A. "Minister as Prophet? Or as Mother? Two Nineteenth Century Models." In *Women in New Worlds*, vol. 1, edited by Hilah F. Thomas and Rosemary Skinner Keller, 88–101. Nashville: Abingdon Press, 1981.

Harkin, Michael E. Introduction to *Reassessing Revitalization Movements: Perspectives from North America and the Pacific Islands*, edited by Michael E. Harkin. Lincoln: University of Nebraska Press, 2004.

Hayford, Charles W. *To the People: James Yen and Village China*. New York: Columbia University Press, 1990.

He Yuehan, ed. *Malaixiya jidujiao weiligonghui huaren nianyihuui wushiwu zhounian jinian tekan* [*Annual Meeting of the Methodist Church of Malaysia 55th Anniversary Special Publication*]. Penang, Malaysia: Lee and Sons, 1992.

Hefner, Robert. *Conversion to Christianity: Historical and Anthropological Perspectives on a Great Transformation*. Berkeley: University of California Press, 1993.

"Hengyang fenxing dahui jilue [Brief Description of the Hengyang Revival Meetings]." *Zhenguang* [*True Light*] 33, no. 3 (March 1934): 62–63.

Henriot, Christian. *Prostitution and Sexuality in Shanghai: A Social History, 1849–1949*. Translated by Noël Castelino. Cambridge: Cambridge University Press, 2001.

Henry Sloane Coffin Collection. Series 2: Sermons, Addresses, Lecture Notes, 1903–1962, box 9, folder 127. Burke Library, Union Theological Seminary, New York.

Hershatter, Gail. *Women in China's Long Twentieth Century*. Berkeley: University of California Press, 2007.

———. *The Workers of Tianjin, 1900–1949*. Stanford: Stanford University Press, 1986.

Het Utrechts Archief, Utrecht, the Netherlands.

Hindmarsh, D. Bruce. *The Evangelical Conversion Narrative: Spiritual Autobiography in Early Modern England*. New York: Oxford University Press, 2005.

Hing Ai Yun. "Resistance Narratives from Mothers of Married Daughters in Singapore." In *Motherhood: Power and Oppression*, edited by Andrea O'Reilly, Marie Porter, and Patricia Short. Toronto: Women's Press, 2005.

Hinghwa Annual Conference. *Official Minutes of the 24th Session of the Hinghwa Annual Conference of the Methodist Episcopal Church.* Shanghai: Methodist Publishing House, 1928.

————. *Official Minutes of the 25th Session of the Hinghwa Annual Conference of the Methodist Episcopal Church.* Shanghai: Methodist Publishing House, 1929.

————. *Official Minutes of the 26th Session of the Hinghwa Annual Conference of the Methodist Episcopal Church.* Shanghai: Methodist Publishing House, 1930.

————. *Official Minutes of the 27th Session of the Hinghwa Annual Conference of the Methodist Episcopal Church.* Shanghai: Methodist Pub. House, 1931.

Hinghwa Methodist Church, 75th Anniversary Souvenir Magazine, 1911–1986. Singapore: 1986.

Hinrichs, T. J., and Linda L. Barnes, eds. *Chinese Medicine and Healing: An Illustrated History.* Cambridge, Mass.: Bellknap Press of Harvard University Press, 2013.

"A History of the Pentecostal Movement in Indonesia." *Asian Journal of Pentecostal Studies* 4, no. 1 (January 2001): 131–48.

Ho, Herbert Hoi-lap. *Protestant Missionary Publications in Modern China, 1912–1949: A Study of Their Programs, Operations and Trends.* Hong Kong: Chinese Church Research Centre, 1988.

Hockelman, Anna. "The Story of a Thirty-Nine Day Revival." *Latter Rain Evangel* 26, no. 10 (July 1935): 19–21.

Hockman, William. "Missionary Department." *Moody Bible Institute Monthly* 28 (November 1927): 110.

Hong Junbao. "Song Shangjie xiaozhuan [Short Biography of John Sung]." *Zhonghua yu jiaohui [China and the Church]* 13 (September–October 1983): 13–18.

Howard, Ella. *Homeless: Poverty and Place in Urban America.* Philadelphia: University of Pennsylvania Press, 2013.

Hu Zhenyou. "Minbei xiejinhui lingxiuhui gaikuang." *Xinghua bao* 33, no. 46 (December 2, 1936): 28–33.

Hughes, Jennie, ed. *Bethel Heart Throbs of Grace Triumphant.* Shanghai: Bethel Mission, 1930.

————, ed. *Bethel Heart Throbs of Revival.* Shanghai: Bethel Mission, 1931.

————, ed. *Bethel Heart Throbs of Surprises.* Shanghai: Bethel Mission, 1932.

————. "Bethel Summer Bible Conference." *Bible for China* 53 (September 1931): 12–13.

————. [Hu Zunli]. "Juantou yan." *Shengjie zhinan yuekan [Guide to Holiness]* 6, no. 1 (January 1934): 1–2.

Hunt, Robert. "The Churches and Social Problems." In *Christianity in Malaysia: A Denominational History*. Edited by Robert Hunt, Lee Kam Hing, and John Roxborogh. Petaling Jaya, Selangor Darul Ehsan, Malaysia: Pelanduk Publications, 1992.

Hunt, Robert, Lee Kam Hing, and John Roxborogh, eds. *Christianity in Malaysia: A Denominational History*. Petaling Jaya, Selangor Darul Ehsan, Malaysia: Pelanduk Publications, 1992.

Hunter, Alan, and Kim-Kwon Chan. *Protestantism in Contemporary China*. Cambridge: Cambridge University Press, 1993.

Hunter, Jane. *The Gospel of Gentility: American Women Missionaries in Turn-of-the-Century China*. New Haven: Yale University Press, 1984.

Inouye, Melissa Wei-Tsing. *China and the True Jesus: Charisma and Organization in a Chinese Christian Church*. New York: Oxford University Press, 2019.

———. "Miraculous Mundane: The True Jesus Church and Chinese Christianity in the Twentieth Century." Ph.D. diss., Harvard University, 2011.

Interview with David Howard Adeney. Collection 393. Billy Graham Center Archives, Wheaton, Ill.

Ireland, Daryl R. "Becoming Modern Women: Creating a New Female Identity through John Sung's Evangelistic Teams." *Studies in World Christianity* 18, no. 3 (2012): 237–53.

———. "John Sung: Revitalization in China and Southeast Asia." Ph.D. diss., Boston University, 2015.

———. "John Sung's Malleable Conversion Narrative." *Fides et Historia* 45, no. 1 (2013): 48–75.

———. "The Legacy of John Sung." *International Bulletin of Mission Research* 40, no. 4 (October 2016): 349–57.

———. "Unbound: The Creative Power of Scripture in the Lives of Chinese Nazarene Women." *Wesleyan Theological Journal* 46, no. 2 (2011): 168–92.

Jeffrey, Mrs. D. I. "Dr. John Sung." *Alliance Weekly* 73, no. 47 (November 19, 1938): 744–46.

Jewell, J. A. "The Development of Chinese Health Care, 1911–1949." In *Health Care and Traditional Medicine in China, 1800–1982*, edited by S. M. Hillier and J. A. Jewell, 28–65. Boston: Routledge, 1983.

"Jiaohui yu fenxing yundong [The Church and Revival Movements]." *Zhonghua gui zhu* 155 (April 1, 1935): 19.

"Jidujiao budaotuan: qing Song Shangjie boshi jiangyan [Christian Evangelistic League Invites Dr. John Song to Speak]." *Tianjin dagong bao*, section 3 (April 15, 1934): 10.

Jing Wu. "Wuhu erjie jiaoqu fenxinghui [Wuhu Second Street District Revival Meeting]." *Xinghua bao* 28, no. 13 (April 8, 1931): 28–29.

Jiushizhounian ganen tekan [Special 90th Anniversary Thanksgiving Publication]. Hong Kong: 2011.

Johnson, Paul E. *A Shopkeeper's Millennium: Society and Revivals in Rochester, New York, 1815–1837*. New York: Hill and Wang, 1978.

Johnson, Todd M., and Gina A. Zurlo. *World Christian Encyclopedia*. 3rd ed. Edinburgh: Edinburgh University Press, 2019.

Joiner, Thekla Ellen. *Sin in the City: Chicago and Revivalism, 1880–1920*. Columbia: University of Missouri Press, 2007.

Jones, Francis P. *The Church in Communist China: A Protestant Appraisal*. New York: Friendship Press, 1962.

———. "John Sung." *China Bulletin* 5, no. 4 (February 1955): 2–3.

———. "John Sung." In *Encyclopedia of World Methodism, L–Z*, edited by Harmon B. Nolan. Nashville: United Methodist Publishing House, 1974.

Jordan, David K. *Gods, Ghosts, and Ancestors*. Berkeley: University of California Press, 1972.

"Juantou yu." *Shenghie zhinan yuekan [Guide to Holiness]* 3, no. 4 (April 1931): 1.

"Kaifeng jinlihui shijitang fenxing dahui jilue [A Brief Account of Kaifeng Shiji Baptist Church's Revival Meetings]." *Zhenguang [True Light]* 32, no. 5 (May 1933): 70–71.

Kam Louie, ed. *The Cambridge Companion to Modern Chinese Culture*. Cambridge: Cambridge University Press, 2008.

Kampung Koh Pioneer Methodist Church, 85th Anniversary, 1902–1987. N.p., 1987.

Kang, Xiaofei. "Women and the Religious Question in Modern China." In *Modern Chinese Religion II: 1850–2015*, vol. 1, edited by Vincent Goossaert, Jan Kiely, and John Lagerwey. Leiden: Brill, 2015.

"Kartasoera." *Gouden Schoven* 12, no. 20 (October 15, 1939): 19.

Kaye, Barrington. *Upper Nankin Street Singapore: A Sociological Study of Chinese Households Living in a Densely Populated Area*. Singapore: University of Malaya Press, 1960.

Kazeno, Sumiko. *The Role of Women in Singapore: Collaboration and Conflict between Capitalism and Asian Values*. Midoriku, Japan: Kazeno Shoboh, 2004.

Ke Shejie. "Song Shangjie boshi [Dr. John Sung]." *Taiwan jiaohui gongbao* 611 (February 1926): 23–24. Accessed June 20, 2014. http://www.laijohn.com/archives/pc/Song/Song,SChiat/model/Koa,Skai.htm.

Kele Paofan. *Xingan Puxian*. Taipei: Hyweb Technology, 2006.

Kepler, A. R., to H. A. C. Hildering. September 28, 1938, File 6493, Raad voor de zending (1102–2), Het Utrechts Archief, Utrecht, Netherlands;

A. C. Hildering to the National Christian Council of China, October 29, 1939, file 6493, Raad voor de zending (1102–2), Het Utrechts Archief, Utrecht, Netherlands.

Kiehn, Peter. "The Legacy of Peter and Anna Kiehn." Unpublished manuscript, biography, Kiehn Collection (file 192-61), Nazarene Archives, Kansas City, Mo.

———. "A Sketch of Our Work in China." *The Other Sheep* (October 1923): 16.

Kleinman, Arthur. *Patients and Healers in the Context of Culture: An Exploration of the Borderland between Anthropology, Medicine, and Pscyhiatry*. Berkeley: University of California Press, 1980.

Kraemer, Hendrik. *Van Godsdiensten en Menschen* [*About Religions and People*]. Nijkerk, Netherlands: G. F. Callenbach, 1940.

Kwok, D. W. Y. *Scientism in Chinese Thought, 1900–1950*. New Haven: Yale University Press, 1965.

Kwok, Pui-lan. "Chinese Women and Protestant Christianity at the Turn of the Twentieth Century." In *Christianity in China: From the Eighteenth Century to the Present*, edited by Daniel H. Bays. Stanford: Stanford University Press, 1996.

———. "Claiming Our Heritage: Chinese Women and Christianity." *International Bulletin of Missionary Research* 16, no. 4 (1992): 150–54.

Ladd, Tony, and James A. Mathisen. *Muscular Christianity: Evangelical Protestants and the Development of American Sport*. Grand Rapids: Baker Books, 1999.

Lake Geneva Student Conference. *Lake Geneva Student Conference, June 12–22, 1925*. United States: Young Men's Christian Association, 1925.

Latourette, Kenneth Scott. *A History of Christian Missions in China*. New York: Macmillan, 1929.

———. *A History of the Expansion of Christianity*. Vol. 7, *Advance through Storm*. Grand Rapids: Zondervan, 1970.

Le Bijou: Ohio Wesleyan University Yearbook, 1924. Delaware: Ohio Wesleyan University, 1923.

Lee, Chun Kwan. "The Theology of Revival in the Chinese Christian Church, 1900–1949: Its Emergence and Impact." Ph.D. diss., Westminster Theological Seminary, 1988.

Lee, Leo Ou-fan. "In Search of Modernity: Some Reflections on a New Mode of Consciousness in Twentieth-Century Chinese History and Literature." In *Ideas across Cultures*, edited by Paul Cohen and Merle Goldman, 108–35. Cambridge, Mass.: Harvard University Press, 1990.

———. *Shanghai Modern: The Flowering of a New Urban Culture in China, 1930–1945*. Cambridge, Mass.: Harvard University Press, 1999.

Lei, Sean Hsiang-lin. "When Chinese Medicine Encountered the State, 1910–1949." Ph.D. diss., University of Chicago, 1999.

Leung, Ka-lun. "The Influence of Revivalists in the Chinese Church." *Jian Dao: A Journal of Bible and Theology* 11 (1999): 105–57.

———. "Song Shangjie de Chongsheng Jiaodao [John Sung's Concept of Rebirth]." *Jian Dao: A Journal of Bible and Theology* 4 (1995): 1–15.

Leung, Ka-lun, and Huang Cailian. "Song Shangjie de Shenglingguan [The Pneumatology of John Sung]." *Jian Dao: A Journal of Bible and Theology* 18 (2002): 159–87.

Li Ruizhou. "Quanzhou xinzu budaotuan [Quanzhou Forms New Evangelistic Teams]." *Xinghua bao* 31, no. 47 (December 5, 1934): 31–33.

Lian Xi. *Redeemed by Fire: The Rise of Popular Christianity in Modern China.* New Haven: Yale University Press, 2010.

Liang Jiasi. "Changsha fuxinghuizhi jiakuang [Changsha Revival's Good News]." *Xinghua bao* 31, no. 21 (July 4, 1934): 25.

Lim, Ka-Tong. "The Life and Ministry of John Sung: Sowing Seeds of Vibrant Christianity in Asian Soil." Ph.D. diss., Asbury Theological Seminary, 2009.

———. *The Life and Ministry of John Sung.* Singapore: Genesis Books, 2012.

Lin Kaizhen. *Shiwu jidutu budaotuan tuangan [Sibu Christian Preaching Band Reports].* Sibu, Sarawak: Xingzhou huanan, 1936.

Lin Yuezhi. "Haila'er budaozhi shengkuang [The Highlights of Evangelism in Harbin]." *Shengjie zhinan yuekan [Guide to Holiness]* 4, no. 1 (January 1932): 36–37.

Lin Yutang. *From Pagan to Christian.* Cleveland: World Publishing, 1959.

Ling Kai Cheng. *Huishou wushinian [Fifty Years in Reminiscence].* Kowloon, Hong Kong: Rock House, 1965.

Ling, Samuel. "The Other May Fourth Movement: The Chinese 'Christian Renaissance,' 1919–1937." Ph.D. diss., Temple University, 1981.

Ling Shiao. "Culture, Commerce, and Connections: The Inner Dynamics of New Culture Publishing in the Post-May Fourth Period." In *From Woodblocks to the Internet: Chinese Publishing and Print Culture in Transition, circa 1800 to 2008,* edited by Cynthia Brokaw and Christopher A. Reed, 213–48. Leiden: Brill, 2010.

"Linggong zuzhifa [Organizing for Spiritual Work]." *Shengjie zhinan yuekan [Guide to Holiness]* 3, no. 7 (July 1931): 26–30.

Link, E. Perry, Jr. *Mandarin Ducks and Butterflies: Popular Fiction in Early Twentieth-Century Chinese Cities.* Berkeley: University of California Press, 1981.

Liu Yiling. *Song Shangjie yanxinglu [Anecdotes and Sayings of John Sung].* Kowloon, Hong Kong: Alliance Press, 1967.

———. *Song Shangjie zhuan.* Hong Kong: Christian Witness Press, 1962.

Lozada, Eriberto. *God Aboveground: Catholic Church, Postsocialist State, and Transnational Processes in a Chinese Village*. Stanford: Stanford University Press, 2001.

Lu, Hanchao. *Beyond the Neon Lights: Everyday Shanghai in the Early Twentieth Century*. Berkeley: University of California Press, 1999.

Lu Ming, "Boteli mingmingde youlai [The Origin of Bethel's Name]." In *Jiushizhounian ganen tekan [90th Anniversary Thanksgiving Publication]*. Hong Kong: Bethel, 2011.

Lu Xun. "Yao [Medicine]." In *Lu Xun quan ji*. Beijing: Ren min wen xue chu ban she, 1981.

Lucardie, B. I. J. "Ingezonden getuigenissen [Testimonies Received]." *Gouden Schoven* 12, no. 22 (November 15, 1939): 13–14.

Luo Weihong. *Christianity in China*. Translated by Zhu Chengming. Beijing: Wuzhou, 2004.

Luo Yunyan. "Xinshenghuo yuandong yu jidutu [New Life Movement and Christians]." *Xinghua bao* 33, no. 41 (October 28, 1936): 4–7.

Lyall, Leslie T. *A Biography of John Sung*. Singapore: Genesis Books, 2004.

MacIntire Papers. Box 383. Princeton Theological Seminary Archives, Princeton, New Jersey.

Malaixiya weiligonghui qishiwuzhounian jinian tekan, 1885–1960 [Seventy-Fifth Anniversary of the Methodist Church in Malaysia, 1885–1960]. N.p.,1960.

Malay Conference. *Minutes of the Forty-Fourth Session of the Malaya Conference of the Methodist Episcopal Church Held in Wesley Church, Singapore, Straits Settlements, January 2–7, 1936*. Singapore: 1936.

Malaysia Message, November 1935.

Manual of the Pilgrim Holiness Church. Easton, Md.: Easton Publishing, 1926.

Marsden, George M. *Fundamentalism and American Culture: The Shaping of Twentieth-Century Evangelism, 1870–1925*. New York: Oxford University Press, 1980.

———. *Understanding Fundamentalism and Evangelicalism*. Grand Rapids: Eerdmans, 1991.

Martin, Brian G. *The Shanghai Green Gang: Politics and Organized Crime, 1919–1937*. Berkeley: University of California Press, 1996.

McClymond, Michael J., ed. *Embodying the Spirit: New Perspectives on North American Revivalism*. Baltimore: John Hopkins University Press, 2004.

McLoughlin, William G. *Modern Revivalism: Charles Grandison Finney to Billy Graham*. New York: Ronald Press, 1959.

Means, Paul M. "From the Editor's Desk." *Malaysia Message* (September 1935): 6.

"Medical Records of Siong Ceh Sung." Medical Center Archives of New York-Presbyterian/Weil Cornell, New York, 1927.

Merkelijn, A. *26 Jaren op het zendingsveld: herinneringen van een missionair predikant* [*26 Years on the Mission Field: Memories of a Missionary Preacher*]. 'S-Gravenhage, Netherlands: D. A. Daamen's Uitgeversmaatschappij, 1941.

Merwin, Wallace C. *Adventure in Unity: The Church of Christ in China*. Grand Rapids: Eerdmans, 1974.

Methodist Church Missionary Files Series. General Commission on Archives and History. United Methodist Church, Madison, N.J.

Midwest China Oral History and Archives Collection. "Cora Martinson." St. Paul, Minn.: Archives-Gullixson Hall, 1980.

Millican, F. R. "Four Methods of Evangelism." *Chinese Recorder* 69 (May 1938): 245–48.

Miss Julian. "The Modern Chinese Girl: A Model Wife and Perfect Mother." *Malay Tribune*, May 9, 1931.

"Miss Utley Continues Revival." *New York Times*, October 4, 1926.

Mission Geographic Reference Files. General Commission on Archives and History. United Methodist Church, Madison, N.J.

Mitter, Rana. *A Bitter Revolution: China's Struggle with the Modern World*. New York: Oxford University Press, 2004.

Monsen, Marie. *The Awakening: Revival in China, 1927–1937*. Translated by Joy Guinness. London: China Inland Mission, 1961.

Morris, Andrew D. "'The Me in the Mirror': A Narrative of Voyeurism and Discipline in Chinese Women's Physical Culture, 1921–1937." In *Visualizing Modern China*, edited by James A. Cook et al. Lanham, Md.: Lexington Books, 2014.

Morse, Wilbur, Jr. "East Asia Crippled by Communism Rev. McIntire Says." *Christian Beacon* 15, no. 1 (February 16, 1950): 5.

Mouw, J. A., W. M. Post, H. Mitchell, W. Konemann, and G. M. Dittmar. "Netherlands East Indies Mission Conference." *Alliance Weekly* 76, no 25 (June 21, 1941): 392–94.

Mukonyora, Isabel. *Wandering: A Gendered Wilderness*. Berne, Switzerland: Peter Lang, 2007.

Nanyang Siang Pau [南洋商報], October 27, 1935.

Nedostup, Rebecca. *Superstitious Regimes: Religion and the Politics of Chinese Modernity*. Cambridge, Mass.: Harvard University Press, 2009.

Nee, Watchman. *Concerning Our Missions*. London: Witness and Testimony Publishers, 1939.

Ng, Janet. *The Experience of Modernity: Chinese Autobiography of the Early Twentieth Century*. Ann Arbor: University of Michigan Press, 2003.

Ng, Peter Tze Ming. *Chinese Christianity: An Interplay between Global and Local Perspectives*. Leiden: Brill, 2012.

Ng, Peter Tze Ming, and Zhang Yongguang. "Nationalism, Modernization, and Christian Education in 20th Century East Asia: A Comparison of the Situations in China, Japan, and Korea." In *Christian Presence and Progress in North-East Asia*, edited by Jan A. B. Jongeneel et al., 57–72. Frankfurt am main: Peter Lang, 2011.

Ng, Vivien W. *Madness in Later Imperial China: From Illness to Deviance*. Norman: University of Oklahoma Press, 1990.

Noll, Mark A., and Carolyn Nystrom. *Clouds of Witnesses: Christian Voices from Africa and Asia*. Downers Grove, Ill.: IVP, 2011.

North China Conference. *The Official Journal of the Forty-First Session of the North China Annual Conference of the Methodist Episcopal Church, August 23–27, 1933*. Beijing: 1933.

———. *The Official Journal of the Forty-Second Session of the North China Annual Conference of the Methodist Episcopal Church Held at the South Gate Methodist Episcopal Church, Tientsin, Hopei, China, August 22– 26, 1934*. Beijing: 1934.

———. *The Official Journal of the Forty-Third Session of the North China Annual Conference of the Methodist Episcopal Church, August 21–26, 1935*. Beijing: 1935.

"Nürenmen qilai!" *Sin Chew Jit Poh* [星州日報], October 5, 1935.

Oblau, Gotthard. "Divine Healing and the Growth of Practical Christianity in China." In *Global Pentecostal and Charismatic Healing*, edited by Candy Gunther Brown. Oxford: Oxford University Press, 2011.

Ohio State Lantern, 1924–1926.

Ohio State University, March Convocation. March 19, 1926. Ohio State University Archives, Columbus, Ohio.

Ohio Wesleyan Magazine, April 1929.

Ohio Wesleyan Transcript, 1921–1923.

Ohio Wesleyan University Seventy-Ninth Commencement. June 8, 1923. Ohio Wesleyan University Archives, Delaware, Ohio.

"Opposes Force in China." *New York Times*, December 4, 1926.

Oral History Interviews. Special Project. Accession numbers 002007, 002239. National Archives of Singapore. Interviews from this project are listed individually in the bibliography.

Osborn, L. C. "God's Blessings at Fan Hsien." *The Other Sheep* (September 1935): 17.

"Ovaltine." *Sin Chew Jit Poh* [星州日報], September 9, 1935.

Pan Naizhao. "Cong Song Shangjie boshi zai meiyimeihui zhiluoyatangde fenxingbudaohui kan jiaohuide chengzhang, yiji jiaohui dui shehui Chujingde huiying." Unpublished paper, Trinity Theological College,

May 9, 2005. Accessed June 27, 2020. https://www.doc88.com/p
-6364178273761.html.

Park, Albert L., and David K. Yoo, eds. *Encountering Modernity: Christianity in East Asia and Asian America*. Honolulu: University of Hawaii Press, 2014.

Parker, Joseph. *Interpretive Statistical Survey of the World Mission of the Christian Church: Summary and Detailed Statistics of Churches and Missionary Societies, Interpretive Articles, and Indices*. New York: International Missionary Council, 1938.

Patterson, James Alan. "The Loss of a Protestant Missionary Consensus: Foreign Missions and the Fundamentalist-Modernist Conflict." In *Earthen Vessels: American Evangelicals and Foreign Missions, 1880–1980*, edited by Joel A. Carpenter and Wilbert Shenk, 73–91. Grand Rapids: Eerdmans, 1990.

"Personals." *Christian Advocate* 84, no. 37 (September 16, 1909): 1478.

"Personals." *Christian Advocate* 91 (July 6, 1916): 897.

"Personals." *Malaysia Message* (August 1935): 2.

Poon, Michael Nai-Chiu, and Simon Chan. *Christian Movements in Southeast Asia: A Theological Exploration*. Singapore: Genesis Books, 2010.

Porkert, Manfred. "The Intellectual and Social Impulses behind the Evolution of Traditional Chinese Medicine." In *Asian Medical Systems: A Comparative Study*, edited by Charles Leslie, 63–76. Berkeley: University of California Press, 1976.

Porterfield, Amanda. *Healing in the History of Christianity*. Oxford: Oxford University Press, 2005.

Prior, Markus. "Media and Political Polarization." *Annual Review of Political Science* 16 (2013): 101–27.

Putney, Clifford. *Muscular Christianity: Manhood and Sports in Protestant America, 1880–1920*. Cambridge, Mass.: Harvard University Press, 2001.

Quanguo jidutu budaotuan baogaoshu [*National Christian Evangelistic League Report Booklet*] 2 (March 1936).

Raad voor de Zending. Het Utrechts Archief, Netherlands.

Rambo, Lewis R. *Understanding Religious Conversion*. New Haven: Yale University Press, 1993.

Rawlinson, Frank, ed. *China Christian Year Book, 1928*. Shanghai: Christian Literature Society, 1928.

———, ed. *China Christian Year Book, 1929*. Shanghai: Christian Literature Society, 1929.

———, ed. *China Christian Year Book, 1931*. Shanghai: Christian Literature Society, 1931.

————, ed. *China Christian Year Book, 1932–1933*. Shanghai: Christian Literature Society, 1934.

————, ed. *China Christian Year Book, 1934–1935*. Shanghai: Christian Literature Society, 1935.

————, ed. *China Christian Year Book, 1936–1937*. Shanghai: Christian Literature Society, 1937.

Records of the General Conference, United Methodist Church Archives—GCAH, Madison, N.J.

Records of the Immigration and Naturalization Service. Record group 85. National Archives at San Francisco, San Francisco, Calif.

Rees, Paul S. *Seth Cook Rees: The Warrior-Saint*. Indianapolis: Pilgrim Book Room, 1934.

Ren Zuotian. "Shanghai boteli huanyou budaotuan [Shanghai's Bethel Worldwide Evangelistic Band Report]." *Shengjie zhinan yuekan [Guide to Holiness]* 4, no. 1 (January 1932): 37–38.

Renshaw, Michelle. *Accommodating the Chinese: The American Hospital in China, 1880–1920*. New York: Routledge, 2005.

"Revival Is Coming." *Christian Observer*. Referenced in "The Coming Revival," *Bible for China* 82 (September–October 1936): 41–42.

Richardson, R. P. "Our Diamond Jubilee." *Bible for China* 82 (September–October 1936): 10–23.

Richey, Russell E. "Revivalism: In Search of a Definition." *Wesleyan Theological Journal* 28, nos. 1–2 (1993): 165–75.

Riss, Richard M. *A Survey of 20th Century Revival Movements in North America*. Peabody, Mass.: Hendrickson, 1988.

Robert, Dana L. *American Women in Mission: A Social History of Their Thought and Practice*. Macon, Ga.: Mercer University Press, 1997.

Rogaski, Ruth. *Hygienic Modernity: Meanings of Health and Disease in Treaty-Port China*. Berkeley: University of California Press, 2004.

Rogers, Richard Lee. "The Urban Threshold and the Second Great Awakening: Revivalism in New York State, 1825–1835." *Journal for the Scientific Study of Religion* 49, no. 4 (2010): 694–709.

"Ruhe daijin fuxing? [How Does One Bring about Revival?]" *Jidutu bao* 4 (February 1936): 10–17.

Ryan, Mary P. *Cradle of the Middle Class: The Family in Oneida County, New York, 1790–1865*. Cambridge: Cambridge University Press, 1981.

————. *Womanhood in America: From Colonial Times to the Present*. 3rd ed. New York: F. Watts, 1983.

————. "A Women's Awakening: Evangelical Religion and the Families of Utica, New York, 1800–1840." In *Religion and American Culture*, edited by David G. Hackett, 147–66. New York: Routledge, 1995.

Sands, Barbara, and Ramon H. Myers. "The Spatial Approach to Chinese History: A Test." *Journal of Asian Studies* 45, no. 4 (August 1986): 721–43.

Sarawak Annual Conference of the Methodist Church. *The Seventy Fifth Anniversary Journal of the Sarawak Chinese Methodist Church, 1901–1975.* Hong Kong: Rock House, 1975.

Schubert, William E. *I Remember John Sung.* Singapore: Armour Publishing, 2005.

———. "Revival in Kiangsi." *Bible Union for China* (May 1931): 49.

Schwarcz, Vera. *The Chinese Enlightenment: Intellectuals and the Legacy of the May Fourth Movement of 1919.* Berkeley: University of California Press, 1986.

Seitz, Jonathan. "Converting John Sung: UTS Drop-Out, Psychiatric Patient, Chinese Evangelist." *Union Seminary Quarterly Review* 62, nos. 1–2 (2009): 78–92.

Shanghai jidutu budaotuan tuankan [*Shanghai Christian Evangelistic Team Report*] 1 (May 1, 1937).

Shanghai jidutu budaotuan tuankan [*Shanghai Christian Evangelistic Team Report*] 2 (June 1, 1937).

Sheehan, Brett. *Trust in Troubled Times: Money, Banks, and State-Society Relations in Republican Tianjin.* Cambridge, Mass.: Harvard University Press, 2003.

"Shenxi jidujiao jinlihui fuyincun chongme xuexiao fuxing." *Zhenguang* [*True Light*] 31, nos. 3–4 (April 1932): 115–16.

Sheridan, James E. *China in Disintegration: The Republican Era in Chinese History, 1912–1949.* New York: Free Press, 1975.

———. "The Warlord Era: Politics and Militarism under the Peking Government, 1916–1928." In *The Cambridge History of China,* vol. 12, part 1, ed. John K. Fairbank. Cambridge: Cambridge University Press, 1983.

"Shi Meiyu yisheng." In *Jiushizhounian ganen tekan* [*90th Anniversary Thanksgiving Publication*]. Hong Kong: Bethel, 2011.

Shih Toong Siong. *The Foochows of Sitiawan: A Historical Perspective.* Sitiawan, Perak, Malaysia: Persatuan Kutien Daerah Manjung, 2004.

"Shuyuanxi tebie budaoji [Special Evangelism Report from Shuyuanxi]." *Xinghau bao* 31, no. 48 (December 12, 1934): 32–33.

Shyrock, John. *The Temples of Anking and Their Cults: A Study of Chinese Religion.* Paris: Librairie Orientaliste Paul Geuthner, 1931.

Sim, Joshua Dao We. "Chinese Evangelistic Bands in Nanyang: Leona Wu and the Implementation of the John Sung-Inspired Evangelistic Band Model in Pre-War Singapore." *Fides et Historia* 50, no. 2 (2018): 38–65.

Sin Chew Jit Poh [星州日報], October 27, 1935.

"Siong-Ceh Sang." National Archives Arrival Investigation Case Files, 1884–1944. San Francisco Records, Records of the Immigration and Naturalization Service, record group 85. 1926. San Francisco, Calif.

Skinner, G. William, ed. *The City in Late Imperial China*. Stanford: Stanford University Press, 1977.

Smith, C. Stanley. "Modern Religious Movements." In *China Christian Year Book, 1934–1935*, edited by Frank Rawlinson, 97–111. Shanghai: Christian Literature Society, 1935.

Smith, Timothy L. *Revivalism and Social Reform in Mid-Nineteenth Century America*. New York: Abingdon Press, 1957.

Smitley, Megan. *The Feminine Public Sphere: Middle Class Women in Civic Life in Scotland, c. 1870–1914*. Manchester: Manchester University Press, 2009.

Sneller, Christopher David. "Let the World Come to Union and Union Go into the World: Union Theological Seminary in the City of New York and the Quest for Indigenous Christianity in Twentieth Century China." Ph.D. diss., University of London, 2015.

Sng, Bobby E. K. *In His Good Time: The Story of the Church in Singapore, 1819–1978*. Singapore: Graduates' Christian Fellowship, 1980.

Sook, Kru, to Mr. and Mrs. Landon via Margaret C. McCord [October 1938, Phet Burl, Thailand], SC/38 Box 94 Folder 9, Wheaton College Special Collections, Wheaton, Ill.

Southern Bell 11, no. 3 (March 1938): 16–17.

Society of the New York Hospital. "Annual Report of the Medical Director of Bloomingdale Hospital, White Plains, New York." New York: Society of the New York Hospital, 1926. Medical Center Archives of New York-Presbyterian/Weill Cornell.

Song Shangjie. "Bihui mianyan [Concluding Remarks]." In *Zhonghua quanguo jidutu budaotuan huananqu chajingdahui baogoshu [The National Evangelistic Association Southern Division Bible Study Meeting Report]*, edited by Cai Jianyuan, 9–10. Fuzhou, Fujian: Shiming Shuguan, 1937.

———. *Chajingji [Bible Study Messages]*. Hong Kong: Bellman House, 1968.

———. "Chengwei shengjie [Becoming Holy]." *Budao zazhi [Evangelism]* 7, no. 5 (September–October 1934): 8–13.

———. "Chuangshijide qi xiaohai [The Seven Children of Genesis]." As recorded by Chen Zhenfan, March 31, 1931. *Shengjie zhinan yuekan [Guide to Holiness]* 3, no. 6 (June 1931): 13–15.

———. "Chuangshiji yu jiaohui lishi [Genesis and Church History]." As recorded by Chen Zhenfan, April 2, 1931. *Shengjie zhinan yuekan [Guide to Holiness]* 3, no. 6 (June 1931): 23–26.

————. "Chuangshiji yu shizijia [Genesis and the Cross]." As recorded by Chen Qiujin, April 3, 1931. *Shengjie zhinan yuekan* [*Guide to Holiness*] 3, no. 6 (June 1931): 31–36.

————. "Chuangshiji yu xinjiuyue [Genesis and the New and Old Testaments]." As recorded by Chen Qiujin, April 1, 1931. *Shengjie zhinan yuekan* [*Guide to Holiness*] 3, no. 6 (June 1931): 15–18.

————. "Chuangshiji yu yuehan fuyin [Genesis and the Gospel of John]." As recorded by Chen Qiujin, April 1, 1931. *Shengjie zhinan yuekan* [*Guide to Holiness*] 3, no. 6 (June 1931): 18–23.

————. *The Diaries of John Sung: An Autobiography*. Translated by Stephen L. Sheng. Brighton, Mich.: Luke H. Sheng, Stephen L. Sheng, 1995.

————. "Dujing make diyizhang [Reading Mark Chapter One]." As recorded by Chen Zhenfan. *Shengjie zhinan yuekan* [*Guide to Holiness*] 3, no. 9 (September 1931): 12–17.

————. *Fenxingji* [*Revival Messages*]. 6th ed. 1935. Reprint, Hong Kong: Bellman House, 1989.

————. *Forty John Sung Revival Sermons*. Vols. 1 and 2. Translated by Timothy Tow. Singapore: Alice Doo, 1978, 1983.

————. "Fujia yu ling'en [Carrying the Cross and Gifts of the Spirit]." As recorded by Chen Zhenfan. *Shengjie zhinan yuekan* [*Guide to Holiness*] 3, no. 12 (December 1931): 31–36.

————. *Fuxingji* [*Revival Messages*]. Bellman House, 1990.

————. "Gelinduo qianshu dishisanzhang [First Corinthians Chapter Thirteen]." As recorded by Liao Guotian, morning, March 30, 1931. *Shengjie zhinan yuekan* [*Guide to Holiness*] 3, no. 6 (June 1931): 3–6.

————. *Gongzuode huigu* [*Review of My Ministry*]. Singapore: Singapore Christian Evangelistic League, 1960.

————. "Hagaishu [Haggai]." *Light in Darkness* 6, no. 8 (June 1935): 41–44.

————. "Hagaishu <Part 2> [Haggai]." *Light in Darkness* 6, no. 11 (September–October 1935): 22–24.

————. "Hagaishu <Part 3> [Haggai]." *Light in Darkness* 6, no. 12 (November–December 1935): 37–41.

————. *Jiangjingji* [*Bible Study*]. 1937. Reprint, Hong Kong: Bellman House, 1987.

————. *Jiangjingji xia* [*Bible Study Part II*]. Taipei: Glory Press, 1988.

————. "Jidutu lingchengzhi xiezhao [A Portrayal of the Christian's Spiritual Journey]." As recorded by Chen Qiujin, morning, July 8, 1931. *Shengjie zhinan yuekan* [*Guide to Holiness*] 3, no. 12 (December 1931): 36–44.

————. "Jingyan [Biblical Feast]." In *Zhonghua quanguo jidutu budaotuan huananqu chajingdahui baogoshu* [*The National Evangelistic Association Southern Division Bible Study Meeting Report*], edited by Cai Jianyuan, 4–8. Fuzhou, Fujian: Shiming Shuguan, 1937.

———. "Kaihui ci [A Word before We Begin]." In *Zhonghua quanguo jidutu budaotuan huananqu chajingdahui baogoshu* [*The National Evangelistic Association Southern Division Bible Study Meeting Report*], edited by Cai Jianyuan, 3–4. Fuzhou, Fujian: Shiming Shuguan, 1937.

———. *Lingcheng zhinan* [*A Guide for the Spiritual Journey*]. 1932. Reprint, Hong Kong: Shengwen Publishing, 1969.

———. "Make di'erzhang [Mark Chapter Two]." As recorded by Chen Zhenfan. *Shengjie zhinan yuekan* [*Guide to Holiness*] 3, no. 9 (September 1931): 17–22.

———. "Make diliuzhang [Mark Chapter Six]." As recorded by Chen Zhenfan. *Shengjie zhinan yuekan* [*Guide to Holiness*] 4, no. 1 (January 1932): 12–18.

———. "Make disanzhang [Mark Chapter Three]." As recorded by Chen Zhenfan. *Shengjie zhinan yuekan* [*Guide to Holiness*] 3, no. 9 (September 1931): 22–26.

———. "Make disizhang [Mark Chapter Four]." As recorded by Chen Zhenfan, July 7, 1931. *Shengjie zhinan yuekan* [*Guide to Holiness*] 3, no. 11 (November 1931): 11–15.

———. "Matai fuyin di liu zhang [Matthew Chapter Six]." As recorded by Chen Zhenfan, March 31, 1931. *Shengjie zhinan yuekan* [*Guide to Holiness*] 3, no. 6 (June 1931): 9–13.

———. "Matai fuyin di wu zhang [Matthew Chapter Five]." As recorded by Chen Zhenfan, March 30, 1931. *Shengjie zhinan yuekan* [*Guide to Holiness*] 3, no. 6 (June 1931): 6–9.

———. "Mingzhi yu shunfu [Knowing God's Will and Obedience]." As recorded by Chen Qiujiin. *Shengjie zhinan yuekan* [*Guide to Holiness*] 4, no. 1 (January 1932): 29–31.

———. *Moshide jidutu dang zhuyide er da wenti* [*Two Important Issues End-Time Christians Should Be Aware of*]. 1936. Reprint, Beijing: Endiantang, 1963.

———. "Noya zao fangzhou [Noah Builds the Ark]." *Budao zazhi* [*Evangelism*] 9, no. 6 (November–December 1936): 7–11.

———. *Peilingji* [*Devotional Messages*]. 1935. Reprint, Hong Kong: Bellman House, n.d.

———, ed. *Quanguo jidutu budaotuan tuankan* [*National Christian Evangelistic League Publication*] (March 1936).

———. "Saoluode meng'en [Saul Receives Grace]." As recorded by Jia Zi'an, evening of April 9, 1935, in Ertiao Presbyterian Church, Beijing. *Light in Darkness* 7, no. 11 (November 1936): 22–27.

———. "Shangdi yu zui [God and Sin]." As recorded by Sheng Cailan. *Shengjie zhinan yuekan* [*Guide to Holiness*] 6, no. 1 (January 1934): 3–8.

———. "Shenglingde xi [Baptism of the Holy Spirit]." As recorded by Zhao Aiguang. *Budao zazhi* [*Evangelism*] 7, no. 6 (November–December 1934): 8–10.

———. "Shituxingzhuan di'erzhang [Acts Chapter Two]." As recorded by Yang Zhicheng. *Shengjie zhinan yuekan* [*Guide to Holiness*] 3, no. 11 (November 1931): 3–7.

———. "Shituxingzhuan disanzhang [Acts Chapter Three]." As recorded by Yang Zhicheng. *Shengjie zhinan yuekan* [*Guide to Holiness*] 3, no. 11 (November 1931): 7–11.

———. "Shituxingzhuan diyizhang [Acts Chapter One]." As recorded by Chen Qiujin. *Shengjie zhinan yuekan* [*Guide to Holiness*] 3, no. 9 (September 1931): 28–33.

———. "Song Shangjie boshi geren jianzheng [The Testimony of Dr. Song Shangjie]." As recorded by Liao Guotian, afternoon, April 2, 1931. *Shengjie zhinan yuekan* [*Guide to Holiness*] 3, no. 6 (June 1931): 26–31.

———. "Song Shangjie boshi jiejing [Dr. Song Shangjie's Explanation of Scripture]." As recorded by Liao Guotian. *Shengjie zhinan yuekan* [*Guide to Holiness*] 3, no. 4 (May 1931): 2–8.

———. "Song Shangjie boshi jiejing: make shijang, shiyizhang [Dr. Song Shangjie's Explanation of Scripture: Mark 10 and 11]." As recorded by Liao Guotian. *Shengjie zhinan yuekan* [*Guide to Holiness*] 3, no. 7 (July 1931): 6–12.

———. "Song Shangjie boshi yanjiangji [Text of Dr. Song Shangjie's Sermon]." *Shengjie zhinan yuekan* [*Guide to Holiness*] 3, no. 3 (March 1931): 3–5.

———. Song Shangjie Diaries. Trinity Theological College, Singapore.

———. Song Shangjie Diary. 1927–1942. John Song Papers. Record group 263. Yale Divinity School. New Haven, Conn.

———. *Wode jianzheng* [*My Testimony*]. 1933. Reprint, Hong Kong: Bellman House, 1991.

———. "Xiangwo chuilingqi [May the Spirit Breathe on Me]." As recorded by Zhao Aiguang. *Budao zazhi* [*Evangelism*] 8, no. 3 (May–June 1935): 10–14.

———. "Yesu zailai [Jesus' Return]." As recorded by Lü Daguang, Moore Memorial Church, 1936. *Lingsheng* 2, no. 5 (May 1936): 15–23.

———. "Yongyuan shifang [Eternally Set Free]." As recorded by Zhao Aiguang. *Budao zazhi* [*Evangelism*] 7, no. 3 (May–June 1934): 11–17.

———. *Yujing gushi* [*Bible Story Illustrations*]. Taipei: Glory Press, 1988.

———. "Zhengwei shengjie." As recorded by Xiao Liangtong. *Budao zazhi* [*Evangelism*] 7, no. 5 (September–October 1934): 8–13.

———. "Zhiyao yangwang yesu [Just Look to Jesus]." As recorded by Xiao Liangtong, November 8, 1933, in Changsha. *Budao zazhi* [*Evangelism*] 7, no. 1 (January–February 1934): 8–11.

———. "Zhude enai [The Lord's Grace and Love]." As recorded by Zhao Aiguang. *Budao zazhi* [*Evangelism*] 7, no. 4 (July–August 1934): 8–13.

———. "Zuidan tuoluo: Yuehan fuyin di bazhang [Casting Off the Burden of Sin: John Chapter Eight]." As recorded by Zhao Aiguang. *Budao zazhi* [*Evangelism*] 7, no. 2 (March–April 1934): 8–12.

Song Siong Chiat [Song Shangjie]. *My Testimony: Being the Autobiography of Dr. John Sung (Song Siong Chiat) the Chinese Evangelist*. Translated by E. Tipson. Kuala Lumpur: Caxton Press, 1936.

Song, Tianzhen (Levi), ed. *The Diary of John Sung: Extracts from His Journals and Notes*. Singapore: Genesis Books, 2012.

———, ed. *The Journal Once Lost—Extracts from the Diary of John Sung*. Translated by Thng Pheng Soon. Singapore: Genesis Books, 2008.

———, ed. and comp. *Lingli Jiguang* [*The Diary of His Spiritual Life (of John Sung)*]. Edited and compiled from the diaries of John Sung. Hong Kong: Eng Yu Evangelistic Mission, 1995.

———, ed. *Shi'er fude de riji* [*The Journal Once Lost*]. Kowloon, Hong Kong: China Alliance Press, 2006.

Spence, Jonathan. *The Search for Modern China*. New York: W. W. Norton, 1990.

Staff Records (Cases). Vol. 5: Bloomingdale Hospital, 1926–1936. Medical Center Archives of New York-Presbyterian/Weill Cornell.

Statistical Atlas of Christian Missions, compiled by a sub-committee of Commission I of the World Missionary Conference. Edinburgh: World Missionary Conference, 1910.

Stevens, Sarah. "Figuring Modernity: The New Woman and the Modern Girl." *NWSA Journal* 15, no. 3 (2003): 82–103.

Stickmann, Michel. *Chinese Magical Medicine*. Edited by Barnard Faure. Stanford: Stanford University Press, 2002.

Strand, David. "'A High Place Is No Better Than a Low Place': The City in the Making of Modern China." In *Becoming Chinese: Passages to Modernity and Beyond*, edited by Wen-hsin Yeh, 98–136. Berkeley: University of California Press, 2000.

———. *Rickshaw Beijing: City, People and Politics in the 1920s*. Berkeley: University of California Press, 1989.

Su, John E. *Shenren Song Shanghjie* [*Dr. John Sung—the Godly Man*]. Hong Kong: Heavenly People Depot, 1959.

"Summary of Results of Revival Meetings Held by Dr. John Sung in Singapore in September." *Malaysia Message* (November 1935): 14.

Sung, Siong Ceh. "The Constitution of Organo-Magnesium Compounds and the Mechanism of Grignard Reaction." Ph.D. diss., Ohio State University, 1926.

Tay Poh Luan (Mrs.). Interview. February 27, 2000, access number 002239, reel 3. National Archives of Singapore.

Tay Poh Luan (Mrs.). Interview, February 27, 2000, access number 002239, reel 4. National Archives of Singapore.

Taylor, Jay. *The Generalissimo: Chiang Kai-shek and the Struggle for Modern China.* Cambridge, Mass.: Belknap Press of Harvard University Press, 2009.

"Tebie qishi [Special Announcements]." *Shengjie zhinan yuekan [Guide to Holiness]* 6, no. 1 (January 1934): 64.

Telok Ayer Methodist Church, 120th Anniversary Thanksgiving Service. Singapore: n.d.

TenHarmsel, Wayne. *China's Registered Churches: Flourishing in a Challenging Environment.* Eugene, Ore.: Wipf and Stock, forthcoming.

Thomas, George M. *Revivalism and Culture Change: Christianity, Nation Building, and the Market in the Nineteenth-Century United States.* Chicago: University of Chicago Press, 1989.

Thomson, James C. *While China Faced West: American Reformers in Nationalist China, 1928–1937.* Cambridge, Mass.: Harvard University Press, 1969.

Thornberry, Judith. "Women in China." *Church and Society* 65, no. 3 (January–February 1975): 38–45.

"Tianjin xiangcun lianhe budaotuan gaikuang [Tianjin Villages' Evangelistic Teams Cooperate]." *Xinghua bao* 32, no. 14 (April 16, 1935): 25–26.

Tipson, E. Preface to *My Testimony: Being the Autobiography of Dr. John Sung (Song Siong Chiat) the Chinese Evangelist,* by Song Siong Chiat. Translated by E. Tipson. Kuala Lumpur: Caxton Press, 1936.

Tong Chee Kiong. "Religion." In *The Making of Singapore Sociology: Society and State,* edited by Tong Chee Kiong and Lian Kwen Fee. Leiden: Brill and Times Academic Press, 2002.

Tow, Siang Hwa. Foreword to *John Sung My Teacher,* by Timothy Tow. Singapore: Christian Life Publishers, 1985.

Tow, Timothy. *John Sung My Teacher.* Singapore: Christian Life Publishers, 1985.

Trewartha, Glenn T. "Chinese Cities: Numbers and Distribution." *Annals of the Association of American Geographers* 41, no. 4 (December 1951): 331–47.

Tyrell, Ian. *Woman's World, Woman's Empire: The Woman's Christian Temperance Union in International Perspective, 1880–1930.* Chapel Hill: University of North Carolina Press, 1991.

United Methodist Church (U.S.). *Missionary Files: Methodist Church, 1912–1949*. Wilmington, Del.: Scholarly Resources.

Unschuld, Paul U. *Medicine in China: A History of Ideas*. Berkeley: University of California Press, 1985.

van de Ven, Hans J. *From Friend to Comrade: The Founding of the Chinese Communist Party, 1920–1927*. Berkeley: University of California Press, 1991.

van den End, Theo. *De Nederlandse Zendingsvereniging in West-Java, 1858–1963: een bronnenpublicatie*. N.p.: Raad voor de Zending der Ned. Herv. Kerk [etc.], 1991.

van der Veer, Peter. *Conversion to Modernities*. New York: Routledge, 1996.

van Hoogstraten, S. A. "Dr. John Sung in Soerabaia." *De Opwekker* 84, no. 10 (October 1939): 544–49.

Vanderpool, Harold Y. "The Wesleyan-Methodist Tradition." In *Caring and Curing: Health and Medicine in the Western Religious Traditions*, edited by Ronald L. Numbers and Darrel W. Amundsen, 317–53. New York: Macmillan, 1986.

Veldman, Jeannette. "To God Be the Glory." Western Theological Seminary, W89–102, Veldman, Jeannette (1901–1994), Papers, 1912–1989, Joint Archives of Holland, Holland, Mich.

Wakeman, Frederic. *Policing Shanghai, 1927–1937*. Berkeley: University of California Press, 1995.

Wallace, Anthony F. C. Foreword to *Reassessing Revitalization Movements: Perspectives from North America and the Pacific Islands*, edited by Michael E. Harkin, vii-xi. Lincoln: University of Nebraska Press, 2004.

———. "Revitalization Movements." *American Anthropologist* 58, no. 2 (April 1956): 264–81.

Wang, Ming Tao. "Is Dr. George Sherwood Eddy an Evangelist?" Translated by M. A. Hopkins. *China Fundamentalist* 7, no. 4 (April–September 1935): 18–21.

Wang, Wenzong. "Yin Rexian." In *Salt and Light*, vol. 2, edited by Carol Lee Hamrin, 123–42. Eugene, Ore.: Pickwick Publications, 2010.

Wang Fumei. "Putian jidujiaohui (xinjiao) zhi yanjiu (1863–1949 nian) [A Study of Protestant Christianity in Putian (1863–1949)]." M.A. thesis, Fujian Normal University, 2002.

Wang Yongxin. "Wang Mingdao yu Song Shangjie: Liangwei butong eryou xiangtongde ren [Wang Mingdao and Song Shangjie: Two Different but Similar Men]." *Jinri huaren jiaohui* [*Chinese Churches Today*] (August 1983): 4–9.

Weiligonghui. *Shalayue jidujiao wushizhounian jiniankang* [*Fiftieth Anniversary of the Methodist Church in Sarawak*]. 1950. Reprint, Sibu,

Malaysia: Malaixia jidudiao shalayue weiligonghui huaren nianyihui wenzi shiyebu chuban, 2002.

Welch, Holmes. *The Practice of Chinese Buddhism, 1900–1950.* Cambridge, Mass.: Harvard University Press, 1967.

Wells, H. G. *Outline of History.* New York: MacMillan, 1920.

"When 684 Souls Were Saved." *Pentecostal Evangel* 1380 (October 19, 1940): 11.

Wiese, H. A. "Blind Receives Sight, Dumb Speaks." *The Other Sheep* (May 1936): 21–22.

———. "China Crusaders." *The Other Sheep* (August 1935): 12.

Wiese, Katherine. "A Bible School Student." *The Other Sheep* (February 1942): 23.

Williamson, H. R. "Evangelistic Work in China To-day." A four-part essay that appeared in the May, July, July–August, and September issues of the 1938 *Christian Recorder.*

Wong, Aline K. *Women in Modern Singapore.* Singapore: University Education Press, 1975.

Wong, May. Interview, access number 000093, reel 8, National Archives of Singapore.

Wong Meng Lei, ed. *The Methodist Episcopal Church in Borneo, 1911–1930.* Sibu, Sarawak, Malaysia: Board of Christian Literature, Sarawak Chinese Annual Conference, Methodist Church in Malaysia, 2002.

Wu Delei [Uldine Utley]. "Dazhongde jidu [Christ for All People]." Translated by Chen Renbing. *Budao zazhi* [*Evangelism*] 7, no. 1 (January–February 1934): 53–57.

"Wubai yu ren chajing dahui [Five Hundred People Study the Bible at Big Meeting]." *Xinghua bao* 32, no. 10 (March 20, 1935): 32–33.

"Wuyun lingxiu fenxing budao [Five Year Movement: Devotion, Revival, Evangelism]." *Zhenguang* [*True Light*] 30, no. 5 (May 1931): 80–82.

"Wuzhou kongqian weiyoude fenxing budaohui [Wuzhou's Unprecendented and Never-Seen-Before Revival Evangelistic Meetings]." *Zhenguang* [*True Light*] 32, no. 7 (July 1933): 69.

"Wuzhou kongqiande fenxing budao dahui [Wuzhou's Unprecedented Revival Evangelistic Meetings]." *Zhenguang* [*True Light*] 31, no. 7 (July 1932): 85–86.

Xin, Yalin. *Inside China's House Church Network: The Word of Life Movement and Its Renewing Dynamic.* Lexington, Ky.: Enoch Press, 2009.

Xing, Jun. *Baptized in the Fire of Revolution: The American Social Gospel and the YMCA in China, 1919–1937.* Bethlehem, Pa: Lehigh University Press, 1996.

Xingzhou jidujiao budaotuan tuankan, 1935–1936 [*Singapore Christian Evangelistic League, 1935–1936*]. 1936. Reprint, Singapore: 2000.

Xingzhou jidujiao budaotuan tuankan, 1946 [Singapore Christian Evangelistic League, 1946]. Singapore: 1946.

"Xinjiapo fengqi yunyongzhi budaotuan [Singapore's Evangelistic Teams Channel Enthusiastic Response]." *Xinghua bao* 32, no. 41 (October 23, 1935): 26.

Xinjiapo jidutu budaotuan jinxi jiniankan [Singapore Christian Evangelistic League Golden Jubilee Souvenir Magazine, 1985]. Singapore: 1985.

Xinjiapo jidutu budaotuan yingxi jiniankan [Singapore Christian Evangelistic League, Silver Anniversary]. Singapore: n.p., 1960.

"Xinshenghuo yundong juxing daibiao dahui [New Life Movement Holds Representative Meeting]." *Tianjin dagong bao*, April 15, 1934.

Yang, C. K. *Religion in Chinese Society: A Study of Contemporary Social Functions of Religion and Some of Their Historical Factors*. Berkeley: University of California Press, 1961.

Yang, Fenggang, Joy K. C. Tong, and Allan H. Anderson. *Global Chinese Pentecostal and Charismatic Christianity*. Leiden: Brill, 2017.

Yang, Fenggang. "Lost in the Market, Saved at McDonald's: Conversion to Christianity in Urban China." *Journal for the Scientific Study of Religion* 44, no. 4 (December 2005): 423–41.

Yao, Kevin Xiyi. *The Fundamentalist Movement among Protestant Missionaries in China, 1920–1937*. Lanham, Md.: University Press of America, 2003.

Ye Xiaoqing. "Regulating the Medical Profession in China: Health Policies of the Nationalist Government." In *Historical Perspectives on East Asian Science, Technology and Medicine*, edited by Alan K. L. Chan, Gregory K. Clancy, and Hui-chieh Loy. Singapore: Singapore University Press, 1999.

Yeh, Wen-hsin. *Shanghai Splendor: Economic Sentiments and the Making of Modern China, 1843–1949*. Berkeley: University of California Press, 2007.

"Yesu zailai tujie [Explanatory Drawing of Jesus' Return]." *Shengling bao* 10, no. 1 (January 1935).

Yi yao zhi ye zheng wen ji. Di san jie ["Old Style" versus "Modern" Medicine in China: Which Can Do More For the Health and Progress of the Country, and Why?]. Shanghai: Wei sheng jiao yu hui, 1926. A compilation of student essays, by various student authors, on the question of Chinese medicine versus "modern" medicine.

Yip, Ka-che. *Religion, Nationalism, and Chinese Students: The Anti-Christian Movement of 1922–1927*. Bellingham: Western Washington University, 1980.

Yu, Chin Cheak. "Uncovering Seeds for Awakening and Living in the Spirit: A Cross Cultural Study of John Sung and John Wesley." Ph.D. diss., Claremont School of Theology, 2001.

Yu Chun-fang. *Kuan-yin: The Transformation of Avalokitesvara*. New York: Columbia University Press, 2001.

Zarrow, Peter Gue. *China in War and Revolution, 1895–1949*. New York: Routledge, 2005.

Zhang Douwen. "Wuchu lianhe budao dahui [Five Districts Cooperate in Large Evangelism Meeting]." *Xinghua bao* 32, no. 16 (May 1, 1935): 28–30.

Zhang Fuji, ed. *Xinghua weiligonghuishi [Hinghwa Methodist History]*. Putian, China: Weiligonghui, 1947.

Zhang Jing. "Fuxingdahui shengkuang [Highlights of the Big Revival Meeting]." *Xinghua bao* 28, no. 14 (April 15, 1931): 31–32.

Zhao Zichen. "Wode zongjiao jingyan." *Shengming* 4, no. 3 (November 1923).

"Zhongguo gongchandangzhi wajie [The Collapse of the China Communist Party]." *Xinghua bao* 8 (March 14, 1931): 41–42.

Zhongguo jiaohui wenxian. Shanghai Municipal Archive, China.

Zhonghua quanguo jidujiao xiejinhui [National Council of Churches in China]. *Fenjin budao yundong tonggao*. Shanghai: 1937.

———. *Jiaohui yu qingnian shiye* [The Church and Youth]. Shanghai: 1930.

———. *Womende jiaohui* [*Our Church*]. Shanghai: 1937.

"Zhongshan doumen jiaohui xinchun lingxiuhui [Zhongshan Doumen Church's New Year's Devotional Meetings]." *Zhenguang* [*True Light*] 34, no. 4 (April 1935): 72.

Zhou Cezong. *Research Guide to the May Fourth Movement: Intellectual Revolution in Modern China, 1915–1924*. Cambridge, Mass.: Harvard University Press, 1963.

Zhou Dedu. "Zhonggau zongzhu tongbaoshu." *Budao zazhi* [*Evangelism*] 10, no. 2 (February 1937): 8–11.

Zhu, Jianfei. *Architecture of Modern China: A Critique*. New York: Routledge, 2009.

Index